Conversations with Mary Gordon

Literary Conversations Series

Peggy Whitman Prenshaw
General Editor

Conversations
with Mary Gordon

Edited by
Alma Bennett

University Press of Mississippi
Jackson

Books by Mary Gordon

Final Payments. New York: Random House, 1978.
The Company of Women. New York: Random House, 1980.
Men and Angels. New York: Random House, 1985.
Temporary Shelter: Short Stories. New York: Random House, 1987.
The Other Side. New York: Viking, 1989.
Good Boys and Dead Girls and Other Essays. New York: Viking, 1991.
The Rest of Life: Three Novellas. New York: Viking, 1993.
The Shadow Man: A Daughter's Search for Her Father. New York: Random House, 1996.
Spending: A Utopian Divertimento. New York: Scribner, 1998.
Seeing Through Places: Reflections on Geography and Identity. New York: Scribner, 2000.
Joan of Arc. New York: Viking, 2000.

www.upress.state.ms.us

Copyright © 2002 by University Press of Mississippi
Manufactured in the United States of America

10   09   08   07   06   05   04   03   02   4   3   2   1
∞

Library of Congress Cataloging-in-Publication Data

Gordon, Mary, 1949–
    Conversations with Mary Gordon / edited by Alma Bennett.
        p.   cm.—(Literary conversations series)
    Includes index.
    ISBN 1-57806-446-5 (cloth : alk. paper)—ISBN 1-57806-447-3 (pbk. : alk. paper)
    1. Gordon, Mary, 1949–   —Interviews.   2. Novelists, American—20th
century—Interviews.   3. Irish Americans in literature.   4. Catholics in literature.
I. Bennett, Alma.   II. Title.   III.   Series.

PS3557.O669 Z464   2002
813'.54—dc21
    [B]   2001046782

British Library Cataloging-in-Publication Data available

Contents

Introduction

Mary Gordon has given dozens of interviews since the resounding success in 1978 of her first novel *Final Payments*. If she has been hounded by questions—after all, this is a person who insists, "interviews are absolutely my idea of hell"—it is because, as interviewer Susan Bolotin points out, Gordon answers them. And there is rarely anything perfunctory or testy in those answers, even to unprepared interviewers (who privately enrage her) or to formulaic questions (which she often steers toward more substantive issues). As I quickly discovered in late October of 1994, when I arrived for the first of three interview sessions, Gordon is open, engaging, and engaged. But that engagement never quite masks what she later described to me as a constant struggle with the "daily splitting" of her time and energy, with a desire for a pure, uninterrupted life of the mind and spirit versus "a life of ordinary happiness," filled with her family and friends, daily exercise, volunteer work, board meetings, good food, and conversations.

Struggle notwithstanding, once an interview begins, she is remarkably generous. Gordon's interviewers also can count on her articulateness, candor, and strong opinions. A case in point is Sandy Asirvatham's recounting Gordon's response to a *Newsday* writer, just before the pope visited New York in 1995: "But true to form, the article's representative Catholic novelist [Mary Gordon] answered in a highly unorthodox manner, if not quite blasphemously: 'I wouldn't want to say anything to the pope,' Mary Gordon began, 'because he doesn't interest me particularly. He's not important to me; he's not someone who dwells in my imagination.' "

Still, what makes a Gordon interview something to be reckoned with is not her candor. It is the moral and mental courage, the informed risk-taking, behind the candor. More important than her courage is Gordon's fierce intelligence, which, in multiple guises, keeps breaking into exchanges. She has, for instance, a superb sense of timing and delights in quick up-takes, which unfortunately cannot be replicated in a written interview, but can be surmised from radio and filmed conversations. Then there is her habitual awareness of form: the form of her sentences and explanations, of the momentum and direction of the interview itself.

Closely connected is her intellectual rigor, a brilliant specificity that shows up in a penchant for precise terms and well-structured arguments. As Susan Bolotin puts it, "Ms. Gordon speaks easily, with the clarity of someone who performs daily blitzkriegs on equivocation. She tosses off a definition of a moral person—someone who is 'highly moral while always being afraid he is immoral'—as matter-of-factly as some might define a table to a child." In response to Madison Smartt Bell's query about this skill, Gordon pointed out that she is both attracted to and repelled by the Scholastic tradition. Describing herself as anti-Scholastic, "as always being hybrid, as always being a mutt, as always being a synthesizer," she attributes an incisive intelligence to her heritage: "There is a dualism that I think comes from being Irish, that comes from the very structure of Christianity that I both love and have to fight against. There's a clarity of terms that I adore, but that very clarity of terms can exclude too much." The explanation typifies her intellectual patterning; at the same time, it confirms novelist Margaret Drabble's observation that Gordon is always reaching for "a sense of wholeness, for the possibility of inclusion rather than exclusion, for a way of connecting the differing passages of existence."[1]

As if to demonstrate this and perhaps to keep intellectual rigor in its place, Gordon's interviews are filled with moments in which she will pivot from riveting verbal precisions to sentences of extraordinary lushness or droll understatement. Or she will veer away incrementally from a serious discussion and end up with an almost ludicrous aside. Only later does one realize that each step of Gordon's diversionary tactic grounds the serious topic in important ways. For example, in the middle of trying to convince interviewer Edmund White that "it's more fun to be religious; it may be more *honest* to be secular. Nothing is more interesting than religion," she segues to her current reading obsession, Simone Weil, and Weil's disturbing denial of pleasure, and then plunges into: "I love show business. Just the other day I went to Radio City and really enjoyed that unspeakable show with the Rockettes as nuns dancing and kicking in the form of the Cross. Oh, it's all so confusing."

Gordon's seriousness, wit, and intellectual and theological acumen are hallmarks of her public utterances. But there's no mistaking the voice that is a central presence throughout her interviews, and one of the highest priorities in this volume: Gordon's voice as an artist, a writer, a reader, an intense participant in and scholar of American and European letters. Perhaps because, as John Auchard puts it, "Mary Gordon appeared on the literary scene [in 1978, with her first novel, *Final Payments*], not as a promising apprentice but as an accomplished and mature writer,"[2] whom critics immediately began to recognize as "one of the most gifted writers of her generation,"[3] her earliest interviewers wasted no time in asking Gordon about her formative influences, mentors, other writers, critics, and her craft. Obviously stunned by the success of *Final Payments*, the 28-year-old author at first seemed somewhat tentative, guarded. By the spring of 1980, however, there is nothing *sotto voce* about her literary insights. For instance, in the Diana Cooper-Clark interview, published in *Commonweal* in early May, Gordon has found her public literary voice, and it is commanding, opinionated, erudite, dauntingly articulate. Intertwined with discussions of *Final Payments*, she dismisses the comments of most of her critics. She mentions some of the preoccupations in her forthcoming second novel (*The Company of Women*, published in late 1980): women and their habit of abdicating responsibility for their inner lives to men. She offers a refreshing take on the function of a novel: "If it's accidentally instructive, that's all to the good. But its main function is to be beautiful and, in some sense, true in a very large way I can't even begin to explain. . . . I don't think it makes people any better. If that were true English departments would be moral paragons of this or any age." She blazes through discussions of novelists she loves—Virginia Woolf, Jane Austen, Charlotte Brontë, Thomas Hardy, George Eliot, Ford Madox Ford—and contemporary novelistic approaches that put her off: "I never want to read *Finnegans Wake*; *Finnegans Wake* is about language, it's not about people"; "I don't particularly like the Barth, Vonnegut, Barthelme trip where literature is about literature." She moves through a definition and examples of the religious novel, and an astute explanation of why there is no Catholic school of letters in American literature. She talks about how she uses Roman Catholicism as a metaphor, a symbol, in her work, explaining how any such symbol must "have a kind of [communicative] thickness to it, something that has to build up over time for people really to be able to respond to it." And, particularly valuable to her readers, she discusses her craft, her love of formal beauty and balance, of "a well-made piece of work." She explains that she an anti-Romantic Classicist. She admits that what she likes best about her work is an ability to write "really smashing sentences." She worries about "a narrowness of range" and her inability to write about physical violence and to give her male characters viable sexual identities.

Such a performance, at the start of her career, raised the ante for subsequent interviewers, but not every interview is created equally. Not every interviewer can offer Gordon the most opportune venue. Still, and without exception, the world of letters and of the mind plays a major role in her interviews.

When tracked across more than twenty years of interviews, Gordon's public conversations reveal not only a writer's life-in-progress, but also how a little girl from Valley Stream, Long Island, became a master of her craft and an acclaimed author, despite the early loss of her father, despite her subsequently feeling trapped as a child in a punitive familial environment and in poor schools. One learns, for example, about the formative influence of her father, a writer who felt that she was brilliant and who left her with an intellectual mandate and model and the confidence that she could achieve anything, be anything. One also learns about her training as a poet, the invaluable mentoring she received at Barnard College (Anne Prescott, Janice Farrar Thaddeus, and Elizabeth Hardwick), the stylistic mentoring of Virginia Woolf's novels, and the enragingly chauvinistic treatment she received during her graduate work at Syracuse University—an experience that inadvertantly led her away from poetry and to fiction. Her discussions of novelist Margaret Drabble's role in the publication of Gordon's first novel are fascinating. Explanations of her aesthetic and theological grounding in Catholicism also clarify the process involved in, as she once phrased it, her "getting here from there."

Her staying power as a major writer is substantiated in published works which, to date, include five novels, three novellas, a collection of short stories, two collections of essays, a memoir, a biography, some thirty short stories and eighty essays, and dozens of reviews. Parallel evidence of her status in American letters is found in her persistent presence in high-profile interviews that continue to inform her maturation as an artist, her shifting literary genres and interests, her looser stylistic approaches, her passionate literary opinions (which, in the case of postmodernist writers and even Updike, are mellowing), and her teaching.

Regarding the latter, when one reads the 1997 interview by Sandy Asirvatham, one of Gordon's former students—who points out that Gordon is a tough "straight-shooter" when critiquing the work of her writing students at Barnard College and Columbia University—one remembers other Gordon interviews that reflect her keen attention to the difficulties that women writers of her and earlier generations have faced and continue to face. Perhaps the most thorough of these discussions is found in the 1985 "Margaret Drabble-Mary Gordon: Writers Talk About Ideas in Our Time."

A self-described "red-alert feminist," and "feminist writer," Gordon, as she tells Le Anne Schreiber, has always dedicated herself to writing "about issues that are central to women's lives, to write about them beautifully and in high style. I'm so aware of how I was liberated by the women's movement, and I feel a sense of vocation in putting in the style of the great tradition the issues that consciousness has opened up to me." The women's movement has not always appreciated her efforts. A case in point is her third novel, *Men and Angels* (1985), a novel about women and children. That same year in England, in the "Margaret Drabble-Mary Gordon" film, Gordon talked at length about the angry responses of many feminists who felt that by the novel's "suggesting that it was possible to enjoy one's children, that it was possible not to see them as a terrible barrier to achievement" she had betrayed the feminist cause. More recent, and rather bewildered, feminist criticism has hovered around her 1998 novel, *Spending: A Utopian Divertimento*, which champions a woman's sexual pleasure and career and whose protagonist, a painter, is involved with a commodities broker—her male muse, model, financial backer, and lover.

Such reactions serve as reminders that Gordon is stubbornly dedicated to inclusivity, to writerly ways in which she can pursue the whole of life. That pursuit continues to emerge in her work. But it has always been an overt and dominant aspect of the auto/biographical preoccupations that fill her interviews. Questions about this have followed Gordon, ever since Edmund White began her first published interview in 1978 with, "O.K. let me ask you the vulgar question: how autobiographical is your book [*Final Payments*]?" More than two decades later, the question persists. Gordon once laughed and told me, "If you use the real names it's non-fiction. If you change the names it's fiction. The rest of that is total crap." Elsewhere, she has insisted that "the question of whether there is a different method for fiction and nonfiction . . . is the kind of thing that makes me want to take to my bed with the vapors."[4] Vapors and genres aside, much of Gordon's work is deeply informed by autobiographical and familial material. This in itself is not unusual. Writers habitually plumb such sources, but, unlike Gordon, few reveal them. As Madison Smartt Bell admitted to Gordon, "All writers, I think, have secrets that kind of give them power. Frequently these secrets are formed in childhood. I have secrets of that kind that drive my work. I would never tell them to anyone." However, the degree of Gordon's auto/biographical candor and obsessions and of her fiction-non fiction manipulations suggests a nexus of work and life, one in which, as Gordon confirms to Asirvatham, "I cannot divide a self from a writer."

Nowhere is that clearer than in her interviews. Using an instinctive mnemotechnic, she habitually calls up places, people, images, and anecdotes from her life in ways that move beyond perfunctory answers to even the most formulaic biographical questions. In a sort of jealous economy of time and opportunity, Gordon seems to employ "remembrances of things past" in her interviews, not only to do her duty as a public person, but also to explore the language, parameters, and validity of memory. When Canadian radio interviewer Eleanor Wachtel said to Gordon, "You always look back," Gordon shot back, with laughter, "You don't expect me to look forward, do you? You think I'm crazy!" If Gordon's is a conflicted public exploration of the past—because it has everything to do with her art as well as her public and private personae—there's nothing conflicted about her artistic dependence on *Mnemosyne* [memory], the mother of the Muses and, unbeknownst to the ancient Greeks, of distinctive interviews.

Thus, while the twenty-five interviews selected for this volume track the evolution of and attention to Gordon's work, they also trace the evolution of her auto/biographical preoccupations and the ways in which those preoccupations invariably make their way into her work. For example, the central concerns of Gordon's 1985 novel, *Men and Angels* (1985), mirror hundreds of her interview comments; these exchanges, in turn, offer a sort of pointillistic doubling: a "Portrait of the Artist [Gordon] as Young Mom" (to borrow an interview title).[5] Like Anne Foster, the novel's protagonist, Gordon is as deeply committed to motherhood, friendship, and her professional career as she is to ethical and gender issues. Such resonances give us glimpses into the highly charged interface between Gordon's craft and life—in other words, into her art. Coincidentally, *Men and Angels* also gives her interviewers a brand new topic, her burgeoning interest in painting. The ensuing questions and answers illuminate a number of her subsequent essays and particularly her novel, *Spending* (1998).

Perhaps the most striking demonstration of the ways interviews track the evolution of Gordon's auto/biographical preoccupations is found in *The Shadow Man: A Daughter's Search for Her Father.* By the time Gordon's wrenching memoir was published in 1996, we have on hand eighteen years of interviews in which she talks about her father, David Gordon, who died when she was seven years old and who, as the 1978 Nan Robertson interview records, once gave her Robert Louis Stevenson's *A Child's Garden of Verses* inscribed in seven languages, each of which said, "To my daughter, Mary Catherine, with love from her father. I love you." Three years later, the ten-

year-old daughter began a biography of her father with the sentence, "My
father had one of the greatest minds I have ever known."[6] Although the project trailed off on page twenty-eight, its careful format and ambition document
her early decision to follow in her father's professional foot-steps: she would
be a writer when she grew up.

By late 1994, that daughter's interviews begin to chronicle her discovery
of harrowing facts and fictions in her beloved father's identity. The man she
identifies in her interview with Edmund White as "an extraordinary man," a
Harvard-educated intellectual, and Jewish convert to Catholicism, and whom
she discusses proudly for the next sixteen years was, in fact, a mediocre
writer; a self-taught, high school drop-out; a man born in Lithuania with a
different name, birth year, and mother tongue, Yiddish, a language he never
acknowledged; an immigrant son and brother, who walked out of the lives of
his family in Ohio. Worse still, David Gordon's publications reflected a self-
hatred so profound, an anti-Semitism and ultra-conservatism so virulent and
nasty that by 1994 Mary Gordon, with great anguish, begins using the words
"insane" and "evil" in interview discussions of her father, even while she
holds on resolutely to the love and intellectual encouragement he had given
her.

As several interviews record, Gordon was well aware that her excruciating
investigation and transformation of that investigation into *The Shadow Man*
were pivotal points in her life and career. Obviously Gordon had to come to
terms with a complex second loss of her father. As she explained to Terry
Gross, in a 1996 WHYY *Fresh Air* radio interview, "I feel that I am a less
fathered girl now and more of a woman who doesn't define herself so much
by him, that I'm more alone and now the next however many years of my
life are a task in which he has less and less of a place. . . . I'm not primarily
a daughter anymore." Nor was she the person she thought she was, a person
whose identity had always been bound up with the model of her father as an
intellectual and writer. She went on to confess to Gross that she erupted
angrily when her friends and agent pointed out that his work was not interesting, that she is the writer her father never was.

Equally traumatic in terms of her life as a writer, especially as a novelist,
was her loss of faith in memory which, in her words to Gross, is "the gilt-
edged stock that [you believe] you can constantly get dividends from. Then
you find out you bought a swamp in central Florida." That her mother was
suffering from profound dementia in an Upper Manhattan nursing home in-
tensified Gordon's obsession with memory, with the loss and ruination of

memory. As a response and at the same time she was completing *The Shadow Man*, which addresses the double parental loss, she was writing a seeringly honest essay for the *New York Times Magazine*, "My Mother Is Speaking from the Desert." Gordon was also talking to friends and interviewers about her decision to give her father "a local habitation and a name" by having his body disinterred from its unmarked place in the Gagliano family plot and reburied in a newly purchased Gordon-Cash plot. That process subsequently became the conclusion of *The Shadow Man*. And in 2000—in what may turn out to be the final chapter of her shared mourning—Gordon published a collection of essays, *Seeing Through Places: Reflections on Geography and Identity*, the first chapters of which seem to bring a certain closure to her childhood and parents and to the artist's fears regarding memory.

These types of intricate connections between Gordon's familial life and craft have helped dictate the selections for this volume. Another priority has been to include as many interviews as possible that are structured in a question-answer format, since essay-type interviews, by their very nature, contain fewer passages of the artist's words. Nevertheless, the essay-interview style lends itself to valuable accounts of contextual and biographical details. Some interviews include both techniques, often with persuasive results. And in the case of the filmed Drabble-Gordon conversation, for example, the two writers decided to take turns speaking at length directly to the live audience. Thus varied formatting has also been an important factor. It may be helpful to mention that, for the sake of either continuity or economy, station break materials in radio and television interviews and several passages Gordon read from her works have been deleted.

I also have tried to include not only a sampling of the various interview venues—i.e., journals (printed and on-line), magazines, newspapers, radio and television shows—but also an adequate record of the evolving ways in which Gordon has been approached by interviewers. For instance, while Robertson described Gordon as having a "little girl voice" and a personality as "fresh and cheery as a daisy," such phrases seemed ill-suited to the young writer's formidable articulateness and intelligence and soon disappeared. Still, each interviewer's decisions about whether or not (and if so, how) to reference Gordon's demeanor, appearance, surroundings, and/or family make for some fascinating absences and presences in the interviews.

Another persistent problem for Gordon's interviewers is well represented in this volume's selections: how to label her. In addition to be recognized as one of her generation's finest writers, Gordon has been called a Catholic writer, a feminist writer, "her generation's preeminent novelist of Roman Catholic mores and manners," "a kind of collective contemporary American Mother," a neo-realism novelist, "a mesmerizing storyteller," a master novelist of both the Irish-Catholic immigrant subculture and the family saga genre, "Tolstoy in Queens," and a "humane, masterly novelist." The difficulty in labeling her and Gordon's own resistance to labels (particularly that of a "Catholic writer") are acerbated by her chameleonic surprises. For instance, who else in contemporary American literature would work on a comic, erotic novel, *Spending* (1998), a biography of *Joan of Arc* (2000), and a somber, auto/biographical essay collection, *Seeing Through Places: Reflections on Geography and Identity* (2000) at the same time? Perhaps the best approach to a Gordon labeling may be that of Madison Smartt Bell as cited in Asirvatham. Before Gordon gave a reading in Maryland, Bell drolly introduced her as "arguably the pre-eminent Jewish-Irish-Catholic-American novelist." Whatever one calls her, Mary Gordon, like her interviews, is an important voice to be reckoned with—perennially.

I first must thank Mary Gordon for the 1994 and 1995 interviews in New York City and her on- and off-the-record candor, for access to her manuscripts and records, for her 1996 lectures and conversations in Clemson, for her support of this book, and her friendship. I next want to thank all of the interviewers, publishers, and media companies for their permissions to reprint material in this book. I also am grateful to Clemson University and the Department of English for a sabbatical semester and to the reference librarians and interlibrary loan staff of Clemson University's Cooper Library for their resourcefulness. I continue to appreciate Frank Day of Clemson University who introduced me to the work of Mary Gordon and then edited my subsequent book, *Mary Gordon* (1996). For the *Conversations with Mary Gordon* project, the expertise of Seetha Srinivasan of the University Press of Mississippi was enormously helpful, as was her interest in Mary Gordon. I count my friends and family as the encouraging constants in my work and life. I am particularly indebted to my mother Caroline Weir Bennett and my late grandmother Ida Dorroh Bennett who—in their vastly different styles—first showed me the power of conversations.

Notes

1. Drabble, Margaret. "The Limits of Mother Love." *New York Times Book Review* (31 March 1985), 31.

2. Auchard, John. "Mary Gordon." *American Novelists Since World War II*, Second series (Detroit, MI: Gale Research Company, 1980), 109.

3. Allen, Bruce. "First Novels." *Sewanee Review* 86:4 (Fall 1978), 616.

4. Erdrich, Louise and Katrina Kenison, eds. *Best American Short Stories 1993* (Boston: Houghton Mifflin, 1993), 367.

5. Dudar, Helen. "Portrait of the Artist as Young Mom." *Wall Street Journal* (1 April 1985), 20.

6. First quoted in Bennett, Alma. *Mary Gordon*. (New York: Twayne Publishers, Inc./Simon & Schuster, 1996), 7.

Chronology

1949   8 December. Mary Catherine Gordon born in Far Rockaway, New York, to David and Anna Gagliano Gordon. Grows up in Valley Stream (Long Island), New York.

1955   Begins parochial school: Holy Name of Mary School (grammar school through the eighth grade), Valley Stream.

1956   Death of father, David Gordon, at Bellevue Hospital, New York City. Anna and Mary Gordon move to maternal grandmother's home in Valley Stream.

1963   Begins parochial high school: Mary Louis Academy, Jamaica Estates, New York.

1967   Receives scholarship to Barnard College of Columbia University.

1971   Graduates with B.A. degree in English from Barnard. Spends summer in Europe. Receives scholarship to graduate writing program at Syracuse University.

1973   First publication, "To a Cow" (poem) in *American Review*. Completes M.A. degree in English and Creative Writing from Syracuse University. Thesis: "Living With a Body" (collection of poetry). Enrolls in Ph.D. program in English at Syracuse University.

1974   Marries James Brain, Professor of Anthropology at the State University of New York, New Paltz. Begins teaching English (1974–1978) at Dutchess Community College, Poughkeepsie, New York.

1975   First fiction publication, "Now I Am Married" (short story), in *Virginia Quarterly Review*.

1976   "Now I Am Married" receives Balch Award.

1977   Separates from James Brain. Moves to New Paltz, New York.

1978   *Final Payments* (first novel) named one of the outstanding books of 1978 by the *New York Times Book Review* and nominated for the National Book Critics Circle Award.

1979 *Final Payments* receives 1979 Janet Heidinger Kafka Prize for best novel written by an American woman. Divorces James Brain. Marries Arthur Cash, Professor of English at the State University of New York, New Paltz, and biographer of Laurence Sterne. Appointed Visiting Professor, 1979–80, Department of English, Amherst College, Amherst, Massachusetts.

1980 *The Company of Women* (novel). Birth of first child, Anna Gordon Cash.

1981 Receives 1981 Janet Heidinger Kafka Prize for *The Company of Women*.

1983 "The Only Son of the Doctor" included in *Prize Stories 1983: O. Henry Awards*. Birth of second child, David Dess Gordon Cash.

1984 Receives honorary doctorate, Belmont Abbey College, Belmont, North Carolina.

1985 *Men and Angels* (novel). Receives a Literary Lion of the New York Public Library Award.

1987 *Temporary Shelter* (short story collection).

1988 Adjunct Professor, teaching fiction, Barnard College. Receives honorary doctorate, Assumption College, Worcester, Massachusetts.

1989 *The Other Side* (novel). Receives honorary doctorate, State University of New York, New Paltz.

1990 Appointed Millicent C. McIntosh Professor of Writing, Barnard College. Appointed Adjunct Professor, Graduate School of the Arts, Columbia University. Receives Barnard College Woman of Achievement Award.

1991 *Good Boys and Dead Girls and Other Essays* (essay collection). "Separation" included in *Best Short Stories of 1991*.

1992 Receives a Lila Wallace-Reader's Digest Writers' Award.

1993 *The Rest of Life: Three Novellas*. Awarded a Guggenheim Fellowship. "Abortion: How Do We Really Choose?" included in *Best Essays by American Women*. "The Important Houses" included in *Best American Short Stories 1993*.

1994 Receives honorary doctorate, Saint Xavier University, Chicago.

1996   *The Shadow Man: A Daughter's Search for Her Father* (nonfiction memoir).

1998   *Spending: A Utopian Divertimento* (novel).

2000   *Seeing Through Places: Reflections on Geography and Identity* (essay collection). *Joan of Arc* (biography).

Conversations with Mary Gordon

Talking with Mary Gordon

Edmund White / 1978

From the *Washington Post Book World*, 9 April 1978, E1, E4. © 1978
Edmund White. Reprinted by permission.

After Edmund White turned in his review of Mary Gordon's novel *Final
Payments, Book World* asked him to interview the author. Their conversation
took place over dinner in a New York restaurant.

Q: O.K. let me ask you the vulgar question: how autobiographical is your
book?

A: I welcome the vulgarity, because no one will believe me that it's fiction.
My father died when I was seven, not recently (I'm 29 now). And unlike
Isabel I have not lived a life of sacrifice. But the book, I think, comes out of
a moral preoccupation with sacrifice. Though I'm not willing to immolate
myself, I think it's scary the way people today have a nasty Freudian assumption that sacrifice is really sick. Something valuable has been lost.

Q: If you respect sacrifice so much, then why does your heroine decide at
the end of the book not to stay with Margaret, that dreadful woman she had
intended to help?

A: When Isabel served her *father* she was happy. You see, I think sacrifice
for someone you love is pure joy, the highest form of love, but sacrifice for
someone you loathe is just egotism.

Q: Are you religious?

A: Yes. I was brought up as a strict Catholic. I'm well into a new novel,
one that's a bit more experimental but that also deals with religion. I read
theology for pleasure. Are you religious?

Q: I say I'm an atheist, though friends accuse me of being a crypto-Catho-
lic. But I think it's more fun than being secular.

A: No, it's more fun to be religious; it may be more *honest* to be secular.
Nothing is more interesting than religion. Right now I'm reading Simone
Weil; she's become an obsession. She also disturbs me because of her denial
of pleasure. Just now I had some time to kill and I was having a drink in a
bar, reading Simone Weil, but there was someone on television singing,

"When I'm not near the girl I love, I love the girl I'm near," and half of me wanted to sing along with that silly, wonderful song. I love show business. Just the other day I went to Radio City and really enjoyed that unspeakable show with the Rockettes as nuns dancing and kicking in the form of the Cross. Oh, it's all so confusing.

Q: Where did you grow up?

A: On Long Island in a working-class neighborhood right next to Kennedy airport. But I was a very ambitious child. Two of my girlfriends and I decided we would go to college; that was almost unprecedented at my high school. And we all succeeded! I got a scholarship to Barnard. That changed my life, especially when I took creative writing from Elizabeth Hardwick. I think she's the greatest prose stylist in America now. At that time I was writing nothing but poetry, but Lizzie kept telling me, "You're a prose writer, honey," in that charming Southern drawl of hers. She was also a wonderful role model for me; until I met her I had no idea how to be a woman writer.

Q: How did you begin to write prose?

A: I think I was afraid of the length of fiction. But finally a woman friend took me in hand. She gave me a blue-book and told me it was like an exam; I had an hour to write a story. So I filled up the book—and I've been going ever since.

Q: And the novel? How did it come to be published?

A: I was in London for a year with my husband. He's an anthropologist and we were there for his sabbatical. I was very lonely. One day I saw Margaret Drabble on television, and I liked her so much I wrote her a letter. She phoned me the next day and invited me to dinner—extraordinarily generous of her. We became friends and later I showed her *Final Payments*, which I was just finishing. She put me in touch with her American agent, who took me on as a client. Then, when I was back in the States, I showed the manuscript to Elizabeth Hardwick. She liked it, but she said, "Why did you write a first-person narrative in the third person?" You see, at that point it was all "she" rather than "I"; guess I was afraid of the "I." The idea of converting the entire manuscript into the first person seemed overwhelming, but Lizzie told me it would be easy. She sat down with me and did two pages; I rewrote the whole book quickly. It was instantly snapped up by Random House. Do you see how important my woman friends have been to me?

Q: That's one of the things I liked about your book, the very human feminism. Mary, where do you live? Do you work?

A: I live in Poughkeepsie and teach composition and creative writing there at a community college. The work is sometimes a bit defeating. Most of the students are going to be welders or X-ray technicians, and they're just not used to the most essential thing in reading literature—the habit of introspection.

Q: Tell me about your background.

A: My father was an extraordinary man. He was a Jew who grew up in, of all places, Lorain, Ohio. His family—uncles, aunts—sent him to Harvard. He dropped out, went to Paris in the '20s, was a part of the high literati. Slowly he became, like Ezra Pound, disgusted with modern culture. He came back to the States and believe it or not started a girlie magazine. It was called *Hot Dog*. But then in the 1930s he sympathized with the Franco side in the Spanish Civil War—and *that* led him to convert to Catholicism. He gave up the girlie magazine and started one right-wing Catholic periodical after another. They all folded after a few issues. And he married my mother, his romantic ideal: a working-class Irish Catholic girl. Although he died when I was seven, he managed to start teaching me French, Greek, philosophy; in a way he was not sexist at all. I was to be his intellectual heir. When he died, there I was, a morose, plain child who read all the time.

Q: And your mother?

A: We love each other very much, but she doesn't read my work. She's not a reader. We have our own fun—playing canasta, for instance. And for a person without much education, she leads a remarkably sophisticated spiritual life.

Q: How do you feel about all the attention you're getting, the fact that *Final Payments* is a Literary Guild selection and that there's a big paperback deal in the offing and that so many critics have flipped over your novel?

A: It's all terribly strange. I thought I might reach just a few people, be published by a small press. . . . It's almost embarrassing.

A Young Author Probes Old Themes

Nan Robertson / 1978

From the *New York Times*, 31 May 1978, sec. III, 1, 8. © 1978 by the
New York Times Company. Reprinted by permission.

All of a sudden, this first novel called *Final Payments* has surged up out of
the "me generation" of self-absorbed, navel-contemplating, dropout American children, and has knocked the critics for a loop.

Its themes, written with authority and wit, are self-sacrifice, morality,
death, old people and the power of the Catholic religion. Its heroine has given
up 11 years of her young life to nurse her stroke-ridden, hellfire-Catholic
father with saintlike devotion. His death, when she is 30, frees her to pursue
her own life in the outside world. She ultimately embraces self-fulfillment
after a final act of mortification for a loathsome crone who had once been
her father's housekeeper.

The author is Mary Gordon. She is a 28-year-old sprite out of Queens with
a little-girl voice and a personality as fresh and cheery as a daisy.

"I haven't sacrificed very much in my own life so I feel shy talking about
it. I've thought a lot about it, though," she confided in an interview at Random House, her publisher, only hours away from rushing off for four days in
Paris with one of the two girlhood friends she recreates with such tenderness
in the novel. She decided to talk about sacrifice anyway: "As a teen-ager I
did voluntary work in a nursing home for one week, which shows how de-
pendable my emotion for old people is in real life. It really did depress me.
They wanted so much—I just felt their desire for connection and for love was
so overwhelming that I felt swallowed up by it."

Her mother, Anna, is another case altogether: "She's full of courage, full
of endurance. She's badly crippled from polio she got at the age of 3. She
has worked every day of her life as a legal secretary since she was 18; she
was one of nine children who put her brothers through college and her sisters
through nursing school. She supported my father, who stayed home and took
care of me. And she's always being kind to absolutely bone-crushingly boring people—she's always helping out the drips of this life. And yet she's so
cheerful and funny."

4

Miss Gordon's own father, David, died when she was 8 years old, "but to this day," she said, "I remember the years with him with clarity and aliveness and luminosity."

"My father was a gentleman and a scholar," she continued, "and he bred me to be a lady and a scholar. He spoke seven languages, he read Greek with his meals, he was besotted with me, his only child."

He was also feckless, a ne'er do well, a Jew from Lorain, Ohio, who converted in late adulthood to fanatic Catholicism, adored Senator Joseph McCarthy, the Rev. Charles E. Coughlin and, she said, "kept starting doomed little right-wing magazines with articles like 'Roosevelt: The Anti-Christ.' "

"He was fantastically literate," Miss Gordon said, "but he had a terrible disrespect for books, ripping pages out for the passages he liked. He was dazed out about the physical world, he didn't live in it. He forgot about a urinalysis he was supposed to have and carried the little bottle of urine around in his pocket for a week. I don't know how I ever was conceived—it must have been an act of God."

Her parents quarreled constantly about money. "Our financial condition was dire," she said. "They had nothing in common but their phenomenal religiosity."

They sent her to Irish Catholic schools in Valley Stream, L.I., and in Queens with the "incredibly ignorant nuns of that day," Miss Gordon said.

"How can parents not know how enraged a bright child can be in a bad school?" she asked.

For a long while she was, however, docile and obedient. "Those are not skills that are useful in adult life, like shorthand and typing," Miss Gordon said wryly. "I was a terrible prig. I wrote religious treatises and poetry for my own edification. I read the lives of saints over and over. I loved the virgin martyrs. It was so full of high drama and gore—you know, like St. Catherine being broken on the wheel."

Then, she said, "The minute I hit puberty my thing with religion went right out the window. It was shocking how God lost me to Joseph Montalbano, the 12-year-old boy across the classroom who won the science fair."

With her mother's approval, she invited boys to parties at her house. They danced and smoked cigarettes, scandalizing the neighbors in the Rosary Society. She coaxed droves of classmates to pop bubble gum at their desks: "My ambition was to drive the nuns screaming bonkers."

Yet despite her rebellions, in her fiction and in her life, Miss Gordon said she considers herself religious and goes to mass every Sunday.

A scholarship to Barnard—"I knew my mother wouldn't let me go away and it was clearly the only classy school in New York"—brought her finally "to a place where there were people like me, where what I valued, they valued." Her years there were the turbulent ones between 1967 and 1971.

She became radicalized by Vietnam, took part in the Columbia student revolt of 1968 and, she said, "shouted 'up against the wall' like all the others."

"But when I helped occupy a building," she added, "I'd wonder if I could get out to catch the 4:32 train back to Long Island so Mother wouldn't worry about me."

The novelist Elizabeth Hardwick taught her at Barnard and urged her to switch from poetry, her lifelong preference, to prose. "I fought prose," Miss Gordon said. "A poem is just a few words, manipulated very carefully. I was terrified to have so many words. I couldn't imagine how anyone could control them." Most critics have commented on the poetic clarity and intensity of Miss Gordon's book.

It was Miss Hardwick who later read the manuscript of *Final Payments* and urged the author to change the voice of the protagonist, Isabel Moore, from the third to the first person.

Miss Gordon began writing the novel in 1975 at Dutchess Community College in Poughkeepsie, N.Y., where she still teaches English. Her husband, James Brain, an Englishman 20 years older, whom she met while she was a graduate student at Syracuse University, teaches anthropology at the State University of New York in New Paltz.

Miss Gordon said she admired Graham Greene "immensely," as well as another Catholic novelist, Mary McCarthy. She read Charlotte Brontë's *Jane Eyre* at least "50 times when I was a girl, the same with *Little Women*, and I identified with Jo, of course." The author also sprinkled her conversation with references to Thomas Hardy, George Eliot, Henry James, Colette, Simone de Beauvoir, and Virginia Woolf, on whom she has done "five-sevenths of a doctoral dissertation started at Syracuse."

Her father "wouldn't read much that was done after the Reformation," she said.

"You know, Shakespeare was O.K. for a Protestant," she recalled his saying once. "Chaucer was his perfect embodiment of the Christian sensibility and Dante was an ideal."

But the daughter's most prized possession still is her father's early birthday gift of Robert Louis Stevenson's *A Child's Garden of Verses*.

"He inscribed it to me in seven languages," she mused, her voice catching with emotion, "and in each, it said, 'To my daughter, Mary Catherine, with love from her father. I love you.' "

An Interview with Mary Gordon

Diana Cooper-Clark / 1980

From *Commonweal*, 9 May 1980, 270–73. © 1980 Commonweal Foundation. Reprinted by permission.

Diana Cooper-Clark: How do you feel about the critical response to *Final Payments*? Did you find it particularly perceptive?

Mary Gordon: I thought Wilfrid Sheed's review in the *New York Review of Books* was. And that was about it. Every now and again somebody says something that you like to hear, but it turned out that only the Sheed review was instructive to me.

DCC: In your view what is the function of the critic?

MG: To make known good things that are around so that people want to read them. I don't think about criticism in terms of setting standards. For me the ideal critic would be Virginia Woolf—somebody who says, "This is wonderful. You really should read this for this particular reason."

DCC: Do you believe in such a thing as the "function" of the novel, of literature?

MG: Pleasure. If it's accidentally instructive, that's all to the good. But its main function is to be beautiful and, in some sense, true in a very large way I can't even begin to explain. Again Virginia Woolf, "What I want to do is to tell the truth and to create something of beauty." I think that's what the novel is supposed to do. I don't think it makes people any better. If that were true, English departments would be the moral paragons of this or any other age. And anyone who has taught for two minutes knows that they are not. I am very attracted to formal beauty. I like a well-made piece of work. I like balance, so that's very important to me. I'm by nature a Classicist. I am by nature anti-Romantic.

DCC: How do you define the religious novel? I know you were doing a course on the religious novel last year. Now I'm thinking for instance that Paul Tillich, the Protestant theologian, defines the religious as something of honesty and ultimate concern, and he said that a rock by Cezanne is more religious than Christ on the cross by a sentimental German painter named Uhde. How do you feel about that definition of the "religious"?

8

MG: I think it's nonsense because it devalues both the religious experience and the experience of Cezanne. All beauty is not religious in its nature, and all aesthetic or heartfelt responses are not religious, and I don't like that kind of sloppiness. For me the religious novel would be something which had a relationship to God at the center of it. No, I don't think that swimming in the ocean is as religious an act as contemplative prayer, which is not to say that one is more valuable than the other. If you call everything religious, then nothing is religious.

DCC: And so *Final Payments* would not be a religious novel by that definition, or would it?

MG: Well, it's certainly not a religious novel in the way that one of Mauriac's would be, or one of Bernanos's, but I think that Isabel is searching, trying to come to terms with her religious life. I would not say that her path of self-identification is a religious path, but in that she is so formed by religion and really sees everything in metaphors of Catholicism so much, I think it is.

DCC: And to pick up that point of using Roman Catholicism as a metaphor, do you think that the more secular world that we live in today has anaesthetized people to the symbolic world, to the understanding or the sensibility of the symbolic, and has this changed writing styles, writing approaches?

MG: What's happened doesn't have to do with secularism, it has to do with communication. A symbol has to have a kind of thickness to it, something that has to build up over time for people really to be able to respond to it, and I think the whole tenor and tempo of the age is something . . . the symbol of our age would have to be something very evanescent because we're not interested in things that accrete over time, that build up meaning over time, and also if everybody's getting the same kind of stimuli all over the world, which people are now, I don't think there's going to be very much chance for the particular symbol . . . I don't think it has much to do with religion, I think it has to do with the speed at which we live and our terrible disregard for history, because a symbol only takes on meaning as it attaches to the past.

DCC: Wallace Fowlie has stated: "American literature is quite thoroughly non-Catholic. There has never been in this country that would resemble a Catholic school of letters or movement in literature." Do you agree?

MG: Yes, I do. Sure, it makes a lot of sense. The Catholic church in America is an immigrant church. And immigrants were worried about making money and surviving, and learning was a threat to the family. The more you learned, the more likely you were to leave home. The Catholic church in America has been phenomenally anti-intellectual. To go to school and to study philosophy or literature or art is very different because it's learning that won't get you anywhere, except out of the community. And they're right. What is touching and moving is the loneliness of the immigrant experience, always feeling an outsider, always defining yourself as "not Protestant," and ever later on as "not Jewish," knowing that you somehow never had access to the real power, and kind of looking in with your nose pressed against the window. Also I think that's very much a feature of Catholicism in America.

It's also a profoundly anti-sexual tradition, and that's a big problem with it in a way that the French Catholics really aren't and the Italian Catholics really aren't. Irish Catholicism is very anti-sexual, and the sexy people get out of the church; they have to. What you're left with is a marvelous ascetic type who stays in the church, or a person like Flannery O'Connor who's a virgin through and through, one of those wise and fierce Antigones. They can stay and be quite interesting and quite admirable, but the sexual people have to get out.

DCC: Who do you consider to be the best Catholic writers?

MG: Bernanos, I think, is the greatest. And Mauriac, who's very great, Flannery O'Connor, although she's a Catholic writer who never writes about Catholics. . . . Graham Greene, a wonderful writer.

DCC: How about somebody like Waugh or Muriel Spark? Do you consider them Catholic writers?

MG: Well, they'd like to be considered Catholic writers. I don't know. I have a lot of trouble with Muriel Spark. She's awfully thin to me. And Waugh was a brilliant stylist, and I even like *Brideshead Revisited*, which about three people in the world do.

DCC: The Christian in our society must confront certain essential paradoxes of her faith. On the one hand, she is taught the need to lose one's life in order to save it. The lives and writings of the saints and ascetics illustrate this impulse toward retirement and withdrawal. On the other hand, the Incarnation, by which God became man, and dwelt among men in the world and in history with all of its evils, defies this withdrawal. Therefore the Christian lives both in heaven and earth. Does the character of Isabel in any way embody this paradox?

MG: Yes, it's something I think about all the time. It's a terrible paradox: having a body even as Christ had a body with affections and needs and connections and yet knowing or sensing somehow that there's this angelic realm that you might almost have access to if you just give up this body. But it seems to be that the impulse of charity comes from going out. I've always wondered how a contemplative can fulfill his obligation in charity because in some ways it's a profoundly egocentric life. You spend all of your time getting rid of your flesh and the hell with everybody else's flesh; if they're starving and leprous, that's their tough luck.

DCC: Carl Jung believed that religion binds humanity together. Do you agree?

MG: No. I think it probably separates men, one from the other. If you got two people together talking about religion, they'd usually disagree, but if you got people talking about the way they felt about their children, they'd probably agree. Human affection is much more universal than religion.

DCC: What is the meaning of Isabel's sacrifice? She has given up her life for her father, but she makes that statement "not with self-pity but with extreme pride." But sacrifice in the book, especially with Margaret, seems to be more than the "pride of sacrifice," the "romance of devotion," the idea of martyrdom.

MG: What was very important to me was to make the distinction between genuine sacrifice motivated not only by love but by affection which seems to me to be of immense importance in life. The kind of sacrifice that Isabel practiced in relation to Margaret is a kind of theft, sacrifice for its own sake without any movement of the heart. Sacrifice as an abstraction is hateful unless you really want to. Certainly there would be points when the person is physically appalling to you at that particular time. But unless you have a memory of a stirring in the heart, I think you have no right to sacrifice.

DCC: What do you like best and what do you like least about your work?

MG: What I like best is that sometimes I think I write really smashing sentences. What I like least is that there are certain things that I just can't do. I fear a narrowness of range. I can never write about violence. Physical violence. I'm not very good at young men, men who have a sexual identity. And I wish I were better. But Flannery O'Connor says that everything that is important to a writer she learns before the age of eight and I was brought up in a very female-centric world. But I wish . . . I find men so incomprehensible that I can't write about them very well.

DCC: In his review, Peter Prescott said that the best men and the most convincing in *Final Payments* are the invalid father and the alcoholic priest, both of whom are "unsexed." You do agree with him?

MG: Yes. I have to do something terrible to my sexual men in order to understand them *(laughs)*. I can't write sympathetically about a normally sexed man.

DCC: I would like your opinion on various attitudes toward the contemporary novel. First, the whole death of the novel debate between, for example, Cheever and Fowles who assert that the novel is alive and, well, versus Vidal and Capote who maintain that it is a dying art form and that journalism, magazines are taking over. What do you think about all that?

MG: I haven't thought much about it. I think that Capote and Vidal write journalism because they can't write novels, and infinitely would rather be writing novels but they can't, they're blocked. So I don't know; I suppose people don't need novels very much now, and that's sad, but I think it's their attention span.

DCC: Robert Scholes. I don't know if you're familiar with him; he's an academic modernist, he's a scholar and he advocates fictional fabulation, structural fabulation. This is the world, the Barth theme world, that would go beyond and ignore historical reality is order to create self-sufficient worlds like Pynchon, Gaddis, etc.

MG: Let them do it as long as I don't ever have to read it. I just find it totally boring. I'm interested in the novel as a form of high gossip and the more the novel gets away from gossip, the less I'm interested in reading it. I want to know about Jane and Mister Rochester. I want to know about Dorothea and Elizabeth Bennet. I want to know what happens to Sue Bridehead. I don't particularly like the Barth, Vonnegut, Barthelme trip where literature is about literature. I wouldn't want to say that they are wrong, that's not the way novels are to be written. I could change my mind in ten years. I never want to read *Finnegans Wake*; *Finnegans Wake* is about language, it's not about people. I think novels should be about people. Novels that are basically tricks to show us what writing a novel is really about, I'm not interested in. On the other hand, Virginia Woolf's my favorite novelist, and it seems to me she does all the stylization you could ever want to do, but doesn't move away from character, and so I think if they're crabbing they should just go and read Virginia Woolf and shut up *(laughs)*.

DCC: How about Anaïs Nin and her notion of abstraction and the future of the novel?

MG: She's such a dumb . . . I just can't understand all that.

DCC: Which writers in the past do you admire, then?

MG: My favorite novelist is Jane Austen, and then I love Charlotte Brontë, and I love Hardy, and I love George Eliot, and I love Ford Madox Ford. He's one of my favorites. I think I'm going to have to put him third after Woolf and Austen.

DCC: Would you consider any of these major influences to the point that you say that they influenced you in style or content?

MG: Virginia Woolf did. I was writing a dissertation on her when I was writing *Final Payments*, and I was copying out—I never finished it—but I was copying out passages of her novels in the afternoons, and I was writing my own work in the mornings, and I learned so much about prose writing from her.

DCC: Does your writing draw heavily from your own life? I'm thinking of *Final Payments* and short stories like "The Thorn," "Now I Am Married," "The Other Woman."

MG: I feel more free to be autobiographical in short stories than in novels. Somehow talking about yourself for ten pages is okay, but talking about yourself for three hundred pages is a bit much. *Final Payments*—I've said this a million times—is not about me, but I'm tempted to that setting, the setting of Irish Catholicism. But if you write a good novel, who cares where it comes from? Virginia Woolf says about Charlotte Brontë: "always to be a governess and always to be in love is no advantage in a world in which most people are neither." On the other hand, we have *Jane Eyre* and *Villette* and I'm terribly glad we do. I don't care that she was being autobiographical. I care about the novel.

DCC: Virginia Woolf said there's such a thing as a female sentence. She never expanded on it. But there are people who are working to create a feminist criticism. And a lot of female artists insist that female metaphors, for example, are very different. . . .

MG: It might be true, but it's nothing I think about. I mean, I wonder about it, but I certainly don't wonder about it while I'm writing. I think it's much more simple than that; I think that women have a proclivity, women are trained to be more associative, and they're trained to be more interested in human relations, and so that's what they're going to tend to write about in their novels. That's what I'm interested in, and because I think other things are trivial, I'm perfectly happy with that. I don't read many novels that don't have women in them, I don't read many novels about men shooting up other men and finding out what their penises are for. That bores me to death. I'll read about what happens in the drawing room in Somerset by the hand of Jane Austen for fifty years, but don't ever ask me to read Conrad again.

DCC: Well, you have met with tremendous success, and Graham Greene said something marvelous: "For the serious writer as for the priest, there is no such thing as success."

MG: Except in practical terms, if you have some money you have more time, and that's important. But on a profound level it's perfectly true: the only thing that matters is what you're doing in front of the page, and this has nothing to do with what anybody thinks about it.

DCC: Diane Keaton took an option on *Final Payments*. Can mediums be transferred? John Cheever says no.

MG: I don't think about it. If they make a movie I have nothing to do with it.

DCC: You would prefer it done well, but—

MG: Sure, but if it means that I could buy a house in Cape Cod, I would like to have a house in Cape Cod. I would feel terrific responsibility for anything I wrote. But because it's a different medium, I feel no responsibility for it. Even if they did it well, it wouldn't be mine anymore, so good luck to them. I just don't want to hear about it.

DCC: What is the role of an editor? You have published in *Redbook, Mademoiselle*, etc. Is there any kind of critical help on their part? Or is it a *fait accompli* when the story is submitted?

MG: You have to be very tough. If they say, "we are going to cut out the whole middle paragraph because we have an ad for shampoo there," you just have to say, "Well, you can't do that." They cut things up and you just have to be ferocious.

DCC: That's outrageous. Isabel feels that her father's stroke cleanses her sin and is "the mechanism of forgiveness." What is the nature of her sin?

MG: Betraying her father.

DCC: Well, that leads me to the next question. The relationship between Isabel and her father is emotionally incestuous. They are "connected by flesh"; her sexual relationship with David is a kind of punishment because her father is not jealous; she says that she has "borne the impress of his body all my life"; and she keeps Margaret from her father and is jealous that he has sent her money, written to her and sent her Christmas presents; she's angry at Eleanor's confession that she had sexual fantasies about her father; Isabel says: "I loved him more than anyone else"; her father says: "I love you more than I love God. I love you more than God loves you." What part does this play in the motion of Isabel's life?

MG: Well, it's overwhelmingly clear. I do want to say that there is something overwhelming about their love for one another and not quite right. Romantic and compelling as it is, there's no way for her to be an adult as long as her father is alive. So although it is very attractive because it is so all-consuming, it is in some sense damaging to her as what we would call a healthy person. But she manages to survive it because there is that love there. Another writer that I love is Tillie Olsen, and one of the messages of Tillie Olsen that has been very instructive to me is that even "warped" love is somehow life-giving and in the end it will probably come out okay. I do believe that in some sort of very primitive way. That love, that any passionate attachment is all to the good.

DCC: In your excellent article on Archbishop Lefebvre, I felt that the modern world disappoints you. It is Kresge's not Balmain's. Is there a world where words like "sublime," "miracle," "mystery," "immutability," "the impossible," are realized and compatible with "certainty" and "authority"?

MG: Probably, but it would be such an awful world that I would never want to live there. People do such terrible things in the search for certainty and sublimity. You could say that's what the Nazis were looking for. That really is the root of totalitarianism. I think one must hunger for that and yet not try to put it into practice. But as a hunger it makes you much more interesting.

DCC: In reference to your next book, you said that you "want to be talking about women and their spiritual mentors, and the female habit of abdicating responsibility for their inner lives to the men—priests, lovers—who in one way or another compel them." Could you expand on that?

MG: I think we've always thought that anything not rooted in the flesh is the realm of men. So that if a woman had aspirations to be anything but rooted in the flesh, she had to go to another man for it. And he would tell her what she was really like. She would never go to another woman because she was mucking around in the same "unsublime" area. And this kind of habit of women saying "tell me what I'm like" to a man and believing him against all sorts of evidence, and then being willing to radically change your life is a very big pattern in everything from professors and students, to husbands and wives, to the Manson family, and it just seems to have very strong ramifications. Women believe that men have all the interesting data in some way. I hope it's changing now.

Mary Gordon

Barbara A. Bannon / 1981

From *Publishers Weekly*, 6 February 1981, 274–75. © 1981 Publishers Weekly. Reprinted by permission.

On a very cold afternoon in January a PW interviewer waits in the Random House offices to talk with Mary Gordon whose new novel is *The Company of Women*. It is a cozy scene, books along one wall, armchairs and sofa, soft lights, a thick rug on the floor. This last will prove useful.

Gordon comes in, most unaffectedly carrying a large, downy duffel bag and her three-month-old daughter, Anna, named after Mary Gordon's mother. The immediate need is for Anna to have some nourishment, so she is nursed during the interview except when her diapers are being changed. Out of the duffel bag comes a quilted pad that makes a comfortable cushion on the rug. Anna is a most amiable child, and her rapport with her mother is evident and constant—from happy sounds to wide smiles.

Mary Gordon's first novel, *Final Payments* (also Random House), received excellent reviews and was a candidate for a National Book Critics Circle award. It dealt with a grown daughter's response to her father's death—and much more besides.

"I was interested in the phenomenon of women who take care of their families," Gordon says. "For my generation to have to do that is an anomaly, both a genuine and a false sacrifice."

The new novel, *The Company of Women*, introduces five women whose lives revolve around a charismatic Roman Catholic priest and depicts with irony and insight the way in which the spiritual "daughter" of them all (the actual daughter of one of the women) makes it on her own. She does not do so, however, without a funny and savage encounter with the drug-sexual scene of the 1960s, centered on a professor named Robert.

"Elizabeth Hardwick told me I had to tone Robert down," Gordon says. "She told me: 'He's just too awful. *No one* would sleep with him the way you've written about him.' I made some changes."

Gordon talks about her own family background easily. She is married to Arthur Cash, a professor at the state university in New Paltz, New York. It is

17

for her a second marriage, a first child. "Yes," she says with a broad grin, "I was absolutely delighted it was a girl; now I feel free to have a boy."

In an essay Gordon wrote, "I discovered that what I loved in writing was not distance but radical closeness . . . the company of other women writers. Men are not as good at being friends with one another as women are."

The Roman Catholic background is very much there in both of Gordon's novels. It is a major experience in her life out of which she is writing, and yet it is one to which readers with no such personal affiliation can respond.

Gordon's own father was Jewish. He was converted to Roman Catholicism in 1937, when he became an ardent supporter of Franco in Spain. "My father was a writer and a right wing Catholic," she says. "He was quite well educated. He went to Harvard for a year, but all of the publications with which he was associated would inevitably fold. He romanticized working-class Catholicism. (Have you read Georges Bernanos—marvelous novels but a hateful man?) My father wanted me to be scholarly. He died when I was eight."

"I went to Catholic schools in Long Island and Queens. Then I practically ran away from home—not literally, but it seemed that way—to commute to Barnard College in Manhattan.

"My mother is the daughter of Irish and Italian immigrants. She had polio as a child, and she walks with braces and a cane. She works for a law firm, drives a car, has lived in the same house for 60 years. My parents met through a Roman Catholic priest. The metaphor of Catholicism, the Catholic way of looking at the world, these are in my bones. It is my framework of language."

Readers of The Company of Women should know that Charlotte, the resilient, tough-talking, supportive and strongest woman in the novel is modeled on Anna Gordon, Mary's mother. "I wrote a line for Charlotte, and about two months later my mother actually said the exact same thing," Gordon says in baffled delight.

Talking about the published history of her two novels, Gordon says, "I had met Margaret Drabble in England. Peter Matson was her agent, and it was through her that Final Payments came to him. It went to Viking and Knopf written in the third person. Then it came to Anne Freedgood at Random House, and she suggested writing it in the first person. It was finished soon after."

Gordon has taught writing courses for five years at community colleges and at Amherst. "I think you teach tricks," she says of the experience. "You cannot teach people to have an interesting mind. You cannot give them an ear. You can tell them craftsmanly tricks and give them some kind of map of self-criticism. You can make them see that writers are real people, too, and that there is a certain way in which a writer looks at literature."

Anna Cash's diapers have been changed now, and she is showing signs of wanting a more interesting environment than the Random House rug.

Gordon sums up what she wants to achieve in her own writing, in both novels and short stories.

"What I want to accomplish is to tell stories about real people, to tell the truth about human beings in human situations, the way in which people live their lives. What has evolved in the role of contemporary women writers is the receptiveness of the audience to *what* they have to say. Now those writers have to think about how *well* they want to say it."

Bundling up Anna, about to take her to spend the evening with her grandmother while she and her husband go to a performance of *The Dialogues of the Carmelites*, Gordon explains how she feels at this moment in time. "I find it much easier to be a mother than a writer; no moral judgments have to be made about an infant. It is a much simpler mode of life, quite enchanting and obsessive."

A Talk with Mary Gordon

Le Anne Schreiber / 1981

From the *New York Times Book Review*, 15 February 1981, 26–28. ©
1980 the New York Times Company. Reprinted by permission.

As a child in Queens, Mary Gordon imagined that she would grow up to be
a very elegant writing nun: "I thought I'd write poetry in my habit and lead
a very disciplined life. A very cool life." As a kind of self-styled training,
she wrote religious treatises with titles that ended in question marks, like
"What is Prayer?" by Mary Gordon, age 8. But visions of the cool life ended
with childhood, and although Miss Gordon at 31 still admits the allure of a
life of single-minded devotion, she says that she has chosen instead "a life
of ordinary human happiness."

On one recent snowy afternoon in New Paltz, N.Y., ordinary human happiness seemed to consist of a loaf of fresh bakery bread, a generous supply of
Pepperidge Farm butter cookies and a steady flow of heat from the wood-
burning stove in the kitchen of an odd, neo-Victorian home that reminds its
owners of "The House of Usher." Sitting contentedly in her mother's lap
was three-month-old Anna, wearing what her mother calls her "papal nun-
cio" look, "smugly satisfied and judgmental."

"I'm giving myself six months to just live in a moronic haze of milk,"
says Mary Gordon, who also remarked that she desperately wanted her first
child to be a girl. Arthur Cash, Anna's father, is giving himself a year's leave
from his position as chairman of the English department at the nearby state
university to help his wife with the baby. Like the heroine of her new novel,
who wants to spare her daughter the burden of being "the family hope,"
Mary Gordon wants to bestow upon Anna the most ordinary of childhoods,
free from the extravagant literary and religious expectations that daunted her
heroines and herself. And indeed there is a very standard version of "Pat the
Bunny" on the book shelves in the nursery. Next to it, however, is a five-
volume set of C. S. Lewis, that purveyor of literate, Christian allegories for
children.

The romance of religion is very seductive. In the interview that follows,
Mary Gordon talks about this and the other concerns that are central to her
fiction.

Q: Are you still a believing Catholic?

A: I consider myself a Catholic, I have a real religious life in a framework which I think of as Catholic. But I don't think John Paul II would be real pleased with it. . . . I think one of the things that helped me in life is Flannery O'Connor's statement that you must remember that in this day and age one must suffer because of the church and not for the church.

Q: What is most troubling to you about the church?

A: The issue that is the most upsetting to me is the failure to ordain women, because the church's other positions—on birth control and abortion, for instance—which are quite crazy, at least have some moral root, if skewed. But the prejudice against ordaining women has no possible moral root under any interpretation. I thought that nun who stood up to the Pope was one of the bravest people I have ever heard of, because I know what that weight of authority is, and that weight of tradition. It's one of the things I was writing about in *The Company of Women*, the relationship between the male spiritual authority and the female.

Q: Do you see the relation of the women to Father Cyprian as typical of relations between women and their mentors?

A: Yes, definitely. It seems to me one of the things that most interested me in *The Company of Women* is female powerlessness in relation to male power, the phenomenon of women who are very powerful with each other and very powerful in their own lives and powerful in their outside accomplishments, but who will suddenly buckle to the authority of a male mentor, whether it's a priest or professor or a lover. Women with a kind of zeal to abandon the powerfulness of their lives to a male who claims authority. I think it's very pervasive, and I think it's a big problem in relations between men and women. So I did think that the relationship between Father Cyprian as a priest to these women as believers was very archetypal.

Q: Felicitas reads and rereads *Jane Eyre*. Was the relationship between Jane Eyre and Rochester the model for the relation of Felicitas and Cyprian?

A: Yes, and I even have Cyprian at the end weakened by age in the way that Brontë really did a job on poor Mr. Rochester. I mean he's blind and symbolically castrated. Of course he's going to be good at the end—he has no other choice. . . . And the pleasure that Jane has at the end! Of coming back to a blind, crippled Mr. Rochester and saying, "Yes, well now I'll take over."

Q: And yet Cyprian, though weakened at the end, remains at the center of your heroine's life.

A: I think for her it has to be that way, because I really make her a very radical case. But what I think is the positive side of people like Cyprian is that they stand for a kind of absolute standard and passion and uncompromis-ingness and some notion of the ideal. Without which I think life is very impoverished. . . . That's what I wanted to say . . . that what he stood for, that wonderful, crazy, destructive but somehow very compelling sense of the ideal, would be at the center of her life. Once she had de-idealized the human casing of it.

Q: Cyprian remains mentor to Felicitas, but she describes her mind as better than his, more supple.

A: Well, because I think that absolutists never really have first-rate minds—they're too rigid—but they are passionate minds. And so I think that contact with that sort of absolutism, tempered by experience or compassion or mercy or gorgeous common sense, in the end makes the best sort of mind, the best sort of soul to have.

Q: The heroines of both your novels come to a rather sudden and absolute rejection of the possibilities of romantic or sexual love. Are we to understand this as a wise choice?

A: Both of my heroines have been in some way damaged by male author-ity. And so they've been rendered unfit for ordinary life. I think I was clearer about that with Felicitas than I was with Isabel in *Final Payments*. She sees ordinary life as a definite comedown from the exalted ideal that she grew up with, and I want that to be seen as a kind of damage that is done these women. And it is the damage of any kind of romance. I think romance believed too strongly too early is damaging. Whether it's the romance of sexual love or the romance of religion or the romance of political purity. It is damaging.

Q: How autobiographical are your heroines?

A: I think I'd be less than honest if I said they're nothing like me. They're not me. But there is at once the "there but for the grace of God go I" feeling about them and the envy of their kind of absoluteness, which I have not chosen for myself and which I really try to work against. And so it is a way of my having the absolute life without living it, without living the kind of life which obviously upsets me.

Q: Has there been any framework of values you've been exposed to as an adult that has the resonance for you that Catholicism does?

A: No. But feminism comes closest to it. Absolutely. But precisely because feminism is postulated on democratic theories, it breaks down very often into a kind of infighting, which is how I see the movement right now. We're all going off in about 55 different directions. And there's not the cohesion . . . And the thing about the church, which is why it's so resonant, is that it does seem there is an essential core that seems to last and to go on, to retain its language, to retain its ritual, to retain—I like to think—some central values that are immutable. Whereas anything that is modern in conception—because the modern sensibility demands change all the time—doesn't have the resonance that builds up over time.

Q: How much hold upon your imagination did notions of the Immaculate Conception, the virgin birth, the lives of the virgin martyrs, have?

A: Well, the Immaculate Conception happens to be my birthday. I think the whole notion of purity has been—and is—very important to me. Now I've redefined it from a narrow and, I think, wrong definition of it as sexual chastity. Purity and chastity seem to be two extremely different things. But I think that ideal of unencumberedness, of commitment, of passion, is very much with me, and very much came out of those images of the virgin martyrs. That notion of an unencumbered, devoted, directed singular life has always been very much in my imagination, although I don't live that way. I can't.

Q: Did you think about writing in terms of a vocation?

A: Yes, absolutely. From early childhood I knew what I was going to be, and I felt it demanded devotion and discipline, and it had to have the same kind of purity as a religious vocation. . . . I think the image of the nun is something that every Cathoic girl works against and with or plays off in some way. Which is very different from other religious traditions. You do have the notion of a woman, without men, living a very pure centered life which has nothing to do with the domestic.

Q: Would you call yourself a feminist writer?

A: Sure. What is terribly important to me, deeply important—and this is where I feel a sense of vocation—is to write about issues that are central to women's lives, to write about them beautifully and in high style. . . . I'm so aware of how I was liberated by the women's movement, and I feel a sense of vocation in putting in the style of the great tradition the issues that consciousness has opened up to me. Not to use Leavis's phrase, because his "great tradition" and mine are different. But to keep standards of beauty and excellence in writing, to follow in that tradition, but to use the insights that I've been given because of my great good fortune in having been a young adult when the women's movement was first starting out.

Q: Is writing about women in what you call the high style a way of bestowing value upon that experience?

A: Yes. It's a way of being faithful to the worth of that experience. And it's also a way of not allowing high style to become atrophied, because new experiences are fed into it. If this tradition which I value so enormously is going to continue to be lively, it has to use its grace, its elegance, its precision to come to terms with experiences that are new.

Q: To write with grace, elegance and precision, do you have to struggle against the temptation to be polemical, to be angry?

A: Yes. For instance one of the things that I had a lot of trouble with was the character of Robert in *The Company of Women*. In the first version, he was so awful that a friend of mine said nobody would have gone to bed with him. I mean, it's just that nobody's that horrible. Felicitas has to like him; there had to be something about him that made her fall in love with him for whatever skewed reasons. But I'm so angry with that kind of man—and that kind of abuse of sexuality and power—that it was hard for me to remember the ideals of . . . well, what you really have to do is create a character who is neither a hero nor a villain, but who makes sense in some human terms. I think my temptation is not so much to polemic as to vitriol, and I have to work against that.

Q: Do you think it's harder for you to create a lover than a father?

A: Oh, infinitely. I'm not very good at writing about sexual men. The only men that I write about well, I desex somehow, and it is a failing of mine, a way in which my consciousness, what I know about the world, gets in the way of my art. . . . Some of my best friends are men. I do love men. I have had wonderful relationships and deep friendships and things like that, but I can't write about that. I just can't do it. Because my sense is so much that the overall structure is so perverted, and that a perverted attitude toward women is so much the norm for men.

Q: Are you going to return to the terrain of Catholic girlhood and to these issues between men and women in your next novel?

A: In my next book, I'm not putting anybody's childhood in, and so I'm really consciously working very hard at trying to achieve the same kind of richness of texture in some other place. I don't know whether I can do it yet. I just started. . . . I'm hoping to write something which opens out to the world a little bit more. And to find a language which is less the language of memory, less the language of childhood, but that has its own density and its own shape. I think it's going to be hard. But I think I have to do it if I'm not going to be self-indulgent. I can't keep repeating myself all the time. I guess. Sometimes I think I can.

Moral Aerobics

Susan Bolotin / 1985

From *Vogue*, April 1985, 232, 234. © 1985 Susan Bolotin. Reprinted by permission.

Interviewers have plagued Mary Gordon with questions about the autobiographical in her fiction ever since the celebrated publication of her first novel, *Final Payments*, in 1978. Ms. Gordon believes it was "the rubric of Catholicism" in both that book and her second, more difficult novel, *The Company of Women*, that made "people's latent voyeurism more respectable. Catholicism seemed like a very exotic, foreign terrain," she says. "They assumed that whatever religious life I might have was theirs to ask about in a way they wouldn't have dared ask about my sexual life. To me it's just as intimate."

With the publication this month of *Men and Angels* (Random House), Ms. Gordon will see her theory tested. The story of a woman—wife, mother, art historian—who becomes the object of an unlikable younger woman's obsessive affection, this novel has nothing to do with Catholicism, though, as Gordon points out, "the failure of love is certainly a religious theme."

My suspicion is that the shift in theme won't inhibit the curious: writers will continue to explicate her text, and her life, looking for the real Mary Gordon. Once again, she's written a compelling, literate, and probably commercial novel of ideas. And once again, the issues that trigger those ideas resonate with Mary Gordon's own experience—as wife, a mother, a writer.

Can one love the unloveable? Anne, the book's heroine, wonders. ("What made me want to write this book," Ms. Gordon says, "was knowing a couple of young women who were quite damaged, and who clearly needed me to love them, and for whom I could feel nothing but revulsion. I closed off love to them, and there was nothing I could do about it.") Can one balance a professional life and a maternal one? Anne needs to know. (Ms. Gordon, who is thirty-four, has borne two children—as well as two books—since *Final Payments*.) Can one push out the traditional limits of friendship and marriage? ("The history of women is the history of a great deal of thwarting. It's very wicked.")

But there's another reason people ask Mary Gordon questions: she answers them. She is open, intelligent, opinionated, passionate, committed to conversation; a joy. She assumes intelligence in her interviewer much as she supposes that her readers care as deeply as she does about ideas, character, politics, ethics.

"I always have been something of a fatalist," she says. "I think that's a very Irish perspective. But every novelist has to believe that character is more important than outside events, or he or she would not be a novelist—unless you were someone like Gorky. Even with Defoe, or Fielding, or Tolstoy, or Thackery, who include a lot of the outside world in their books, the reason we read the novel is to find out about the inner workings. As the outside world impinges, it impinges on that particular individual, whom we know in a very inner way."

Ms. Gordon speaks easily, with the clarity of someone who performs daily blitzkriegs on equivocation. She tosses off a definition of a moral person— someone who is "highly moral while always being afraid he is immoral"—as matter-of-factly as some might define a table to a child. It is no surprise, then, that both *Final Payments* and *The Company of Women* were, quite specifically, full of absolute judgments about what makes a life well-lived. *Men and Angels* is just as decent—"I was very interested in the problem of charity," she says, "what in the early Christian community was called *caritas*, doing well by those in need"—but the judgments passed are somehow softer, more humane.

"Maternity makes you much more humble about the moral life," Ms. Gordon explains. "The most important things in my life are the feelings I feel for the children; no abstract moral idea could compromise that or could have anything like their potency. I think about it all the time: what would I sacrifice the children for? If I were in Germany, what would I have done?"

How would she have solved *Sophie's Choice*, I wonder. "I'd have killed all three of us," she answers instantly. She stops to laugh at herself: "My husband thinks I'm insane to think about these things all day, but I've made him promise that if he's ever in the situation, he will save the children—never me or him."

Ms. Gordon brings a similar artlessness to her opinions about feminism. ("I can't imagine how anybody who has a daughter could not be a feminist.") She knows she is lucky never to have had to sublimate her desire—her *need*—to produce valued and valuable work to her urge for maternity.

"Most of the conflicts that women have about work and domestic life are largely invented by a society that doesn't give a damn if women either contribute to the society or get something out of it," she says. "People can't afford not to work, and it makes me furious, absolutely enraged about the world, that the conflict could be so easily solved—if parents could share child care, if people could have more flexible working arrangements, if people could have places to put their children in that didn't terrify them. The conflict *must* be solved: it's one of the most immoral things in our society.

"It's very unnatural for *one* woman to be in *one* house with two or three children all day long. It's very crazy-making. It gives you the illusion that you have more power over your children than you really do, and it makes you feel powerless in the outside world. The price one pays for not having a life in the outside world is that mothers become tyrannical; they don't want to let their children go."

Both *Final Payments* and *The Company of Women* dealt with troubled and intense relationships with fathers (of the familial or clerical but always difficult type). And in *Men and Angels*, Anne confronts her crisis of ethics and choice during a year when her husband—and the father of her children—is in France on a sabbatical. It seems fair to ask Ms. Gordon if she's perhaps letting fathers off easy in her scenario of tyranny.

"Yes," she agrees. "But it's so much harder for a man to be good than it is for a woman. Automatically more powerful, men have much more opportunity to misuse power. There are immense exceptions, but I think that men are brought up, or have been in the past, to be less conscious of the feelings of other people.

"If you told a man that being nice to his kid could be a turn-on, he would think you were nuts. Tenderness is *so* sexy. But the truly sexy thing about a man is to love women. There aren't very many who do, and so that rarity makes it more valuable."

I've fallen into the trap of treating Ms. Gordon as a social commentator rather than a novelist, and I apologize. Ever the lady and always the good sport, she reassures me: "What else are you going to ask?"

"Well, whom do you read?" I mutter, trying to save face. "The three writers I read over and over again are Virginia Woolf, Jane Austen, and Ford Madox Ford. There is so much beauty in those sentences, and the people are so interesting. I'm not a great Proust fan—I recognize that the sentences are beautiful, but are these people I care about? Not a whole lot—but I get a physical pleasure from reading those other sentences. There is a great human sympathy and a real artistic perfection drawing together.

"Among contemporary authors, I find myself attracted to women, because I think we're doing the most interesting work. The tendency of the novel is to get more abstract and removed and cold, and we are fighting that, on the whole. There are these bad specters—Ann Beattie is one. The other, John-Updike-kind of bad specter is to be as macho as you please, but to use a kind of fake lyricism, as if that wipes out everything.

"John Updike never writes about a genuine inner life, but he uses a sentence that takes up four lines, and that is supposed to be poetry; well, it's not. I don't know why people don't nail him. He's so horrified by the female body, I feel like saying to him, 'Well, then, stop fucking these women if they are so disgusting. Stop *doing* it, and then telling us how loathsome the whole thing is. Just shut up, or go do it with a guy, but just stop already.' It makes me crazy."

For her next novel, Mary Gordon will again change venues. "It sounds like a TV mini-series, but it's going to be about a woman, now in her nineties, who emigrated from Ireland. She's dying, and it's about how the experience of immigration affects different generations, and how it still has an effect on my generation, but how I think we'll really be the last. It's been done for the Jews, but I don't think anybody's talked about the experience of Irish immigration—except for schlock novelists." Always the moralist, Ms. Gordon smiles. "I think it's too good a subject for them to have."

Margaret Drabble and Mary Gordon: Writers Talk Ideas of Our Time

Margaret Drabble and Mary Gordon / 1985
Clare Doylan, introduction

Transcription of video from *Writers in Conversation* film series, The Roland Collection of Films on Art. Copyright 1985 The Institute of Contemporary Arts. Printed by Permission.

Clare Doylan *(reads from Mary Gordon's novel,* Men and Angels):

People who were interested in the achievements of women wanted the grossest facts: Whom did they sleep with? Did they have babies? Were their fathers kind to them? Cruel to them? Did they obey or go against their mothers? Infantile questions. Yet one felt one had to know. It gave courage somehow. One had to believe that the price was not impossible for these accomplished women, that there were fathers, husbands, babies, beautifully flourishing beside the beautiful work. But there so rarely were.

Doylan: Someone once remarked to me that the biggest polarization was not between men and women but between women with children and women without children—for the reason that people normally have either children or a career. Our next two guests both have wonderful, wonderful careers and children *(begins laughing)*—I don't know how wonderful their children are, but I suspect they are. They are going to talk about using children or motherhood in their work.

As writers, these guests really need no introduction at all from me. Mary Gordon achieved instant acclaim with her first novel, *Final Payments*, which deals with the guilts and influences of a Catholic upbringing. And she has written two more novels, *The Company of Women,* and her newest and just published one, *Men and Angels*. The quote with which I introduced this is from her new book, *Men and Angels*. Margaret Drabble is one of our most eminent living writers: novelist, biographer, and most recently editor of the new edition of the *Oxford Companion to English Literature*. And she is also a heroine to a generation of women who have read her work as Bible as well as literature. Everyone will be delighted to know that she is now at work on a new novel, and we're greatly privileged that she has taken time off from this work to be with us today. Margaret Drabble and Mary Gordon.

Both Drabble and Gordon speak without notes directly to the audience.

Margaret Drabble: Mary and I decided that we will both speak fairly briefly and read a passage out of our work each, and then hope that we would get some responses from you, some questions and discussions from you.

I am very much a woman who has written while producing a family. I wrote my first book while I was expecting my first baby. I wrote my second book while I was expecting my second baby. I wrote my third baby while I was expecting my third baby. And then I decided that that was enough babies, and I would keep on with the books. I must say writing my fourth book was extremely difficult because, by that stage, I had produced a little superstition for myself, that there was a complementary action going on between the book and the baby. My fourth novel, *Jerusalem the Golden* [1968], was particularly difficult and sticky to write. Of course, looking back I now realize that was partly because I had three small children under the age of five, who were constantly tripping me up when I was trying to get on with the novel. I did also find, as I became more self-conscious about my own work, that I was looking back through the tradition of the woman's novel to find how other women had written about children, about childbearing, what their experiences of it had been. And of course, looking back to the nineteenth-century woman's novels, I didn't find very many women who had had children.

In the nineteenth century there were distinguished women novelists, but most of them were women who had not themselves had children. One thinks of George Eliot or the Brontë sisters. They were not themselves mothers. The only eminent nineteenth-century novelist, perhaps I could say, who did have children was Mrs. Gaskell [Elizabeth Cleghorn Gaskell]. She had, I think, five children. And I did find something eminently sympathetic in her work, when I came to it, because I could tell that she was writing about some areas of experiences that the other women weren't touching on.

When one looks at Jane Austen's descriptions of children, one can feel from her a kind of perfectly permissible recoil. In *Persuasion* [1818], there's a scene where one of the nieces or nephews climbs on Anne's back and messes up her hair. One feels that Jane Austen didn't really enjoy that kind of experience. Although she was everybody's favorite aunt, sometimes they went too far. Similarly with Charlotte Brontë. One feels that she didn't enjoy being a governess. The only other job a woman could do, apart from writing, was being a governess. She didn't like little children. They tormented her. She took her revenge in some of her descriptions of children.

Mrs. Gaskell enjoyed it more because she had her own children, which—as Mary and I probably agree—is a great way of converting one to liking children. You like them because you've got to, because they're there. And only in Mrs. Gaskell did I find the kind of descriptions of how babies behaved. In *Mary Barton* [1848] there's a description of breastfeeding, which I think is one of the earliest descriptions of breastfeeding in fiction. There's a description of spoon-feeding where the husband, whose wife has died, is trying to feed this two-year-old. And he's shoving the spoon into the baby's mouth, and the baby keeps making its mouth all square, and the food runs out. One feels this is a description by someone who really knew what it was like.

One has to wait a long time before one finds other writers who have that familiarity with the domestic details of childhood and who consider maternity an important subject. It is interesting to note parenthetically that Mrs. Gaskell started writing—I've always found this interesting—when her little boy died of either measles or scarlet fever and her husband (who has always had a bad press, but in fact I think he was a generous and sensitive man) said, "Why don't you write a book to take your mind off your grief?" So her writing career, in a sense, sprang out of a child substitute, and I've often felt myself . . . Even Jane Austen said that her books were her babies. So there is not a contradiction between the two, but often a parallel between the two.

After Mrs. Gaskell, there is a long, long gap when there didn't seem to be any women writing sympathetically about children. There were poems by Christina Rossetti about lost children, fairy babies, but nothing very practical and familiar. Virginia Woolf did not have children. Dorothy Richardson did not have children. One feels there was a tradition of choice. As Clare said, there was a choice. You either did one career or the other. It wasn't expected that you should do both.

What happened, I think, in recent decades was that an educated generation of women—who had been educated by Virginia Woolf to demand equal rights, freedom, true equality—had decided that they *would* be equal, and they would do both. They would have babies, and they would have careers. And in the late '50s, early '60s, you had the protests of the women who found that they couldn't do it. Although on paper they could, although in their heads they could, in practice there weren't enough hours in the day, their husbands were uncooperative, they were constantly exhausted, they never got enough sleep.

That particular feeling of frustration and false position, I think, erupted in a clutch of novels, of which perhaps the focal one, as Fay Weldon said earlier today, was Doris Lessing's *The Golden Notebook* in 1962. But surrounding *The Golden Notebook* there were several other novels. There was Nell Dunn's first novel. There was Penelope Mortimer's *The Pumpkin Eater* [1962], which was about a woman who had so many children she didn't know what to do and whose husband obliged her to have a hysterectomy because he was having an affair with the *au pair* girl. It's rather a crude summary of the plot, but that in fact is what happens. There was Edna O'Brien's first early novels about sexuality and then about marriage and children. There were Sylvia Plath's poems about breastfeeding. I've looked for a long time to find somebody describing what it was like to get up in the early morning. And there is Sylvia Plath's very tender, not at all depressing or violent poem, "Morning Song," in which she describes getting up in her floral, victorian nightgown and feeding the baby.

So it's as though there was a mixture of celebration of the writing woman's new role and *fury* that one couldn't actually do the two things very smoothly together. I published my own first novel in 1963, which was when this new kind of domestic realism was being produced. I hadn't then read *The Golden Notebook*, and when I read *The Golden Notebook* two or three years later, it was a revelation that one could say all these things: one could describe a life that was both a literary life, a life of friendships and politics, *and* a life that included bringing up difficult children with difficult husbands, vanished husbands, difficult lovers. This was real, and the novel managed to survive the stress that produced it.

Since then there's been a flood of women novelists treating this kind of domestic material. And most of these women have had children and have written also about the experience of incorporating children into this modern style of life, very different from the life of Jane Austen and Charlotte Brontë. The kind of muddle that we get into is a different kind of muddle altogether. We're now free to describe what it's like to give birth to a baby, we're free to describe what it's like to try to feed a baby. We're free to describe the fury that one sometimes feels with one's own dearly beloved children. The taboos have been lifted in that area.

I remember in Doris Lessing's Martha Quest series, there's a description, which is really remarkably similar to Mrs. Gaskell's, about trying to spoon-

feed an angry toddler. The scene consists of Martha Quest trying to feed a
baby in a high chair. And watching this scene is an older male friend of
Martha. Martha is trying to appear, as we all do, the perfect mother, loved by
her child, expert at all the domestic chores. The baby doesn't want its food,
doesn't like it for some reason and is shutting its mouth. The food is dribbling
down. Martha is trying more and more to have a conversation with the man,
and in the end, she ends up by getting a hold of the child's head and ramming
the spoon in. And then she feels she has failed on every front. And I think
that many people would recognize the truth of that kind of situation. It may
be a small domestic incident, but to many people, it is a true confrontation.
Mary has written of such scenes in her latest novel, *Men and Angels*.

It is very hard to decide—as Don Thomas was saying about sex—how
important one should allow one's children to be in one's books, the experience of one's children. It's a very common experience. It doesn't involve
everybody. Some people are bored by descriptions of children. Some people
consider it an exclusive maternal sorority of people who are only interested
in talking about breastfeeding and antenatal clinics and postnatal clinics.
Nevertheless for a period of one's life, the period when one's going through
it, it is extremely important. It is a kind of sisterhood. I remember being
astonished myself by my interest in talking about washing machines and
disposable nappies and breastfeeding and hours of sleep. This kind of subject
matter. I now feel I don't have to write about it in quite the same way. I tend
to leave railway compartments when I see a baby in them these days, instead
of looking at it with great interest. But for a period of my life it was a very
important spring in my work. And I'd like to finish these comments by reading a passage from my novel *The Millstone* [1966].

*Before reading from pages 146–151, Drabble sets up the context of the
long passage, during which she mentions:* And so I wrote this book which
was about the experience of having a baby and the terrible way it exposures
you to grief and sorrow. You're given a hostaged fortune. You are opened up
in a way you never thought you'd need to be.

(after reading, applause)

Mary Gordon: I decided to write a novel that had to do with mothers and
children in writing *Men and Angels*, which I began writing about two weeks
before my first child was born and finished writing when my second child
was six months old. So I wrote the entire thing through a glaze of pregnancy
and lactation [and a miscarriage between the two children], which, if some

people don't like it, could be the reason why. And one of the things that was difficult for me—because I am a person who likes to feel I am by nature not someone who takes a great deal of pleasure thinking I've done something new. I love being in the *derrière garde*. No pleasure to me in breaking new ground—I kept looking, with a kind of desperation, for models of writing about children that I could feel comfortable with, safe with, so I didn't feel I was doing it alone.

Luckily I had Maggie Drabble's models to guide me. But I tried to look back in history and I found a very peculiar thing, which was that there were two kinds of writing about children, one of which was written from the child's point of view . . . and one of which could have been extraordinary. People like Henry James, paradoxically enough, whom one thinks of being born bald and middle aged with a weskit, writes extraordinarily about children. His novel *What Maisie Knew* [1897] I learned a tremendous amount from, precisely because it was so unnatural in its writing about children. One of the things I learned in reading James was that a great mistake that some of these contemporary novelists, I thought, had made in writing about children was that they tried to make the children sound as children sound in real life, which transfers very, very badly to paper. You merely then get a series of precocious monsters or idiots. And I looked at a particular sentence in *What Maisie Knew*, and it gave me a great sense of liberation, because the sentence went, "And Maisie realized that she began to shade over into the edge of consciousness." Now very few five-year-olds are capable of formulating those exact words.

I felt a similar liberation in reading Virginia Woolf's *The Waves*, when the six-year-old Jinny says to herself, "I want a fiery dress. I want a fulvous dress." Again, "fulvous" is not a word which springs immediately to the mind of your average pre-schooler. But it worked perfectly in the context, precisely because the convention of naturalism had been dashed in favor of a more poetic truth.

Katherine Mansfield was a similar inspiration to me because she had moved away from feeling constrained to describe children as if we felt a responsibility to tape-record the conversations that we'd heard on the bus. She moved into the realm that I think is more true to the reality of a child's consciousness, which is an extremely dense, sensual, and poetic kind of texture which is, I think, the way that children live, which distinguishes them from us. They don't have a kind of editing mechanism, which tells them: This is important to my getting through the world. This is not important. I will jettison it. They experience things in a sort of unedited but very packed way. And in reading those novelists who backed away almost deliberately from the domestic detail—who are the opposite of Mrs. Gaskell in a particular way—I felt that I had learned an important lesson, which made me not afraid to write about children.

I think there's been a kind of counter-phobia on the part of women who have children about writing about children—as if we felt that men thought, "Well, after all, that's all they think about," so therefore we better write about the nature of the novel or the nature of violence or sado-masochism or something. So I was frightened to write the novel. And of negative reactions I've had both to this novel and to a piece I wrote about mothers and children that was published in *Cosmopolitan*. It was first published in the *New York Times*. I seemed to press the button of a fantastic anger in women who were very angry that I was suggesting that it was possible to enjoy one's children, that it was possible not to see them as a terrible barrier to achievement and freedom and all those things we had fought and bled and died for in the years of the revolution. I got extraordinarily angry letters from people who felt I had betrayed the cause of feminism, because I had tried to write about this, to me, very potent and evocative and very sensual relationship between mothers and children. I felt that the extreme sensuality of a mother's relationship with her children had not been written about, and it was something I was very interested in writing about. The truth of it is: it's a much more physical than intellectual relationship. You have these wonderful, beautiful, delicious pieces of flesh. It's like what Winston Churchill said about beautiful women: no matter how badly they behave, they still go on being beautiful. Your children are like that. It's probably the reason we don't drown them. *(audience laughter)* Because even when they have thrown the mashed potatoes on the floor for the fiftieth time, they still have this terrific skin. *(audience laughter)* I really wanted to write about that, and I had found no models for that. And so I was rather frightened to do that.

That kind of counter-phobia, I think, was an unfortunate fall-out—not of feminism, because I think if feminism hadn't happened no one would think it was really alright to write about mothers and children in this particular way because the tyranny of a writing world, largely dictated largely by the interests and concerns of men, is a hierarchy which says violence, disassociated sexuality, the outside world are the interesting and things to write about and devalues the experiences of women.

I felt that I was really trying to work between two poles. I felt I had Norman

Mailer sneering at me from one corner, "Who wants to hear about that?" And then on the other hand I had Virginia Woolf sort of saying, "Do you really think you can do it?" on the other corner. It was very daunting and very frightening. And I felt that I had a kind of tremendous urge to render the complicated life of both children and mothers in a way that I had missed on the whole in literature. I kept being afraid of cuteness. I was afraid of cuteness. I was afraid of sentimentality. And I was always frightened every time I wrote about these children that I was going to fall into one or another pole. On the other hand, I said to myself: I'm writing a novel about mothers and children; I have to put some mothers and children in, after all. But it was a very frightening thing.

What I tried to learn from James and Woolf and those rather more mandarin masters was to remember to include the complicated life of the child, which included—besides this tremendous sensual component—a moral and intellectual component. So, not to be afraid to give the children a multi-edged personality while, at the same time, trying to avoid precocity. Precocity, it seems to me, is a surface flaw, a desire to make people seem interesting without really looking at the layers of the contradictions that make them interesting.

One of the other things that I wanted to write about in this book was the conflict—which I think is a very straightforward one, and not mythic, and not manageable, but really a matter of time—between work and familial love. I really get very angry at the notion that children are little succubi that steal your breath in the night, and that's why you can't write if you have children. You simply can't write when you have children because you're tired and you don't have enough time. I think that has to be said very strongly. On the other hand, there is a matter of a tension. If you have a life lived in the way that I do, and the way any woman who writes and has children [does], if you divide up the day like that, there's that awful interface between the working life and the domestic life, which is very hard to get through. You're all right when you're doing one thing, and all right when you're doing the other, but when they start to spill over, it becomes a problem. And this is something I wrote about in this scene:

Gordon reads from Chapter Two, pages 15–18.

I'll just read one more scene in which I try to show some other aspects of this [mother-child] relationship. There is a character in this book named Jane who is a childless woman and who in fact becomes the mother to my leading character Anne and that she really needed. One of the themes that I try to discuss in the book is that we're often matched up with the wrong parents, by being stuck with our biological parents and in fact with parents being stuck with their biological children. And that somewhere in the world there are often other mothers and other fathers and other sons and daughters who are a much better match. And one of the great good fortunes in life is sometimes they do hook up. So Anne and the children go to visit Jane, who is this sort of pseudo-mother to Anne.

Gordon reads from Men and Angels, *chapter Eight, pages 123–125 (applause)*

Doylan: Thank you very much, both of you. I'm sure everybody's got lots of questions. Would anybody like to start?

Audience Question: Could you tell me please, how, when your children were preschool-age children, how you coped with their demands and those of your writing. Did you have additional outside help?

Margaret Drabble: Well, I used to write sometime with the baby face down on my knee, which they like—the typewriter up here. They would jiggle, and I would type. And I'd get hopeless girls. That's what Mary's writing about, partly, how you get a hopeless girl. Then you spend your time looking after her, worrying about her headaches, writing her love . . . It was dreadful. What about you, Mary?

Mary Gordon: No. I'm very lucky. I take my children off to this . . . although I live in America, I happen to have a strong Lancashire woman as a babysitter. And I take them off at 9:30, and they have whatever life they have with her, which they never tell me about. God only knows. I know it's much tidier than the life they have with me. That's my only clue. So I work every morning and then I pick them up . . . my older daughter is now in school, so it's just my little one. I pick them up at 1:30 and spend the afternoon with them, which is . . . I have the feeling that most people don't do more than four hours of work. I can't go out to lunch with anybody, or fool around, or talk on the phone, or make coffee. So that's hard. And sometimes it's the end of the morning, and I just have to be there at 1:30, and if I'm writing *War and Peace*, it's too bad. And I guess I have to have some sort of faith that it simmers and that it's not burning to a black tar, rather than simmering into a lovely stew. It's very hard. One gets very tired. That's no secret.

   (Remaining questions and answers are not included on film).

Lynn Neary Talks with Mary Gordon

Lynn Neary / 1986

Transcription of *Weekend All Things Considered,* National Public Radio, 2 March 1986. © 1986 National Public Radio. Printed by permission of Mary Gordon and National Public Radio.

Washington-New York telephone interview

LN: Today in the *New York Times,* an ad signed by more than a thousand Catholics [was] directed at the hierarchy of the Catholic Church. The ad accuses the Church of cracking down on dissidents, particularly activists who signed a petition published in the *Times* over a year and a half ago. The petition claimed there was a diversity of opinion about abortion within the Church. Mary Gordon, the novelist and critic, is a practicing Catholic who signed today's ad. She says that the original activists have been harassed by the Church.

MG: There were psychological pressures and there were very real economic pressures placed on people, even people connected with the signers—people who had relatives working in Catholic hospitals, Catholic institutions of other kinds, being threatened with loss of job because their relatives had even signed the petition.

LN: Mary, why do you and other Catholics with similar beliefs remain in the Catholic Church when your positions on such issues as birth control and abortion are so different from the leadership of the Church?

MG: Because I refuse to lose the richness and the truth of the Catholic Church for issues which do not make up the whole of a religious life. I think the tragedy of the Catholic Church right now is that people leave it for issues connected with sexuality, and there's much more to being a Catholic than life lived from the waist down. What in fact the Church hierarchy does is, by placing so much emphasis on a very narrow interpretation of sexuality, they cut many people off from a religious life, because most people who are in the modern world and live as moderns cannot go along with the Church's position on sexuality. Therefore, what the Church does is say: if you don't agree with us on this one small issue, you must leave. Most people do. It seems to me that both the Church and those people lose a lot. I'm not going to let them do that to me.

LN: Do you ever expect the Catholic Church to change its position on these issues—abortion, birth control?

MG: Well, I think that eventually the Church will have to change. Otherwise, there will be no more Church. The Church, unless it comes around to changing, for example, its position on celibacy is going to find itself with a priestless institution. And I think when that begins to change, and the Church is not run by male celibates, many things will begin to change. I don't know if that will happen in my lifetime, but I know that unless people who believe in change bear some sort of witness for the necessity of change, nothing will happen.

LN: Do you ever talk to friends who have left the Catholic Church for the reasons that you've cited, for mainly sexual reasons, and what do they say about your decision to remain in the Church?

MG: They really think that I'm pipe dreaming. They cannot understand what it is about the Church that attracts me enough to stay, because in fact they've become so embittered they've lost all sense of the beauty and the richness of the Church. And they think that I'm really self-deceived or perhaps intellectually or emotionally weak or even childish to want to stay in the Church. And, you know, one understands that position, but to me they have lost something which they need not have lost if the Church were not so intransigent.

LN: Is taking a public stand against a position of the Catholic Church for you personally painful or in any way perhaps frightening?

MG: It's very frightening. One of the things that happens to you when you're a Catholic woman—and I went to Catholic school for twelve years—is that you're taught the rewards and the pleasures of being a good girl. Obedience is rewarded; freedom of thought is not, in the tradition in which I was brought up. So for me it's very, very frightening. I know a lot of people who care for me are very upset by the fact that I would do this, but it is very important to me that one has to be able to live fully as a human being and still have the potential to be a Catholic. So I have to do this extremely unpleasant, rather frightening, thing. I hate controversy. I hate dissent. I would much rather be quiet and, you know, have everybody love me, but I don't think I have that luxury.

Mary Gordon

Annie Lally Milhaven / 1987

From *The Inside Stories: 13 Valiant Women Challenging the Church*, ed. Annie Lally Milhaven (Mystic, CT: Twenty-Third Publications, 1987), 101–18. © 1987 Annie Lally Milhaven. Reprinted by permission.

Mary Gordon, a novelist whom Catholics claim as one of their own, is the author of *Final Payments*, *The Company of Women*, *Men and Angels*, and *Temporary Shelter*. Mourning what she perceives to be a loss of beauty and majesty, she describes the present barren church scene as agitated "busyness," banners with banal statements, and ill-prepared strummers playing on loud guitars. Her view and vision of both women and church are indeed bleak.

Despite her pessimism, she cherishes the Christ figure in Christianity because Christ represents a vision which no other religion possesses. Her ideal of a fully Christian human being is Pope John XXIII. Believing that he—unlike most church leaders—was unafraid of learning, she yearns for his vision of the church and of all people. She, nevertheless, remains in the Catholic church (albeit on the periphery) for her children's sake. The fellowship of left-wing Catholic groups also attracts her because, as she wistfully notes, "They are my people."

Mary Gordon is an ardent admirer of Virginia Woolf and claims, "The beauty of prose and the beauty of appreciation of nature, and the tremendous rhythmicity of her prose was a real inspiration." These words aptly describe Mary Gordon's own artistry.

Where are you in relation to the church?
Gordon: The institutional church is not at the center of my life. I come in and go out of the institutional church as I have more or less patience for it. I have periods where the whole thing makes me so impatient that I lose hope. I feel so alienated. I feel like these bishops and the pope have nothing in common with me; they have nothing to give me and I leave. It's not a great cost to me to be in or out of the church. But I was impressed with these women for whom the church was at the center of their lives—the sisters—

42

they had really taken very courageous stands. But for me it's not such a courageous stand.

Some of the characters in your novels, especially in Final Payments *and* The Company of Women, *have certain Catholic underpinnings.*

Gordon: I think my characters do, and I do. The underpinnings are certainly there. What I'm not sure about is whether the church that formed me even exists any more so that some of the things that were terribly important to me in the church are aesthetic memories.

Such as?

Gordon: Memories of a kind of silence. The ritual provided a kind of solemnity in the sense of formal beauty—the beauty of the prayers, the beauty of the music.

You're talking about the pre-Vatican II church?

Gordon: Yes. I find very little in the current church to feed me aesthetically. I think the ritual, at best, is nondescript. Sometimes it's actively ugly. And so much of what was important to me was that sense of silence and solemnity that I think is gone now. That doesn't mean that I'm going to go back to the silence and solemnity, because the people who seem to be holding onto the ritual which I liked are politically abhorrent to me. And that is a real problem for me. I'm not going to go into some church where they're suggesting that we send money to the Contras [U.S.-backed rebels in Nicaragua] and, you know, excommunicate anybody who uses birth control, so that I can hear "Pange Lingua." So I feel very lost in both camps because I'm a person for whom beauty is very important. That's my life. I am supposed to create beauty, and to be constantly in the midst of ugliness or mediocrity . . . is to me a grief. It's really a grief to hear ugly music, to be in ugly buildings, to hear ugly or stupid or hackneyed language. It hurts me.

You feel quite alienated, then . . . ?

Gordon: Oh, yes. And a lot of people whose politics I love and admire don't seem to have the same aesthetic and ritual and formal sense of beauty.

Who are these people you admire?

Gordon: Well, people very much on the left, and very much concerned with social justice, seem to put together rituals which to me are quite thin, and therefore empty. And so I feel lonely with them in the same way that I'd feel lonely if I were ever to approach the people on the right who have a more formal ritual. I find a kind of physical repulsion to [those on the right]. I feel no ambivalence in relation to them. My ambivalence is to the sort of people on the left whom I admire, but who have lost the sense of solemnity.

So what's the cure for that?
Gordon: I really don't know. I think it's over. I feel very sad. I don't think that we're in an age that can create great public art. We're not in an age of great architecture; we're not in an age of great communal music in the way that either the Middle Ages were, or the German Protestants in the eighteenth century. Modern aesthetics . . . are on the level of the high, very privatist, and on the level of the low, very jangling—there is no religious expression. The *zeitgeist* of the age is not religious. I think we're not going to come up with any more great religious art that I can see.

Are you saying this for the Catholic church or for the whole of Christendom?
Gordon: The whole world, I mean, not just Christianity. But certainly for the West.

You're very pessimistic.
Gordon: I'm very pessimistic, and I really don't know what to do about my children.

How do you feel about having your children participate in a church whose ceremonies have little meaning for you?
Gordon: The children go and there are people jumping around. Nobody's quiet, and nobody's saying anything that has any depth or richness. The language is ugly. The music is exceedingly ugly. Better that there be no music most times, because it's so bad. Much of what formed me as a child was a reflective spirit, a spirit of reflection and spirit of contemplation and a sense of seriousness that I was participating in something quite ancient and quite solemn.

Can you give me an example of . . .
Gordon: I remember Holy Week as a child.

Ah, yes. Tenebrae . . .
Gordon: . . . Absolutely.

Even James Joyce went back to hear Tenebrae.
Gordon: That's right. And Christmas midnight mass. I can't even go now. It's too painful.

Do you think that some of those sentimental memories are exaggerated?

Gordon: I don't think so; I really don't. Because I can hear the music—I have to hear that music which they played then—on records now. I hear those records, and they trigger in me tremendous memories. When I was in London I went to the Brompton Oratory. They were singing "Pange Lingue"; they were doing the Gregorian Mass. Before the sermon . . . because I could hear what they were talking about, I just experienced the old ritual. I was flooded with those very potent memories. I don't know what there is in the church now that is valuable for my children in terms of ritual. There is a kind of spirit of Catholicism. I think I'll keep them in it, because there's nobody like John XXIII anywhere else. There's no image like that in the world, that I can hold up to them as an image of goodness and open generous love and concern.

Do you resonate with any other figure around, for example like Mother Teresa?

Gordon: Oh, no. She just irritates me, quite frankly.

What about figures like Flannery O'Connor, whom we think of as totally Catholic. How do you perceive her?

Gordon: Well, she's a great artist. I personally don't care what it was that made her able to write those stories. I thank God that those stories exist in the world. I think she had a singular experience. Remember she was stricken with a crippling disease at age twenty-four. Who knows what would have happened to her had she moved out into the world. Maybe she would also have been the way she was. But, I don't care. I honor her art. And if it was that strictness of the church that created it, fine. I'm glad of that accident. I have no quarrel with her. I don't want her to be any different. I don't need her to be different. She is [a] genius.

You described many church flaws in your novels. Do you see yourself as a Catholic?

Gordon: It seems to be who I am; it seems to be who my people are. When I go to Catholics for a Free Choice conferences, those are my people. And I see these people have tremendous ideals. The figure of Christ and that kind of love are very, very important to me. I could not give that up. Catholicism and Judaism seem to me the form of continuum to which I'm very attracted, because of the kind of richness and openness to the world which Protestantism lacks.

Judaism, I feel, is blessed in not being cursed with the dualism that is so much a part of Christianity, which I guess is the legacy of the Greeks. There is that figure who gave everything, even unto death on the cross, that I think is unique to Christianity.

But all the first Christians were Jews. Rosemary Ruether suggests that one group pushed the other out of the synagogue.

Gordon: It was a tragedy. It was a terrible tragedy. But I am not convinced that one can be a Jew without having been brought up a Jew. I think it is something much rooted in the family, in the community. It's a much less privatist experience than Christianity. My father was a Jew who converted to Catholicism in a very thoroughgoing way.

What was growing up with two different religions like?

Gordon: Well, my father was more Catholic than anybody. . . . He was extremely anti-Semitic. He was the most anti-Semitic person you'd ever meet. Nevertheless, every night he said over my head a Hebrew blessing. So it was very odd. I did have a slight oral Hebrew memory. But in terms of being brought up with a Jewish feeling, it was Irish Catholicism all the way.

In The Company of Women, *you say you were fascinated by the way women are dominated by men in the church.*

Gordon: I'm fascinated, appalled, horrified by the way . . . by how hard it is for women to be powerful without appealing to a male authority, and by how easy it is for us to give that over—how the instinct to submit to a man is so thoroughgoing and so deep.

But that's not unique to Catholic women.

Gordon: As a matter of fact, I actually think we Catholic women, because of the experience of having nuns who are at least in a somewhat powerful position . . . are better at seeing women as authority figures. I think the whole authority problem is harder for Catholics than for other people. But it's easier for Catholics, in that there's a notion that there was "Sister" as well as "Father." The presence of the Virgin Mary and the female saints, the presence of nuns who had a powerful position in one's life, which was removed from the domestic—they were not like your mother—I think that gives Catholic women actually more access to female community than other women have. The problem with Catholics is we want to obey somebody, and we're not really so particular whether it's a man or a woman.

Are Catholics, therefore, good candidates for the women's movement?

Gordon: Yes, I think we are. Actually, we're quite overrepresented for numbers in NOW. There's a disproportionate number of Catholic women in NOW, compared to our presence in the general population. I think we are good candidates for the women's movement if we can get over our stance of general obedience.

People who know the women in this volume of interviews feel that Catholic women are up against an impossible task. How can women change the Roman Catholic church?

Gordon: I think if the church lasts, then women will prevail. I think the problem with the church is its insistence on a celibate clergy. It's going to run out of clergy. And I think that's what will do it in. And so if the church endures, it's going to have to be very different within forty or fifty years. You're not going to have these celibate males around running things from Rome, because they're not going to have any audience. And so I'm not sure if it will exist. I'm not sure if the church can exist without a powerful hierarchy, and I just don't see young people flocking into seminaries.

As a matter of fact, in 1986, there were 1,847 parishes without a resident priest in this country. Mary Hunt feels that ten years ago, had the bishops put stoles around the nuns, walked them two-by-two up the aisle, and ordained them, they would have stopped the clergy shortage. So now she feels women can create a new church, a women-church.

Gordon: Except, what would be the meaning of this church? Mary and I diverge on these things, too. She is more forward-looking than I am in some ways. What would be the meaning of the sacraments that women-church create?

She's talking about women doing what American blacks did in the 1960s. Many of them in colleges and universities withdrew to be by themselves.

Gordon: And, where are we now? They came back into the mainstream, but, you know, the situation of blacks is worse than it was—economically. I mean blacks are still the underclass, the impermeable underclass. . . . If you're a black child, you still have an infinitely smaller chance of a healthy, productive, safe life than a white child. Infinitely. That's not a model that gives me very much hope.

You are pessimistic about the possibility of women constructing their own theology.

Gordon: The point is very few people want it. For the majority of the people who are still in the church, it's because they want to be attached to the church of their forefathers and foremothers. I mean, we can't even pass the Equal Rights Amendment in this country. And if we think we have problems, what are you going to do with the Third World? If the hope of the church is in Latin countries, what are you going to do with their ethic of machismo? They're going to accept the ordination of women much more slowly than we are. I've talked to women who work in the church in Latin America. They don't see it happening very soon. If it does, it will because of weariness on everybody's part. Maybe the women will be the only ones left.

In the church?

Gordon: Yes. Like what's happening to the Episcopal church. Practically the only Episcopalians you know are people who want to be ordained themselves. They have no congregation. The congregation of twenty-five priests and two people who do not want to be priests. I don't think we're in a religious time. I don't know what that means. I cannot prognosticate in that way.

Theresa Kane has said that although there is much talk about faith, we do not live in a faithful time.

Gordon: No. If you hold up John Paul II and Theresa Kane, people are not going to flock to Theresa Kane. They're going to flock to "big daddy." People in the Third World—I was once in El Salvador—had pictures of John Paul II on every street corner. I'm sure these base communities in Latin America are very moving. The idea of having women leaders is fine, but they don't have that mythical power that the great white father has.

And the women going around doing something informal . . .? Even if those women are there for the people and with them, and living and serving with them, they don't have that mythic appeal. The mythic, the irrational appeal of the church is very, very strong. And I don't see what's going to replace it. I don't *like* it, but I see its importance, and that's what keeps people in, that sense of the irrational. I really think it's over.

You feel that sense of the irrational is appealing to people's unconscious?

Gordon: Yes, I do think that.

What does this have to do with God?

Gordon: One does not go to God for rational reasons. There's no rational reason for belief. Obviously, even if educated people choose to believe, it's not because there are better reasons for belief than for disbelief; there are much better reasons for disbelief than for belief. The whole posture of being a religious person is a posture which you weigh in on the side of the irrational. I think that the new church does not tap deeply enough into the unconscious.

So you feel that the irrational sense is what's missing in the renewed church?

Gordon: Yes. I never thought of that until just now. I think that that's the whole problem. The present church is working on relatively superficial levels of human activity. But the activity that is touched by prayer are beauty, reflection, and a kind of race memory. We've jettisoned all that. And then what do we say to people? What do we give in their place? Try to love Jesus. Give yourself up. Lay down your life for your friend. . . . *Why* lay down your life for your friend? Why should I? Is there a good reason?

Where is your art leading nowadays?

Gordon: I'm writing a novel about Irish immigrants. I've thought a lot about the Irish. I'm reading about their history and thinking a lot about them. I love and I feel very drawn to them. At the same time, I find them appalling at some levels, particularly in America. So I have a real love/hate for them. I think that there is an Irish attachment to both language and nature—the beauties of language and the beauties of nature—that is quite extraordinary. And that makes them a very special and different situation from a lot of people.

Certain pagan cultures were never totally permeated by Christianity. Do you think that your attraction to Irish culture stems from its earlier system of belief?

Gordon: I'm not someone who romanticizes paganism. I think paganism is quite cruel. I get really crazy when people talk about the great matriarchal religions. They were very cruel religions. I'm not saying that patriarchy is not cruel, but there is something about the ideal of justice which is terribly important to human beings. It is something that entered the culture when the mother religions went out of it. Now, a lot was lost, a lot of our connection to the earth, and to nature, and to the moral unconscious was lost. Nevertheless, we don't want to be at the mercy of the unconscious. I don't see nature as a benevolent force.

When did this element of justice enter our culture?

Gordon: I don't know quite enough about it, but certainly the notion of justice was very much of the Jews. With the Greeks also, as they progressed. You can see the difference from Homer's *Iliad*, which is a bloodthirsty, cruel work. The difference between that and the late Greek tragedies is extraordinary. I would much rather live in the world of the tragedies than the world of the *Iliad*. I would rather live in the world of the prophets than in the world of Baal any time, because you have no recourse if justice doesn't have some sort of sway. Not that justice has not been perverted—it has—but unless you introduce that notion of justice triumphing over nature in some way, I think we face a very merciless prospect. Nature is very bleak; nature does not protect the weak.

Many of the women represented in these stories feel that justice is precisely the element women will bring into the church.

Gordon: Because we have been victims of injustice, I think we would be more sensitive to justice. I don't think justice, however, in any deep way is gender-related. I think that there are people of good of both genders who will suffer a great deal for justice. I think it's too hopeful, because the just man or woman is a very rare animal. I don't think there's any magical thing about having ovaries and a uterus. I think there are some things that women are better at. Women are better at having that sort of third ear, alert for the needs of other people. I happen to think that women are very happy because we're trained more sociably; we're rewarded for that more. But I don't think that women are of necessity more just than men. I don't think they're less just than men. I think to be a just human being is difficult and rare.

Therefore it would not make much difference if women became part of the Catholic clergy?

Gordon: It would make a difference in other ways. But I don't think it would necessarily create more justice. It would create more understanding, and it would erase a particular kind of injustice practiced against them. The fact of that bar being lifted would be a triumph for justice. But I certainly don't think that there's any magical way that if there are more women, there will be more justice. You've worked in groups of women, and so have I. One of the things you find out is that there are some ways in which we work together very well, and then one is constantly disillusioned. I always expect women to be better than men.

And some women do not want to be liberated.

Gordon: That's right. And morality is a very difficult thing; we're all very selfish. People like power; men and women. People like having their will;

men and women. And I don't think anything magical happens because you put women together. I wish that I thought that, but I don't. To be a moral and a decent person is a very grueling thing and a very rare thing. There are ways in which women together act better than men because they are not acting for the approval of men. They can sometimes be more natural. But I've seen women be perfectly terrible to each other.

I mean the cruelest people in my family are women. They are more powerful than the men, and they are very cruel. I've always found women more interesting than men; my closest bonds are with women. But I have no romance that they're necessarily nicer. I have a son, and that has really changed me completely about men.

How did he change you?

Gordon: I have a son who is by nature much more loving, much more generous, much warmer than his sister. I adore my daughter; it's not that I love one more than the other. My daughter is a very tough girl. And she walks into the room, takes what she wants, and if she happens to knock somebody over in her path, "toughie for them." But my son worries; if David thinks that I'm not feeling well (he's only three), he says, "Do you have a headache? Are you tired?" He's much more vulnerable than she is. He's much more easily hurt. If you correct her, she will fight you to the death to prove that she's not wrong. If you correct him, he literally lies down on the floor. If you say, "That was naughty," he cries. My daughter wasn't allowed to touch the hi-fi. I said, "Don't touch it." She touched it and I spanked her. She went over and touched it again saying, "I know you're not going to spank me twice. Since I've already been spanked, I might as well do it again." She did that at three.

Where did she get this from?

Gordon: Genes from my grandmother, my mother. Now I'm going to be the tough woman in my family for many generations.

Your mother is a strong woman?

Gordon: She's tough; I don't know how strong she is. She's a combination of being very dependent and rather aggressive. But my grandmother was very tough and very strong. Not a nice woman. Not a tender woman.

Do you think that women who came from oppressive situations are more understanding than women who do not?

Gordon: I don't think so. I'm writing about immigrant women who could not afford to be too understanding because life was very hard. The message they had to give to their children was, "Life is very hard. Better be ready to stand up for it and protect your flanks. Because they'll get you." I think there is a sentimentalism about women. I think that the women who survived were very tough. Particularly the Irish. I didn't know a lot of very tender Irish women, but there was a lot of very tough, admirably strong ones. I didn't get much sense of the tenderness you indicate. Irish men were much tenderer than the Irish women, if they weren't drunk. And I think that's important with the Irish, because so many of the men were alcoholics and walked away. The women had to take over. I also think that Irish women tend to "infantilize" their men.

Who is the opposite of Margaret in Final Payments? *What is your ideal of a good person?*

Gordon: I go back to the image of John XXIII, who seemed to me to enjoy life, to be very open to life, and to have virtue which did not exclude generosity and openness and a kind of pleasure. It's a liveliness. My idea of the good person has to be a lively person who embraces life, as well as being able to deny himself or herself for the sake of others who might be in need. If Christianity could somehow rid itself of this hatred of life, hatred of the world, hatred of the senses, then the ideal of virtue would be much richer and fuller and come closer to my idea of a good person. The good person ought to like to laugh, and ought not to be so exclusionary, so willing to judge and to damn. I think of the face of John XXIII . . . a wonderful face. A face—it was a peasant face—the famous picture of him when he was a cardinal, with a drink in one hand and a cigarette in the other. Generosity is the virtue that is the linchpin of my system of virtues.

So this is the opposite of Margaret in Final Payments. *. . . Do you feel that Margaret is a harsh character because she is a woman?*

Gordon: I don't think there are male Margarets. I think that because women have a smaller arena of power, their cruelty is more pointed. When men are cruel, they hit you; they steal your money; they kill you. So it's very different. One does not choose one over the other. They're both terrible. The "Margarets" don't rape and beat you up and set your house on fire. So their arenas for cruelty are more pointed and in some ways more pernicious. But obviously they are people who steal lives.

Men and Angels *does not focus on the church as much as your earlier novels. Have you moved away from Catholic issues?*

Gordon: I am writing about the Irish now, so there is perforce an inclusion of Catholic issues. But I never know what will be next with me. For the moment I'm very involved with the Irish; so it is also the church. . . . But my Irish people are not very religious; they're kind of angry at the church. They were involved in the labor movement and they feel that the church sold them out, which in fact it did. One of the truly depressing things is to look at the early labor movement and see the number of Irish women who were the "heroes." Mother Jones was an Irish woman, as was Leonore O'Reilly. The early labor movement started with the mills in western Massachusetts which were largely staffed by Irish women. So the heroes of the early labor movement were largely Irish and the church just stomped on them.

Wasn't the church afraid of losing its laborers, as was the case in France?
  Gordon: The church was pro labor as long as labor didn't go too far left, as long as it could labor within the rubrics. Any hint of socialism and the church became really scared. The fact is that there were no Irish women, very few Irish women in labor history after about 1910. Then the field goes to Jewish women. And it's because the church really moved in. Priests gave sermons about how unwomanly it was for women to be involved in these things.

Have you visited Ireland?
  Gordon: Yes, I've been six times. I wouldn't want to live there. I find it very magical. And I'm very drawn to it. Very special, a most sacred, magic place. But I know that if I lived there, it wouldn't be very nice for me. There's some wonderful spirit, but I think the Irish are very tricky. People think that they are openly warm and intimate. But I think the Irish really use language to steel [themselves] against [outsiders], and to distance themselves. And they are very clever at it. Because there are a lot of words coming out, and they're put together very well, you think you're getting information, but you're not getting information.

Do you think the Irish know themselves?
  Gordon: No. I think there's a real premium put on not knowing. But if you know, better not tell. Do they know themselves? Very interesting; I hadn't really gone on that level; it's a very good question. . . .
  I think one of the interesting things most Catholics think is that Irish Catholics are from Mars. It's such a different model from the model of either Jews or Protestants that they find them really alien. There's the guilt, but

there's also a tremendous idealism which both ennobles the Irish and drives them nuts, or causes them to commit suicide. They're always stepping on their own feet. They're always snatching defeat from the jaws of victory. And I think—well, I have a lot of thoughts about the Irish—but I think they love the invisible more than the visible.

The United Nations' ten-year study of the major health problems of the world in the 1970s revealed that the worst international problem was depression. Whether countries are rich, poor, underdeveloped, or developed, they have depression as a major health problem. But two spots are particularly depressed: one is the west coast of Ireland.

Gordon: But there is some real sense of the spirit there, nonetheless. There's a way in which I like the Irish for not running after success and progress. I can't defend that; that's an absolutely indefensible position. They are receptive. And it's funny . . . a new book—Herbie Miller's *Exiles and Immigrants*—gives you the idea that he's angry at Irish immigrants because they weren't pulling themselves up by their bootstraps. One reason is because generosity and hospitality was such a big ethic that they spent a lot of money on funerals and weddings and parties. That is what makes him angry. They're not with the program all the time. There's something in the Irish not being with the program that I like.

What would you say to women like Theresa Kane, Mary Hunt, and Bernadette Brooten?

Gordon: Courage. Better to try than not to try. I don't like to give the idea that they'll win without a fight. What is that phrase, "If we lose hope then all our fears will come to pass." I think they probably have more hopeful natures than I do, and good for them. I genuinely think they're doing a good thing. I don't have much hope, and I don't put my energy there. But I'm moved by their spirit and by their energy. What do they get from that communion that they couldn't get elsewhere? What is the official sanction that they see? I can certainly understand it for those who have been in it for a long time and that's who they are and that's how they define themselves.

The reason that some sisters may stay is, let's face it, social security.

Gordon: That was one of the terrible things about those twenty-four nuns who signed the ad facing the threat of being thrown out.

Were you surprised by public reaction to Geraldine Ferraro?

Gordon: I was tremendously excited when she was nominated. But I'm real mad at her. I think that if she didn't know her husband was involved in those kinds of things, then we'd have to say she's a fool. A public figure has a responsibility to know where her money and her husband's money is coming from. If she doesn't know where her husband's money is coming from, she has no right being vice president of the United States. And she made women look very stupid by saying, "Oh, I didn't know where my husband's money comes from." I means she's not any ordinary housewife. She's a lawyer. She has a responsibility. Also . . . There's no such thing as clean real estate money in New York. . . . She should have known that. Mondale should have known that. And her defense, "I didn't know where my husband's money was coming from," made her look like a dumb broad.

So you're disappointed?

Gordon: Very. And I feel quite betrayed by her. She set us back. Women as political figures will be less credible. It will be a long time before we get a women vice presidential candidate. Unless someone like Jeane Kirkpatrick turns up. I'm not going to be excited if Jeane Kirkpatrick is nominated. But to be a woman who says, "I can do the job that a man can do," and then fall back on, "I didn't know where my husband's money comes from," was just ridiculous. And she made us all look ridiculous.

How did you become this person who you are?

Gordon: I had this sort of magic father. I had a father who loved me above anything else in the world. And thought I was the most important, wonderful, miraculous thing in the world. Even though he died when I was seven, I always had that. It was an incredible strength that he gave me. He gave me literature and languages and music at a very early age, and talked to me seriously. And that was a richness that I'll never lose. The other thing is that I met my two best friends when I was thirteen years old, and these women and I have gone through life together.

Like Liz and Isabelle of Final Payments.

Gordon: No, they're not like that; they're very different. One is actually teaching at Notre Dame, where she is a medieval historian, and one is a doctor. But we gave each other courage as we went out into the world.

It seems that there was something very important in that early love and cherishing with your father and friends . . .

Gordon: And the fact that it did not matter to my father that I was a girl. He never said to me that there are things that you can't do because you are a girl. He taught me Latin at five, he taught me French at four. I certainly didn't get from my family the idea [that if] there was anything that I wanted to do, I couldn't do it because I was a girl. Luckily, I didn't want to be an architect, or a neurosurgeon, or something where I needed training. I just needed to read and write, which I could do in private.

You were only seven years old . . . . did he die suddenly?

Gordon: Yes. Terrible. Terrible. I mean I had five years of my life which were a total daze after he died.

Why did you become a writer?

Gordon: Well, my father was a writer. That's what I was trained to be. It wasn't really a revolutionary act. I was brought up to be that. I never got to be anything else. I was really educated only with women until graduate school. I went to Barnard and then I went to Syracuse. And that was the only place that anybody said you might be as good as a man. It hadn't occurred to me before. Because I'd only been among women.

But he encouraged this world vision and scholarship.

Gordon: Absolutely. I think that was very Jewish. I would not have got it if I were only Irish.

Do you think you have inherited the love of learning from your Irish roots?

Gordon: No. I think that the Irish love of learning was always tainted by the fear of learning. For the Irish, and for Catholics in general, learning, secular learning, is what will push you out of the fold. Therefore, reason is the enemy. Imagine a Jewish *Index.* Imagining the whole idea is incomprehensible. The *Nihil Obstat,* the *Imprimatur* of Catholics—there is always the notion that learning is dangerous.

Whereas for the Jewish person everything is open and one makes a judgment on its merit.

Gordon: But I think we can be romantic about that. Those of us who love Jews can be romantic about Jews. . . . There's a sense for Catholics that learning is a danger. Not only that you have to stay away from anything with sexual content, but anything that talks about freedom of thought is a danger in itself.

Radical Damage: An Interview with Mary Gordon

M. Deiter Keyishian / 1988

From the *Literary Review* 32 (Fall 1988), 69–82. © 1988 The Literary Review. Reprinted by permission.

Mary Gordon lives in an old, grey stone house in New Paltz, a small college town in upstate New York, where her husband, Arthur Cash, biographer of Laurence Sterne, teaches. They have two children, Anna, now seven and a half, and David, four and a half. Her mother lives nearby.

Mary Gordon lectures regularly. Supremely articulate, she speaks as a feminist, a novelist, and a Catholic. She is interviewed for *Once a Catholic*. The collection *Fathers and Daughters* includes a painful consideration of her relations with her beloved father, a virulently anti-Semitic Jewish convert to Catholicism, who died when she was seven.

Her three novels, *Final Payments* (New York: Random House, 1978), *The Company of Women* (New York: Random House, 1980) and *Men and Angels* (New York: Random House, 1985), earned excellent reviews. The occasion of our talk was the publication of her collection of short stories, *Temporary Shelter*, and in anticipation of her fourth novel, tentatively entitled *The Rose Tree*, the story of an Irish immigrant family. She will teach creative writing at Barnard College this fall.

MK: You don't write that many short stories, do you?

MG: I actually write quite a few. Not all of them do I consider publishable. So I have many of them in folders. This collection, *Temporary Shelter*, has twenty, written over the course of a lifetime, over twelve years.

Do you change your mind, decide you like stories you didn't?
Or not like things that I did like. That can be awful too.

I listened to you describe life in New Paltz at lunch. You tell great stories, a sort of comedy of manners.
That's not the kind of story I tend to write so much. The stories are more dense, poetic. Also I feel the luxury to be more personal in the short story.

It's all right to be absorbed by yourself, to write about yourself for ten pages, but to do it for three hundred is enough already.

Your characters take on a compelling life. What if you reject the story?
    Then I'd use the character in another. I've only recently gone back over things I'd written ten, twelve years ago, reworked some, and thought, maybe—that's okay. Some were actually published, and I had to make decisions that I didn't want to include them in the collection.

E. M. Forster says a novelist has to know absolutely everything about a character before he starts to write.
    You have to think you do. As you write them, you're constantly being surprised and learning things. You begin with an illusionary confidence.

Do you begin with characters or a sense of action?
    With characters and a situation and the action to set it up.

You often use elements of fairy tale. In The Company of Women, *good fairies and bad appear to Felicitas's baptismal party; wicked witches appear and disappear.*
    Yes.

And in Men and Angels, *Laura Post, the religious fanatic, slits her wrists in the bathtub. Blood and water come through the ceiling warping the books in the library below. But you don't allow them to be destroyed. Anne dries them out.*
    Well, I'm obsessed by the objective correlative, of the emotional damage being physical damage—of the seeping, lingering. If they were destroyed, you'd get rid of it. You'd get it out of the house. I don't think that kind of thing ever does get out of the house. You do keep it around.

Critics have remarked that in Men and Angels *for the first time you didn't have a religious heroine. But Laura Post is a born-again Christian. And she is mad.*
    Yes. It was a choice that I made because I was interested in that kind of radical damage done to a person who then, because of that damage, is incapable of genuine love but mistakes obsession for love. And I was interested in the perversion of the religious impulse, because I had used the religious impulse differently in other books.

The title story of Temporary Shelter, *set in the household of a Jewish convert of Catholicism, is as involved with religion as* Men and Angels. *You continue that kind of metaphysical problem.*

The immigrant novel will be less so. There is a way in which I'm moving away from it.

In Final Payments, *Isabel chooses to care for her horribly demanding father after he finds her in bed with his student, David. That reads as expiation, not privilege. Then she grows fat, serving the housekeeper-witch. In* The Company of Women, *Felicitas, the unwed mother, serves seven years in upstate New York. But the awful Columbia professor, Robert Cavendish, who regularly seduces students, stays on, unscathed, in New York.*

I do make life harder for my heroines than life generally is for everybody, just because I tend to find that more interesting to write about, on the whole. But I do think those men don't suffer as much as they should or don't suffer as much as they inflict suffering.

In Men and Angels, *you invent a great artist, Caroline Watson, whom critics cheerfully consign to oblivion because her subjects are just women and children. Are you encountering that kind of reaction to your writing?*

To write about women and children is to be immediately ghettoized, unless you're talking about women, children, and sex, and the way that children interfere with sex for women. I think that's why somebody like Sue Miller can be very successful writing about that as long as there's really a man at the center. But, if you really are talking about women and children and you take a man out of the central focus, you're really ghettoized. They think you're writing for *Ladies Home Journal.*

Which makes the focus cleaner and more acceptable.

Right, when it's very dangerous and messy and passionate and frightening and ecstatic and many things—but I simply think it's because motherhood is so threatening to people. It is so overwhelming, and everybody knows that, so they confine it to an inferior status simply because it's so frightening and so potent. That's one thing. The other thing is that there is so much literal drudgery about the care of children that people simply hate it. They want to cast it aside. The two things are at work.

And, of course, you know, you can get a little ridiculous if you do nothing but care for children all the time. I could no more stay home with my kids all day than I could be a neurosurgeon. You have to remember that there's a world out there. And people are right to be nervous, I think, about women whose entire lives are their children.

You don't have any straight mothers in Final Payments.

And I guess I don't have many good mothers. I have good mother substitutes. Although Charlotte's a good mother, she's not exactly a straight mother.

You have wicked Margaret—a marvelous witch.

Yes. That Margaret character, that life denier—the sort of on-paper impeccable woman who can never be found in transgression and yet is an absolute killer—comes up again and again in my fiction.

In that painful piece you did on your father, "David," in Fathers and Daughters, *one gets a very strong sense of the absolute love that you had for each other, complicated by what you found out later as an adult.*

I'm actually working on something about him now. I think because in a way it is such an unbelievable story that I can't use it for fiction. So I want to write more essays about him and about my relationship with him.

Your fictional fathers often have a "murderous importance": "I gave up my life for him. I make that statement not with pity but with extreme pride," Isabel says in Final Payments. *And you praise Father Cyprian, who was killing these women.*

He's both a killer and a tormented, passionately loving man. He set up a relationship, demanded a kind of obeisance that is murderous. I don't deny that. On the other hand, he loved passionately, and I find that redeeming. He didn't love those women well, but he loved Felicitas passionately enough to take her in when she had done what would have been unforgivable to him, and to learn from her, and to change and to accept. I mean he is a changed man.

One of the things that is good about the church is it's a place for people to go who aren't winning in the world's terms to have a kind of shelter and a kind of place. He gave those women that. What you have to ask, to determine whether somebody's a killer or not, is would the people's lives be better without him or her? And I think they would not have been.

In Final Payments, *Isabel spends eleven years caring for her father. Felicitas, in* Company, *spends seven. Cyprian makes her smell manure when she sees something beautiful. There's punishment for sexuality.*

Oh, yes. Oh, yes. That's very strong in Catholicism. Cyprian gave to Felicitas, and prevented her in some ways—it was a double thing. Felicitas was very complicated. In the end, he had to learn from his daughter. I didn't mean that to be a particularly cheerful book. I meant it to be a complicated issue: would Felicitas have been better off without him? Perhaps, but she had a kind of grandeur to her life that she would not have had without him. She put some things together, not everything, maybe, but the best. But she had this very special vision; she's a kind of visionary, and to be a visionary you have to have an extreme life. An extreme life doesn't breed happiness.

Now we're in territory that needs explication for me.

It's like what you want for yourself and what you want for your kids. For yourself, you feel like you can take a certain number of risks, particularly before you have children. What one wanted for one's self when young is not what one wants for one's children. When we were young, we wanted to go off and *be*, and experience things in a very pure and daring way. Well, I want my daughter to be an accountant, just so she's safe.

Felicitas becomes pregnant by one of two possible fathers. Why did you make the father uncertain?

Because I wanted to make it unimportant. It was really Felicitas's child and I didn't want the reader to be thinking of it as the child of any definite man. And I didn't want the reader saying, "Well someday she'll look Robert up and say, 'Don't you want to see your daughter?' " This way she can never do that.

You did a terrific satirical job of ripping apart certain kinds of professors.

Yeah, it was funny. Male critics just said that was totally unrealistic. So many women I talked to said, "I knew him!"

Yes. Then you send Felicitas upstate with the three fairy grandmothers and her mother, and one of your witches, Muriel.

One of the things I do believe is that these women are killers because they're starved. The world is really set up so that a lot of women are very starved.

Felicitas, Isabel, and Anne, your heroines, get furious with themselves because they can't love these unlovable women. You seem to expect them to.

They expect themselves to because the failure of love is such a terrible, terrible dead end for someone who tries to live morally. You cannot even make yourself, after a while, not feel murderous to somebody that you're trying terribly hard to be decent to. And it's a real paradox because I do think that love is the source of any moral vision that's worth anything. Yet so often it's impossible, and so often people who need us most are hardened, the most armed against it. There's nothing you can do about it.

Felicitas is silent for a while, unable to relate to her child. And then you marry her off to this absolute stone.

No, he's not a stone. He's an ox. I made that point. He's not cold.

Nevertheless, to me that kind of thing is hell.

Well, you see, what you have to say about Felicitas is that she is in some sense damaged. She is not going to marry Alan Alda.

How is she damaged?

She has this very extreme life. Her ability to express herself and to find herself was cut short by not the pregnancy but the horror of illegal abortion. Yet in some mysterious way, she is able to recoup part of herself. But not all. Cyprian was a partly killing figure to the part of her that could have had ordinary success, ordinary happiness, ordinary self-expression. So it is a life which had severe limitations on it. What kind of life would that person choose? She could be totally alone with a bunch of old people dying around her, or she could marry somebody that she would meet up with in that life who would give her something that she needed, a kind of very simple humanity and acceptance. She is a visionary of the cloister. She is a visionary of the limited life.

But without its ecstasy. That might appeal on a bad Monday.

Somebody wanted to buy *The Company of Women* for a movie, but she said, "Felicitas has to leave. She has to go back to New York at the end of the movie with her daughter." And I said that she missed the whole point of the book in a very radical way. It's not "An Unmarried Woman." It's not somebody who goes through a rough patch and pulls herself up by her boot straps and goes and works for *Ms.* And most people do have severely limited lives. I mean, life does not always get out of the way so that we express ourselves to the fullest.

Still, it does seem as if you're damning this character—who had potential.

But, you know, I'm very cynical about just having a very good life. I mean, those of us who are out there in the greater world doing everything—we're so exhausted. We're so sort of overburdened. There is no place to rest. I mean, I wouldn't not do it, but every now and then the cloister and a limited life have a real appeal.

A bunch of nuns running one's life?

I don't want a bunch of nuns either, but, you know, decent men want nuns.

I wonder if "Now I Am Married," the five-voiced short story, was an earlier version of The Company of Women *or something you did after.*

That was a very early story. Very, very early. It's the earliest story in the book. I think I wrote that in 1974. It's totally romantic about marriage.

What you also do in Company *and in* Final Payments *and the short stories is real streets, in Sheepshead Bay or Queens, where people really spend time polishing cars and linoleum and stuff like that.*

Because it's so important and hard won.

An Irish family recurs, married sisters and the young crippled Nora. Why the limp?

Well, actually, my mother is a polio victim and a lot of that stuff is family stories. Some of them are my family and some the other. That's *the* thing that was good about my family. They were good storytellers.

That little girl is really a version of my mother. She grows to be an adult in "Delia," where the husband comes back. That actually happened to my mother. And the episode of being turned down at normal school actually happened to her.

And I did have this uncle who was a bootlegger that did have this extremely plain mistress who supported him, whom he then left for somebody else. But she didn't kill herself. There also wasn't a rich WASP woman that he left her for. She was another Irish girl, but she was respectable.

And you collect stories from other people, Sylvie, "Out of the Fray," for one.

What began her? My friend Marv was talking to me about something, and he said, "I have a friend, and her ex-husband said of her, 'She finally has the life she wanted. She finally got to be an old woman.' " And that absolutely grabbed me. But I made up the central people. I had no interest in what they were in real life actually.

But they caught you enough for you to want to retell their story.

But, you know, this is a sort of terrible thing because I don't actually want their story. I want to use parts of their story and retell it in my own way. I might even need a couple of their lines, but then, you know, they can just go off.

Ruth, of "Out of the Fray," is actually sympathetic to Sylvie, the ex-wife—not always the case.

I think I always chose my father over my mother, and that's it. My father is always the star for me and the hero—which is odd for a feminist, but I think maybe in some deep way . . .

Yes, but he died when you were seven. . . . But often you don't bother to redeem the wife.

Well, I'm older now. Maybe I'll change. I guess I never—even though I've been a wife twice now—I've never seen myself as a wife because I wasn't brought up to be a wife. I mean, I was really not brought up to marry. I was brought up to be a secular nun.

Strong friendships between women are central to your work.

Yes. There is an awful way in which I feel men can come and go, but you have these women. I mean, I don't want to live that way, but the strongest bond I have is with my best friend, the friend I've had since I was 13.

Yet at the end of "Out of the Fray," Ruth thinks she'll die if Philip leaves her.

It was shock. She had really tried to live her life as if she could move in and out of her relationship with a man, and she develops a real understanding of what it meant.

You used the lives, the diaries, of real painters, Cassatt, Modersohn-Becker, as sources for Caroline Watson.

Yes. Also I can't paint. I have less talent for painting than for almost anything. But I love painting, so I got to sort of write the paintings I would have like to have painted.

I am terribly concerned with finding the image to render, as Conrad would say, the highest possible justice to the visible world. And to get the right rhythm for the inner life, and the combination of image and rhythm to pin down an internal state is terribly important to me. At least as important as any sort of moral report of the world.

No one would listen, but, of course, you could.

Yes, unfortunately, you really can. Sometimes the most trustworthy moral vision can be rendered in absolutely terrible prose. Often it probably is. I think that people probably with the most acute vision are not tempted by writing it down, because they're acting in the world.

Is writing a temptation?

Yes, I think it's a kind of compulsion or hunger. You can't be writing about the world and acting to change the world at the same time. And I think people whose major concern is really moral are not artists. They're activists. They're serving in some way or another.

Isn't writing an act of morality?

I don't think so. You try to tell the truth aesthetically. I mean, you try to not do what Updike does. And you try not to cut corners and you try not to get away with things that you know you can get away with. And, in that sense, it's moral, but it's a moral good that really leans towards the aesthetic.

What's wrong with that?

Nothing's wrong with it, but I think if you're genuinely—if your first motivation in the world is to relieve suffering, which I think is the height of morality—you go work with Mother Teresa: you're not going to write.

I would be an infinitely better person if I weren't a writer. I mean, now I was born a writer and I have the hunger to, so if I weren't writing, I'd be a really dreadful person given the fact that I have that hunger. But the people that I know who are the really good people in the world are not driven by these hungers to get this stuff down and to record it, to express themselves recording it.

It's a matter of time and attention. You have to be quite selfish to be a writer. As I said, I think there are heroes in the world. I don't necessarily want to hang out with them, but I'm glad they exist.

I find Mother Teresa a very irritating person, but there is no doubt that she does incredible good. And if you've ever been ill in the hospital, the kind of people that really suddenly seem like absolute angels of grace to you are not people you'd want to have a conversation with at dinner. It's a real paradox.

But my perfect saint is Ford Madox Ford because he was really nice and really helped people, and then he wrote these wonderful books.

But you don't like Conrad?

He's a wonderful stylist. I think he has an oversimplified moral vision. Moral choices don't arise like that. And he can't do women. I'm not that interested in a vision that cuts out women. Well, he has Lena in *Victory*; she's sort of romantic and silent, a sex object. And Mrs. Gould in *Nostromo*. But she's not very real, not important. And I don't believe him about moral choices. I think he mistakes the moral and the physical. The extreme states in which very stark choices are made don't interest me very much. I don't think the terms in which he paints the world are the truest terms.

He said a couple of intelligent things, but I just think that any vision that cuts out 53% of humanity is not very comprehensive or trustworthy. And most moral choices are more modulated than Conrad would have us believe.

Who do you feel influences you?

I think I have a new set of influences. I've been reading a lot of Marguerite Duras. There's a German writer that I've discovered that I'm really obsessed by at the moment and that's Christa Wolf. I read a lot of William Trevor. He is a great master to me just for his modesty of execution, a kind of wholeness of response. I read a lot of Louise Bogan.

There's a distillation of her journal called *The Journey Around My Room* which I've been reading kind of obsessively for the past three or four years. When I was a young poet at Barnard, I looked at her poetry and I said, "That's what I want to do." And there's that kind of purity of lyric impulse that I really value, a kind of wonderful severity of line that I adore.

Do minimalists interest you?

I went through a stage where I really let them make me furious and now, I'm really trying to . . . it's interesting; I've become friends with Grace Paley in the past couple of years. She has taught me a lot about generosity and about really not wanting to say, "I'm in and you're out." So I'm trying to be more understanding of what it is they're trying to do. Some of them like Joy Williams, for example, I find quite interesting. I still don't find Ann Beattie interesting. I still don't find Raymond Carver interesting.

I'm not very interested, except that I now have more sympathy with what they're trying to do with prose, because I myself am trying to cut out what I see as a sort of loose connective tissue between vital things. At their best, that's what they're trying to do.

Though I do think there's a turnaround now.

I'm not sure that I like what's on the other side of the turnaround. I don't think it's any better. I mean, I'll take, actually, if I have to choose between Updike and Raymond Carver, I'll take Raymond Carver any day.

What I dislike about Updike is that he's such a liar as a stylist and he really practices false lyricism. He overwrites and . . . he's a kind of professional boy. He has a boy's crudity, a boy's mentality, and he has a boy's notion that if you extend excessive tenderness to an object, that is lyricism. He's a very fraudulent stylist. And he's disgusting about women; he has a real problem about women. He covers that up with a notion that he really does love women, but he doesn't. Updike can never describe a woman physically without putting in some detail which makes a woman's connection to death. For him, women are really corrupt in the flesh. He's a liar, stylistically and morally. When he starts talking about theology, I really want to jump out the window because he's such a coarse theologian.

I think that he lies to himself about women. Or does he know he's lying?
Oh, I don't think he knows. No, he's a deep liar and a successful one. Most successful liars don't know that they're lying to themselves.

Are they? What about John Demjanjuk, the Nazi they tried in Israel? He maintains he isn't the concentration camp guard. Maybe, on some level, he believes he isn't that person.
Oh, I don't think he does.

You think he knows? You think it's just plain outfacing?
Yes. In the most blatant, awful way.

You don't extend the vision in your work to somebody like Demjanjuk.
No, not at all. Because there's private behavior and public behavior, and there is witness, and there is protection of other people. Oh, if, in private, some priest wants to confront Ivan the Terrible, and say, if at the moment of your death you express sorrow, that means something because it's better than not expressing sorrow. Yes, I think that would be something to do. But publicly, we have to say, "You are a killer," and, in order to witness, I think it's terribly important to witness the evil. And sometimes you have to witness to evil by a very radical measure.

By which you mean?
I have absolutely no trouble with Ivan the Terrible being hanged. I think it's right, I think it's just, and I think it's important. I mean, in defense of those who were murdered, who are silent now.
You know, this false forgiveness is a moral problem. I think it's interesting how the Church supported the boy lovers in the two most flagrant killings of young women. Bobby Garland and Robert Chambers. Chambers was living in a rectory and the priest was saying, "He's just a young guy with a lot of energy. What he needs is a basketball." That's false forgiveness.

Aren't you letting the priest off too easy? I think there's something else. They may even revel in the crime.
In the way that perhaps those who forgave Nazis revel in crime, too.

*You've written of Catholic novelists; whose work do you respond to—
Bernanos, Claudel?*

I don't like Claudel. My father did. I found him chilling, forbidding and
hyper-formal. Bernanos, I love Bernanos. *Diary of a Country Priest* really
gets genuine innocence and genuine love, a person that is really on fire with
a very truly and deeply organically felt love for a human being, and a sensitivity, a porosity towards the suffering and the joys of others. The courage of
that love where he can turn to the chatelain, who is responsible for his material well-being, and say, "You hate your daughter." And that is killing. I
believe in that, sort of. There is that kind of pure heart that is granted extraordinary vision into the hearts of others. That I find extremely moving. There
are people extremely motivated. They're on fire with love, and they're very
rare, but I believe in them. Bernanos very convincingly portrays them: people
who have a kind of radical porosity to other human beings, a kind of genius
sensitivity.

I tried to teach that book at Amherst, but the kids just wouldn't buy it.
They just thought he was a masochist.

Who else do you read?

Joyce, *The Dubliners*.

What about Molly Bloom?

I like Molly. She's true as a type. It's not my favorite part of *Ulysses*.

*Edith Wharton said of her that she was a male version of female sexuality;
that she could do it better.*

She didn't. She didn't have the language for it. Actually, Molly isn't really
sexual. She's organic but not really sexual. I think that's the failure. If you
read Colette—that's sex, and the other is a sort of life force. So I don't think
of Molly as about sex. It's about a sort of female principle. If you look at it
that way, it's fine. But you don't get news about female sexuality as you do
with Colette.

I like writing where the sentences themselves are a pleasure to read: Toni
Morrison, Grace Paley. A wonderful writer, I think, is David Plante. I like
Margaret Drabble, Tillie Olsen.

*You do readings with the novelist Esther Broner, a feminist and practicing
Jew.*

O, yes, oh, God, I adore Esther. I adore her. She's a dear, dear friend.

We're gonna take this show on the road; we could make a million dollars. Esther is very important to me. She's just full of life, absolutely full of life.

What fascinates me is your conjunction of Judaism and Catholicism.
   Yes, it's not always an easy conjunction.

Well, for you it's a crucial one.
   Yes, absolutely, because I think that simply being the kind of Irish-Catholic I was brought up among, I could never have written. It was such an interdicting environment, such a silencing environment and, of course, it was very anti any forms of expression. And, I think my father's Jewishness gave me a kind of license to speak. On the other hand, the forms in which I speak were so much influenced by that early both social and religious mode that is very, very Catholic. So I feel . . . well, there's just a very important mix of the two for me.

You're going to have to explain when it comes to Catholicism, because it's like you're crossing over to another island.
   That's why I'm so successful with it. That's why *Final Payments* was so successful, because I was writing about this island that nobody that I knew had visited. The sophisticated had not visited it.

It doesn't always make sense to me.
   Well, no, it probably shouldn't. I think, when hell makes sense, it's a sign that you've lost your mental health.

But you're still a Catholic.
   That's such a complicated issue. It really shifts back and forth, and I feel that I should be allowed to shift. I can change back in the next month. So I don't like to say because it does shift so much.

Your explication in Commonweal *of the Virgin Mary was quite useful. But after Pope [John] Paul II's last visit . . .*
   The pope came, and suddenly, I was the flavor of the month. Everybody was calling me up and asking, "What do you think about the pope?" I never have been happy with the institutional church since Pope John died. And this guy is such a bad egg that it doesn't take a lot of imagination to—I mean, potentially, one could be tremendously devout and religious, people that I know are, and are very critical of this man. He's just a nightmare. He is trying to take everything good that Pope John did and turn it back. He is a

very authoritarian, unimaginative man. He thinks that the world is Poland and it's not.

What are you working on now?

That novel about Irish immigration—four generations. The older people are ninety, and then there are teenagers who make a fleeting appearance. It will start at the present and move back to 1895, then forward and back and forward.

It's just that my books seem to take me longer and longer to write all the time. And yet I can't rush the books. There seems to be a kind of baking time that they need now. You know, it's not that I can't spend as much time on them, it's that they seem to need to bake.

And this fall, you'll teach at Barnard. You haven't taught since Amherst.

Not since '79. I think Barnard is a very special place. It draws a very special kind of young woman who tends to be the kind of young woman of my dreams, somebody who wants to be in an urban situation and wants to be in a female environment. Also, what's very moving about Barnard is, because a certain number of the young women commute, there are always first genera- tion college students in a way a more affluent kind of situation doesn't allow you to have. My friend, Kim McCafflin, who's the head of Women's Studies, says at graduation she's just always in tears because there are these immigrant families there watching their—I mean, now they're Korean, different from what we had—but in a way you really see the tradition perpetuated in a very visible way in a place you wouldn't like Williams or Amherst.

You were a commuting student for two years. Is it going to be like going home?

Yes. Barnard just opened my life. It was wonderful. The most important thing I ever did was go to Barnard.

Susan Stamberg Talks with Mary Gordon

Susan Stamberg / 1989

Transcription of *Weekend Edition Saturday*, National Public Radio, 1 October 1989. © 1989 National Public Radio. Printed by permission of Mary Gordon and National Public Radio.

SS: Vincent McNamara crosses the seas from Ireland to America in Mary Gordon's new novel, *The Other Side*, the story of a family and the distance it travels through three generations of American life. Mary Gordon says the immigrant experience is indelible.

MG: Even as far as my generation was concerned, we sort of thought that we were interlopers, a little bit outsiders, that there was some piece of the pie that the Protestants were getting that we were not quite getting.

SS: You all as Catholics?

MG: Well, as Catholics, as Jews, as people whose grandparents didn't come over on the Mayflower or fight in the Civil War or all that sort of thing. There was a differentness that I think those of us for whom the memory of immigration was still living in the presence of parents and grandparents had.

SS: Here's an excerpt from *The Other Side*:

MG: *(Gordon reads from chapter IV, 240–243, regarding the young Vincent leaving his family and Ireland in 1916 for New York).*

SS: What is it that got you, do you think, so interested in this whole notion of displacement?

MG: I guess I had found that whenever I looked at photographs of immigrants I was sort of struck to the heart by the courage and the pathos of them. And realizing what it must be to actually leave a home, leave a family, leave a whole life, and the strangeness of the new life, the complete unfamiliarity with everything you would come to, and the loss. And it seemed to me as the generations went down, the generation after the people who came over lost a lot of courage and really tried to play it safe.

SS: We have heard other women writing about the immigrant experience on *Weekend Edition* recently: Bharati Mukherjee's *Jasmine* describes the

71

journey from Asia to America, Elizabeth Benedict read from her novel-in-progress about a Jewish family's arrival here. Mary Gordon sees a pattern in all of this: women who began by writing intimate, domestic, personal stories moving on now to bigger histories.

MG: There was so much that needed to be said about the domestic in the late '60s, early '70s, and even through the '70s, because simply it hadn't been spoken about. The inner lives of women were real news. Perhaps the urgency of the immediate description is off us a little bit, and now we may be trying to figure out: How did we get from here to there? Who were these dead people before us? Now the urgency might be to capture the voices of the dying and the dead.

A Conversation Between Tom Smith and Mary Gordon

Tom Smith / 1991

Transcription of *Book Show*, NY Public Radio/New York State Writers Institute, 27 June 1991. © 1991 New York State Writers Institute. Printed by permission.

TS: Welcome to the Public Radio *Book Show*. I'm your host, Tom Smith, of the New York State Writers Institute, which is located at the University of Albany and is part of the State University of New York system. My guest today is one of the most gifted and celebrated writers of contemporary fiction, Mary Gordon. Mary Gordon is the author of four highly-acclaimed novels, *Final Payments, The Company of Women, Men and Angels*, and most recently, *The Other Side*, and a collection of short stories titled, *Temporary Shelter*. And Mary Gordon is also a spirited, shrewd and sparkling essayist and W. W. Norton has recently published her collection of essays, *Good Boys and Bad* [sic] *Girls and Other Essays*. Mary, welcome once again to the Public Radio *Book Show*.

    MG: You just made two mistakes, Tom.

TS: What were the two mistakes?
    MG: First of all, it's not Norton, it's Viking.

TS: Oh, I'm sorry. Viking just published *Good Boys and Dead Girls and Other Essays*.
    MG: And it's *Good Boys and Dead Girls*. You said "Bad Girls."

TS: Oh, oh. Well, we'll examine what I meant.
    MG: Uh-huh, what do we mean by this?

TS: *Good Boys and Dead Girls and Other Essays* which was just recently published by Viking. My apology. Well, anyway, welcome. And listen, *Good Boys and Dead Girls* is a dazzling performance of non-fiction prose: intelligent, lively and wide-ranging in its concern. And the fascinating title essay, Mary, blew my mind because it's strong stuff, and I think it's strong stuff because I think it's true. And let me formulate this into some kind of question.

You say that there's a tradition of American male writers who have been obsessed by what you call "the search for the unfettered self" and hence, lapse into a kind of adolescent solipsism. Now, therefore, American literature tends to be full of female corpses because, and I'm quoting some of your lines from that title essay, "civilization is no place for a boy. He must be able to move and escape from fate." Now, Mary, in this scheme, is the female, are women, the counterpart to fate and hence, the destroyer of freedom and the American dream? Is that really the overview that you're talking about through this tradition?

MG: Yes, I think it is, and I think what you have to begin with is the idea and the ideal that, for Americans, the most desirable character, the most desirable type is a boy. Not a man, but a boy. And a boy who is always on the move, a boy who is not constricted, a boy who is not limited by anything outside the self. Women, in that they are vulnerable, susceptible and attached, are the enemy. And they have to be got out of the way in one way or another, because if a boy is always going to be moving, he cannot attach himself to the cumbrous, encumbered female. So, often he has to kill her.

TS: Now do you think this is a kind of rejection of maturity? I mean, where it comes from in American writers, whether it's Mark Twain or Melville or the writers you focus on in that title essay—Theodore Dreiser, particularly in *An American Tragedy* and Faulkner, particularly in *Light in August*, and John Updike's Rabbit books—do you think this is a kind of rejection of maturity, rejection of adult responsibilty that is peculiar to American males, that, you know, is part of this myth?

MG: I do think both sides of the term have to be examined, "American" and "male," because I think this precisely, as you say, this rejection of maturity, this notion that, rather than live with what you've created, you move on to something else, is a particularly American dream. But when we've talked about American dream we've always assumed male-ness. And one of the factors about mobile America is that if you have children with you or if your're pregnant, you're much less mobile. And so what is it that cuts down mobility? The woman. And if you can't move, if you can't get out, you really have to face what you've done. And I would say living with and facing what you've done is one real good definition for me of maturity.

TS: Yes, yes. As I recall, isn't there a smiliar or at least, analogous, theme that thirty years ago Leslie Fiedler developed in *Love and Death in the American Novel*, where he's talking about this very aspect of the great classics of

American fiction, particularly? I think there was a notorious essay in it called, "Come Back to the Raft Ag'in, Huck, Honey," which [says that] American males simply want to be together. Whether it's some kind of suppressed homosexuality or not is another issue. But whether it's Melville or Twain or Hemingway in *The Sun Also Rises* in a story, when they're up in the mountains things are good and they're fishing. Things are good. They go down and they're in the world of women. Then things get complicated, and death and destruction come into it. And I just wonder if that's really not such a powerful theme. Now you talk about, also, the American idea of innocence in this connection. Do you want to talk about what you think is the peculiar American concept of innocence which is, as you say, "a state of non-pollution"? Not simply being free from moral sin or having done no evil, but some kind of permanent state of election. Do you want to talk about that, Mary?

MG: One of the things that I think is remarkable about the American idea of innocence is that it doesn't seem connected to behavior. So that, in other words, you can behave badly, you can even kill and still be called an innocent. And that, to me, is extraordinarily peculiar. That is, I think, a tremendously Protestant notion of innocence, that goodness is something you're born with and that you don't lose by behaving un-innocently. And I think this is very, very different from a European tradition. So that, if a European innocent loses innocence, he usually is expected to go through some sort of redemptive or expiative process. But that is cut out for Americans. The idea is that you've never lost the innocence; it doesn't have to be regained because it's never been lost, because it's not loseable, because it's not connected to how you act. It's connected to what you were born with, what you were endowed with, in a particular way.

TS: In your theory, then, *Billy Budd*, by Melville, is perhaps the quintessential American text as far as this idea of innocence. Do you see this separated into gender—I'm talking about the American concept of innocence as non-pollution—that either in literature or life or the American culture in general, that the males, particularly the adolescent males, were looked upon as the great innocents and really this is not the case with women characters?

MG: No. I think women characters, the great American women characters, are women of experience. Think of Cather's characters, or Wharton's characters, for example. They're all women who have endured, and what is important, I think, that they suffer and they learn something through suffering. What's remarkable to me is that these boys don't learn. And learning is as beside the point as good behavior is. If you think of someone like Ellen Olenska in Wharton's *The Age of Innocence*, if you think of Antonia in Cather's *My Antonia*, they're all women who endure suffering, and the suffering enlarges them in some way. Even in *The House of Mirth*, Lily does die, but she grows in some way. James's heroines suffer. They suffer, and they take moral responsibility for the world.

TS: I was going to ask you about Henry James who, after all, is an American male writer. Certainly Isabel Archer and Milly Theale and characters such as that seem to have more the European idea of going from innocence to experience. European writers do that—you mention, most acutely, that Hardy's *Jude the Obscure* is antithetical to the American male protagonist in nineteenth century novels. I was wondering, in that title essay, "Good Boys and Dead Girls," you focus on Clyde Griffiths—Dreiser's *An American Tragedy*—Clyde Griffiths who killed Roberta; Joe Christmas in *Light in August* who killed his abolitionist lover, Joanna Burden; and, of course, the Rabbit Angstrom books where this comes about in more complicated ways. Do you see other exemplars in contemporary fiction of this theme that you're exploring? I mean, I suppose Norman Mailer's *The American Dream* is Exhibit A. How about in the work of Roth, Philip Roth? I mean, from *Portnoy's Complaint*, *My Life as a Man*, the Zuckerman books? How do these figure into other contemporary American fiction?

MG: I don't think Philip Roth wants women to die. I have a lot less trouble with Roth's portrayal of women than I do with these other men. First of all, it is comic. I'm occasionally quite offended by it, but it's not hate-filled. And Roth doesn't do what Updike does, which I find completely unacceptable. Roth says, "Look, you know, I really have this problem with women, and here I am, and this is who I am, and you don't have to love me for it." Updike says, "I adore women. You know, I'm really on their side." And [he] creates this kind of pseudo-lyrical, extremely false bubble in which he believes he's being a lovable protector of women. What I find absolutely unacceptable in literature and in life is that somebody wants to kill you and they say, "but you have to love me anyway." And that's something that I think men do and that women fall into. I mean, we do go on loving them, even though they abuse us and kill us. And I guess Roth doesn't say, "you have to love me anyway." He's out there, and he is what he is. But Updike wants it both ways.

TS: I don't know whether you've gone on, since the publication of that essay, gone on to read the most recent and, I presume, the last of the Rabbit books, *Rabbit Is Rich.*

MG: I don't think it's the last. I have a theory. I think that we're going to have *Rabbit Resurrected*! There's a slight possibility at the end that he actually isn't dead, that he can be brought to life. You know, I'm not ready to . . .

TS: Yes. Did you find anything at all redemptive in the last hundred pages? I'm talking about, really, the death of Rabbit and Rabbit's awareness of his death and how that, in some ways, his thoughts about his life and particularly the women in his life . . . was he redeemed at all, you know, in that book?

MG: You know, I didn't think the book was very good. So, first of all, I am a non-innocent reader of Updike . . .

TS: I can see that . . .

MG: And so I don't think you should ask me about Updike.

TS: Okay, I won't.

MG: Because, you know, he could probably write *War and Peace*, and I wouldn't like it at this point. So it's not fair to him. Or to me.

TS: So we'll wait for the possible 2001 AD *Rabbit Resurrected* and maybe talk about it then. Mary, your essays on women writers are particularly wonderful in this collection. They're insightful and acute. Incidentally, I don't want to rule out your essays on male writers, because the one on Ford Madox Ford is one of the best in not only the book, but also one of the best essays I've ever read on Ford Madox Ford, who was one of my favorite writers also. But your essays on women writers, I think, are just terrific—Edna O'Brien and Christa Wolf. I wonder if you'd talk about two of the writers that you have written on who, it seems to me, have had a tremendous impact and influence on your own development and work. And that's Mary McCarthy and Flannery O'Connor, who are very different from each other, but have certain things in common. Do you want to talk about, first of all, Mary McCarthy and the impact, particularly of her memoirs, on your own development?

MG: I think that Mary McCarthy was the ideal literary mother that I dreamed about as a girl beginning to write. She had this marvelous faculty of truth-telling and that sparkling style. And it seemed so bracing and inspiring. It was like a wonderful, shining statue in a green meadow that one could aspire to. And that rigor of hers and the clarity, the classical precision of her thought in her writing were enormously important to me. Also she was Catholic and a bad girl and had left it. And that was extremely encouraging to somebody like me. Because to be Catholic in Protestant America was to feel that you didn't own the country. And you certainly didn't own the language. And your stories were not going to be of any interest to anybody. So she was a very, very important model in that she was a bad Catholic girl. She was very, very encouraging.

TS: I think [of] those two books of memoirs, particularly the first one, *Memories of a Catholic Girlhood*, which had, incidentally, a great impact on me. And particularly the second chapter. The angry, bitter eloquence of the injustice of the tin butterfly episode and others, actually were just cathartic. And her integrity as a writer also must have made a tremendous impact on you. And Flannery O'Connor also, because one of the things that they share, in addition to being Irish-American Catholics, they both have a certain moral rigor, an intellectual rigor that you must have admired very much.

MG: I admire Flannery O'Connor extravagantly, but I don't think she's an influence on me. I always felt very, very different from her. And even her moral rigor is not something . . . it's not a moral world that I work out of. It's very dualistic; it's beautiful in its dualism.

I had a dream about Flannery O'Connor one time. And I dreamed that we were both on a panel together, and she showed up and she looked perfect and her hair was very well-coifed and her dress was terrific. And I came, and my hair was filthy, which is always my nightmare in my dreams—my hair is dirty. (I never dream of being naked; I only dream of having dirty hair.) My hair was dirty, my slip was showing, my notes were in complete chaos. She gave a perfect lecture, and mine was a mess. And she said to me, "You're a mess." Then she said to me, "Your problem is that you don't believe in perfection." And I said to her—because it was my dream and I was directing it, so I got the good lines—I said to her, "No, I do believe in perfection, but we have a different idea of perfection. You think perfection is flawlessness. And I think perfection is completeness." And there is something in Flannery O'Connor's fundamentalist vision that is quite inimical to mine. Although I think she's a great writer.

TS: I must say that I have read Flannery O'Connor many times over the years and used her books in courses. And when I sit down and read, particularly the volumes of short stories, from beginning to end, consecutively, after I'm about three-quarters of the way through, I get a real . . . very edgy feeling, because there's a kind of moral or spiritual smugness that seems to come through those stories. That somewhat, you know what the "right" position is, even through the stories are brilliant. And that's my only negative thing about Flannery O'Connor.

MG: Well, she's an Orthodox. And her work has the strength and the limitations of orthodoxy. And the strengths are, again, the beautiful, shining, classical clarity and the complications. The language is remarkable, the structure is flawless. And she really shows us the complications of evil. She doesn't give us any middle ground. Nor would she want to. She despised the middle ground.

TS: Well, that's what gives her stories power, I think, but maybe if you take too many of them in one sitting, why, you get this feeling. And I think even some other, greater admirers of hers have told me comparable things. Talking about writing in recent years, Mary, you must be really very encouraged by the quantity, the quality, the richness and variety of women writers today, particularly American women writers today. I'm thinking of some of the guests on the *Book Show*—Cynthia Ozick, Grace Paley, Toni Morrison, Louise Erdrich, Anne Beattie, Sue Miller, Jane Smiley—I could go on. This really is, I think, one of the most exciting things about contemporary letters. Once again, not just the number, but the variety of style and concern. Could you talk about that a bit? I certainly include you in that.

MG: I think it's tremendously exciting when I look at exactly what you said: the fact that Maxine Hong Kingston is writing and Toni Morrison is writing and somebody like Cynthia Ozick and even people like Joy Williams and people writing in many different voices, involved in many different enterprises. But not only here—all over the world. I just came back from a State Department tour of Europe, and I found these remarkable correspondences between what women are doing here and what women are doing, particularly in Eastern Europe. And I do feel that there were many years of repressed and untold stories, and now it's our time to tell stories. And enough of us have learned our craft, so that it's really our time. We've got the craft the men used to only have, and we've got the stories to tell. I'm not sure the men have any stories to tell that aren't only about themselves any more.

TS: That's correlated with my next question: Are men getting any better? I mean, you can interpret that various ways!

MG: In life or in art!?

TS: In life or in contemporary American letters . . . do you find more polyphonic voices in men, as compared to women these days?

MG: Interestingly enough, there are some male writers, and the two male writers that I can think of whom I like a lot are both gay. Allan Gurganus and David Plante, I think, are both doing very interesting work. Paul Auster is doing interesting work, I think. You know, there are other kinds of male writers, like Richard Ford, that don't exactly make my blood race, but I can see—you know, it seems to me kind of an old story—but I can see the value of it in a rather distant way. But I do think that a lot of male writing is pretty self-referential at this point. And the reference does not open out to a wider world.

TS: So there's not enough "news" in that tradition. There certainly is in women's writing. Mary, we just have about a half a minute left, and I wanted to ask you another question about some of the essays in *Good Boys and Dead Girls*. Your two essays on abortion are so honest and searching and large-minded. You point out that the anti-choice people have "the great advantage of a monolithic position." Do you have any reflections on the future of legal abortion in light of recent soundings and rulings of the Supreme Court?

MG: Nothing makes me despair more than what the Supreme Court did, because a lot of women are going to die. I can't believe that we'll lose this. We have to fight; every woman and man of good will has got to say no to this insanity.

Mary Gordon
Eleanor Wachtel / 1991

From *Writers & Company: In Conversation with CBC Radio's Elea-nor Wachtel*, ed. Eleanor Wachtel (Toronto: Alfred A. Knopf Canada, 1993), 262–72. © 1993 by Eleanor Wachtel. Reprinted by permission of Harcourt, Inc. and Alfred A. Knopf Canada.

This radio interview (October 1991) from the CBC's New York studio was prepared in collaboration with Sandra Rabinovitch.

Wachtel: The experience of growing up a Catholic has provided material for some of the best literature in English—funny, poignant, even frightening. You've explored this world in your fiction. In fact, you've been described by one critic as the "pre-eminent novelist of Roman Catholic mores and man-ners." Now you're writing about it more directly in your new essay collection *Good Boys and Dead Girls*. Here you observe that there is a silence, an absence of the Catholic voice, in American literature. Is that a role you your-self have chosen to fill.

Gordon: I would never choose a role. For a writer to choose a role is a doomed, perhaps self-defeating and self-deceiving project. As Flannery O'Connor says, you learn everything important that you need to write about by the age of six. By that age, most of what I had learned was imbued with an intense kind of Catholicism, which is what shaped my whole family. So it's not anything I've chosen; rather, I think it was visited upon me.

Wachtel: You grew up in a devout Catholic household, but I was interested to discover that your father, who died when you were seven, was a convert to Catholicism, that he was originally a "left-wing, Jewish intellectual."

Gordon: That's right. He did something that I don't know of anybody else having done and, if for nothing else, that made him noteworthy. My father would be ninety-three in March. He went to Harvard in the middle of the First World War, in 1917 and 1918. He was an enormous liar, and most of the people who knew him are dead, so in a sense I've created a fiction about him, trying to use the facts, but they could be wrong. This is what I put together from what I know and can surmise.

He went to Harvard and he dropped out. He then went to Europe. After that, he seems to have taken a political turn to the right, which was very unusual for a Jew at that time. I was greatly helped by Cynthia Ozick, who told me that probably the experience of having been one of the few Jews at Harvard was so scarring that he wanted to adopt an identity diametrically opposed to the identity expected of Jews. So, after many side-trips in literature and politics, he became a right-wing Catholic. My father had many, many lives (at one point, in the late twenties, he started a girlie magazine), all of which came together in his passionate devotion to the right-wing church.

Wachtel: Did you ever question the spirit behind his conversion? Did you come to understand the strength of his faith?

Gordon: It wasn't until I was at least a teenager that I questioned it. Despite the fact that he was an intellectual, he had a real romance about the working class, particularly the Irish working class. That is the community he placed me in, so I grew up in a world dominated by a very insular, working-class Irish Catholicism. I had no access to any voice that would have led me to question my father's commitment or his choices. In the context of the environment in which I was brought up, his commitment was considered heroic by those who took it seriously; other people just thought he was a nut because he wasn't practical and he didn't make money. But nobody would have questioned the conversion; that would have been honored and valorized.

Wachtel: You're very candid when you say that the only thing your parents had in common *was* Catholicism.

Gordon: That's right. They were wildly mismatched. My mother is Irish and Italian, although the Irish seemed to have drowned out every other ethnic strain. We were brought up in a very Irish Catholic community. She's a very working-class woman. She was a secretary, not very well-educated, certainly not intellectual but highly religious. My father arrived speaking seven languages and giving study groups about Thomas Aquinas to women; they met through a priest. The only thing they had in common was this extremely intense religious life.

Wachtel: And they both loved you more than each other. Did you feel that when you were a child?

Gordon: Oh yes, there was no doubt about that. You didn't have to be subtle to pick it up.

Wachtel: In an essay called "Getting Here from There: A Writer's Reflections on a Religious Past," you talk about the relationship between Catholi-

cism and your writing. You describe the impact on you of some of the rituals
of Catholicism and the way they affected you as a writer. And you say, "The
celebration of mass was an excellent training ground for an aspiring novelist."

Gordon: It was good for a couple of reasons. If you went to daily
mass—as my mother and I did—you were in a very quiet, dark place, very
early in the morning, with some extremely marginal types. What better situation for a novelist: it was made in heaven! When you went to church on
Sunday—this was the fifties, so they were crowded—you got to see the whole
social parade, again in a closed room, where you could be very observant. It
was the perfect place for an observer. Also, there was the aesthetic form of
the Latin mass. One paid a price for that: it was exclusionary and was certainly biased in favour of Western ideas. Nevertheless, it had a kind of auster-
ity and richness of form and language and sensuality that was wonderful
training, that really created a standard of aesthetic formality.

Wachtel: Were you conscious of that at the time?

Gordon: No, I was utterly absorbed in it. Religious Catholics would be
ashamed to talk about the beauty of the mass, as if it were a work of art. It
was utterly functional; it was the vessel that housed the truths by which you
lived. To consider it a species of beauty rather than truth, rather than an
utterly sacred vehicle for a transformation that they believed to be real—they
actually believed that bread and wine were turned into the body and blood of
Christ—to reduce that immensely powerful and important experience to mere
beauty would have been unthinkable. That would have been something people
like my father would have had *complete* contempt for.

Wachtel: How did you overcome that? The church is not necessarily supportive of creative expression, especially by women.

Gordon: My father was enormously supportive of my intelligence. He
trained me to be a little scholar as a very young girl. He taught me to read at
three; he taught me French; he taught me Latin before he died. He always
gave me the sense that I was gifted with words and that I was more gifted
than anybody. It would never have occurred to him that there was anything I
couldn't do because I was a girl. That just was not in the equation. So I grew
up believing myself to be quite gifted. Then the sixties came along, and it
opened up the world. As Pope John XXIII said, "It opened the windows and
the doors." I began to see that there was a larger world, a world to which I
could have access and to which I wanted to have access. I think it was a

combination of personal and historical accidents that enabled me to do this peculiar thing I do with my life.

Wachtel: You always look back. You even find models of heroic women in Catholicism.

Gordon: You don't expect me to look forward, do you? You think I'm crazy!

Wachtel: In "Getting Here from There," you say that the church of your childhood is gone, but there is still something there. How would you describe that?

Gordon: As I say at the end of that particular essay, I don't know where I am. Sometimes I'm in, sometimes I'm out; it depends on whom I'm with and what the church is doing, and how badly they're behaving, and how much toleration I have for their bad behavior. Do I look back? I think most people with a literary sensibility look back, or else they'd be making rock videos. The relationship to the past is one of literature's great subjects.

Wachtel: You've certainly mined it successfully. Where did you find heroic women in the Catholic tradition?

Gordon: One advantage that Catholicism has over other religious traditions is that there was always the example of women who did *not* define themselves through marriage or their sexual or maternal roles. Women like Teresa of Avila and Catherine of Siena who stood up to bishops and popes and who accomplished things that had nothing to do with being sexual or maternal. These were people you prayed to, people children were named after. We also had the figure of the nun, who was unmarried, unconnected to a man, yet who operated in the world. I think that accounts for the disproportionate number of Catholic women who have actually achieved. It's a very double message because Catholicism does go in for a lot of repression. Nevertheless, there was a subtext there, a subversive subtext—though they didn't realize it—of women who did not play the game according to the rules that men set down for the female body. I think there is a way in which Catholic women do have models that are helpful, in a strange way, in counteracting the enormous repression of a church run by celibate males.

Wachtel: You grew up in what you describe as a rather closed community—the predominately Catholic section of Queens—and you have said that it served you well when you did turn to writing fiction, because your natural subject became the secrets of the Catholic world. What kinds of secrets?

Gordon: I think that there was a secret language, and that language created categories of thought. There were ideals of behavior, by which I don't mean rules of behavior but ideals that had one foot in eternity and one foot very solidly on the ground; these were codified and given their own festivals and colors. There was a way of behaving, and there were subversive tactics.

Most of the Catholics I knew became very adept at getting around authority. It's one of the things that Catholics laugh about—how adept a liar being involved in the church makes you, and how you learn all these end runs. But at the center of it, for many Catholics, there was an enormously serious issue, which is, how do you become a saint? How do you save your soul? And that shaped everything in a way that was very unlike other religious traditions.

Wachtel: Is there a way in which it's traitorous to expose the secrets within your own community?

Gordon: Oh, sure. As many people as there are telling me they're very grateful for what I've done in telling their stories, there are others, particularly in my family, who think I'm a slut, because I've opened the door and told what *they* think is a distortion of the truth.

I don't very much like those people in my family who don't like my books, so I really didn't care about their reactions. But there were a couple of very sensitive, thoughtful souls who were really grieved or uncomprehending about what I had done. That was painful, but not enough to stop me. I think I got enough satisfaction out of outraging the bad ones. Also, in a rather touching way, some of the people who were saddened by my work continued to love me. There was some odd bond of understanding there that couldn't be severed.

Wachtel: You write that there *isn't* a tradition, or not much of a tradition, of Irish-American or Irish-Catholic writing. The Irish, you say, like to tell stories, but they don't actually want to reveal anything and they don't value writers. I found this a very surprising notion, but I realize that you're right.

Gordon: People think that the Irish-Americans are like the Irish, and they have these fantasies of the Celtic twilight in Ireland. They forget that most of the writers of the Irish Renaissance were either Protestant or supported mainly by the Protestants. Joyce left Ireland for a very good reason: he wasn't appreciated there. There's an added issue with American-Irish: they left Ireland because they were the practical ones; survival was their business. Telling stories about the clan is not a very great help to survival. They didn't, a lot of them, respect anything that was not going to push them ahead in America.

In addition, because Irish Catholicism has so many secrets, they're a little phobic about expressing *any* emotion.

They're very, very sexually puritanical people, on the whole; they really are phobic about any kind of sexual transgression. Also, the Irish have been very hard hit by alcoholism. Alcoholics have to keep a lot of secrets. I think those are the two major areas of secrecy: sexual transgression, which is bound to happen in such a strict, enclosed system and which the Irish have very little toleration for—they're very different from Mediterranean Catholics in that way—and alcoholism. These are by definition going to create a secretive culture.

Wachtel: You have also written that women are more prone to reveal these secrets, and that for women to write intimately is considered taboo. Yet when this taboo is broken, their work is judged either trivial or an embarrassment.

Gordon: I was brought up short on this topic again when I read the biography of Anne Sexton and thought about the response to her work, which was very intimate and self-revelatory. People were terribly embarrassed by it at the time, in a way that they weren't by the work of Robert Lowell or John Berryman, who were equally self-revelatory. There's something about a *woman* speaking intimately that presses the light of embarrassment, in a way that doesn't happen when men writers do it.

Wachtel: You were schooled in the idea that the writer should strive for distance, but you say that what *you* love to write is "radical closeness."

Gordon: That was the way I was trained. And the values I believed in for a very long time canonized Henry James, for example—whom I adore—as *the* paradigm of how one ought to write. That finished, distant relationship between author and subject matter, and emphasis on formality. My early training in the church made formality and distance things to be enormously desired. Remember, our sacred figure was the figure of the priest, who *never* got close to ordinary life. I think I must have transmuted that ideal of the distant priest to the ideal of the distant artist. Women were the ones who messed about in the muck of life and I didn't want to do that; for a long time I really struggled against that. I thought if I did get too close or too intimate, people would think I was writing like a girl. That was something I was afraid of. Then I realized, I *had* to write like a girl, I *was* a girl; that it would be enormously distorting to try to write like what I was not; and that in fact these models, in their monolithic nature, were extremely distorting and destructive.

Wachtel: You mention that your father wanted to be a writer and was interested in scholarship, in learning, and that that was a form of support for you then. Do you think your father would understand or appreciate your work now?

Gordon: I can't imagine that I would be doing the work I'm doing now, if my father had lived. I think if there is a heaven, he thinks I'm the greatest writer in history. But I would be an enormously different person had he lived; I don't think I would have fought him. I would probably have been seduced into being the good daughter, which is an enormously powerful lure for women. I'm not sure I would have been able to shake it off. I think more women are held back by being good daughters, or good girls, than by many more obvious forms of oppression.

Wachtel: You write that you've also come to realize that you're not only your father's daughter but also your mother's daughter, in terms of influence on your approach to writing: metaphysics from your father's side and the kitchen table from your mother's.

Gordon: Yes, and the more I look, the more I see how difficult a child I must have been for my mother, although I was a very, very good child—I was pathologically obedient. I literally lay in my bed, worrying about it. I was never really disobedient. Now my mother sees my daughter—who tells me exactly what she thinks I'm doing wrong in florid detail, and why there is absolutely no reason for her to brush her hair—and says, "Your mother was never like that. Your mother was such a good child. How come you're such a bad child?" And I say, "Yes, that's right, she's a bad child, thank God!" Although she's not, she's a very good girl. But I was, as I say, pathologically good.

I was really worried about being perfect. In that way, I was an easy child, but my mother must have felt that some bird laid a strange egg in her nest. When I was very young, she must have looked at my father and me and decided, "She'll do better with him." Spiritually, she gave me over to my father, and held back and didn't try to change me, which I think was an act of enormous love. She supported me in an endeavour that she really didn't understand. I don't know whether I could do that for my child. I think it's really extraordinary. My mother also had a lot of pizzazz. She was very snappy, very funny, and she knew how to tell a good story. My father was, too. Thank God, I had two funny parents. But my mother also had a real interest in the dailiness of life that my father didn't have. I think that, too, was a gift to me as a writer.

Wachtel: Do you think that part of your desire to be good had to do with the reality of reward and punishment, heaven and hell, saints and devils, and things like that?

Gordon: Absolutely. I really was in fear for my immortal soul a lot of the time. But there was also the idea of an infinitely loving God whom you were disappointing, whom you were hurting, when He had never done anything but love you. That sense of fear of the Loving One's disappointment was in some ways much more potent than fear of hell-fire.

Wachtel: Although you tell your daughter that the devil is more like the Loch Ness monster, or a banshee.

Gordon: Yes, I cannot, with any conviction, muster up the devil. Although recently, my son—he is having a sleeping problem—kept wanting to wake me up. I said to him, "We really don't want you to do that." I explained the subconscious to my seven-year-old, and I said, "We really want to trick your mind, because there's a voice telling you to sleep, and there's a voice telling you to wake up. We want to trick the voice that's telling you to wake up." He said, "Yes, there's my good voice that says, 'Go to sleep, go to sleep.' Then there's my devil voice that says, 'Try to get into the bed with your mother!' " I really, really didn't tell him that!

Wachtel: You are a feminist with progressive views, and yet you also regret some of the changes that have happened in the church since you were young. How has the feminist in you managed to get along all these years with the Catholic in you?

Gordon: Because there are enough women I know, and men too, who are like me, and because it seems to me I wouldn't be a feminist except for my early training as a Catholic. I was brought up to take issues of justice very seriously. And what is feminism except a desire for universal justice not bounded by gender roles? I don't understand how anybody could be a Catholic and *not* be a feminist. I don't understand how anybody could read the New Testament and support a sexist position. It doesn't seem to me that *I'm* in conflict. I think *they're* wrong, and I'm shocked.

Wachtel: There are a lot of them, though.

Gordon: Well, many people believed in slavery for a very long time. They were wrong. These guys are wrong. Even though there are a lot of them, they can still be all wrong. I don't really see a conflict. I don't know how they can sleep at night. I'm sleeping fine.

Wachtel: Do you still go to church?

Gordon: Sometimes. I can't say it's something that shapes my life in a central way. It's not that I never have a desire to go, or that I feel nothing when I go. I like hearing the gospels read, and I like feeling that I'm in a room with people who at least pretend to believe these words that are of great beauty. I like being in a large room with a lot of different kinds of people. Most of my life now I meet rather upper-class, literate types. I like being in a room with people who are very different from me, all of whom have their hearts tilted towards one thing which, at its best, I find very beautiful.

Mary Gordon

Terry Gross / 1993

Transcription of *Fresh Air,* (WHYY: Philadelphia), National Public Radio, 11 October 1993. © 1993 by WHYY, Inc. Printed by permission.

Gross: Mary Gordon has said that in her new book she wanted to explore what it's like to live in a female body. Her new book also has variations on themes she's written about in previous novels: the complications of romantic love, parental love, and spiritual devotion. Her new book, *The Rest of Life: Three Novellas,* was called "remarkable" in the *New York Times Sunday Book Review.* Before we talk with her, let's hear a reading from the first novella, "Immaculate Man." The main character is a woman who has gone a long time without a passionate sexual involvement with a man, and she's afraid that when or if she loses this particular lover, she'll be alone again and that it will be worse than it was before.

Gordon: *Reads from "Immaculate Man," page 30,* The Rest of Life.

TG: Mary, all three of the novellas in your new book are about women who love men and worry about losing them or, in one case, have already lost him. What were you examining about relationships in the stories?

MG: I think what I'm trying to examine is the place where women really are now. And I guess women of my generation or my cohort really, women, I would say, between 40 and 65. And we're not the women who were denied sexual experience. We're the women who have had sexual experience and then what? So if the story isn't *Anna Karenina*—you know, if we all haven't ended up under the wheels of a train—where have we ended up? It seems to me that the experience of passionate love is a frightening one for both men and women, but especially for women, I would say. Two of my characters, the first two, are in relationships with men presently. One of them is with a man who was a virgin when she met him; he was 43 and still a virgin. And she's afraid that he's only with her because he didn't know any better. And now that he knows better, he'll be with someone else. And my second character is with a man who is constantly putting himself in physical danger. He's a journalist who travels to the hot danger spots of the world, and she's afraid she's going to lose him in death. And I think the reality is that if you are attached to somebody passionately, the loss of them would be a terrible thing. I think that if you do somehow place your body next to the bodily life of a man, it's not that if the man goes away, you stop living, but you live differently. And it's that "differently" that I wanted to explore.

TG: I know when I was young I once woke up one Sunday morning to the sound of my upstairs neighbor dying. And his wife, you know, lived on, became like "the widow" in the building. And I thought, how does someone go on like this, how does a woman who's been married all her life live without a husband? And everyone's attitude seemed to be: end of life, game over, that's it. And I no longer feel that that's exactly what life would be. On the other hand, as you're saying, there would be this terrible loss. It would be a different life. You know what I mean?

MG: One of the things, however, that interests me a lot is how people make another whole life, and it really is a whole life. It's not a fragmented life, it's not a truncated life. I've seen actually a lot of older women who get quite a kick out of their husbands' death *(laughs)*. It's like they're suddenly free, and they're suddenly able to do things that they weren't able to do. I guess what I'm always trying to say is that there's no one way of experiencing it. There are ways of living with men, there are many different ways of living with men, there are many different ways of living without men, there are ways of kind of having part of your life with men and part of your life without men. And it's still a life, and that's enormously interesting to me. What I'm trying to undo is that notion that women are either locked into life with a man (that equals "alive") or somehow cast adrift in this miserable dark sea (and that is being without a man). And it seems to me that both being with a man and being without a man are much more equivocal and partial than people like us have been brought up to expect.

TG: I want get back to the first story, the story you read from. In this story, the man is a virgin. He's a 43-year-old priest whose order has basically died out, and he becomes lovers with a woman just a few years older who works at a shelter for abused women. What interested you in the idea of writing about a 43-year-old male virgin?

MG: Well, nobody believes me *(laughs)* that I was really more interested in writing about a virgin than about a priest. Everybody thinks I'm being coy, but I'm really not. When I was writing the essay, "Good Boys and Dead Girls," I was really exploring the idea of male innocence as seen from a male point of view, and I thought a lot about what innocence might be. And it occurred me to that the paradigm in Western culture for innocence is the female virgin. I mean, we have heard about female virginity 'til we could all die of it. But obviously there is such a thing as male sexual inexperience, not every male baby came out of the womb, you know, Hugh Hefner. So I thought, what would that be like, that sexual blankness for a woman?

TG: You know, there's so much that you can't convey about a book by just kind of summarizing a plot. I was thinking about it when reading the story, because I was thinking on some level the idea a male virgin who is priest in his 40s who falls in love and really desires this woman might sound to someone casually listening like, "oh, the *Thorn Birds!*"

MG: *(laughs)* It should only sell so well. *(pauses)* Yes, it *is*. It's *exactly* like the *Thorn Birds!* Go out and buy it! Quite similar.

TG: The woman character in the story gets really concerned that as her lover gets more experienced and more worldly, not only about sex but about other things in the world, that of course he'll leave. You know, why would he want her now that he's becoming more and more worldly?

MG: One of the things that interests me a lot, and that every woman I know has one version or another of, I simply don't know a woman who doesn't, is the notion: "I'm not desirable enough; there's somebody else out there, anywhere, who could be more desirable." And . . .

TG: And as soon as he finds them, it's all over.

MG: It's all over. All the years I've had, everything that I've done, it'll all be wiped out because he'll see, whoever it is, Michelle Pfeiffer (Michelle Pfeiffer's the one I always fixate on) or somebody. It doesn't matter. I think that so many of us are convinced that in the blink of an eye some strange force will take the men that we love away from us. And I really wanted to play with that, because I don't exactly know if the priest will leave her or not. He might. He might not. But she's really convinced that he will and that becomes a part of the fabric of their love affair, even though he's constantly reassuring her that he loves her and is in fact quite desiring. Nothing silences that tormenting voice, and I think that there are billion dollar industries that are solely devoted to making women feel undesirable. And I think it's a terrible, terrible problem for women.

TG: You're writing about women in love who are mature women and women who feel very physical toward the men they're in love with; they feel that they have physically found the right match as well as emotionally found the right match . . .

MG: Yes.

TG: And I wonder if you think it's any different writing about the physical love of a woman in her forties and writing about the, you know, physical passion of someone in their twenties or teens who is still kind of young and discovering things for the first time.

MG: I think it's enormously different. Somebody once said to me about herself in her teens, "At that point in my life I wasn't interested in enjoying sex; I was interested in having it." And I think that when you're young, just having sex is such an exciting or a different thing or such a proof that you're alive or mature that it's almost . . . I think it becomes a more generic experience. You know the quality of frantic desire that I think marks youth changes, and I think it becomes deeper and it even is experienced in the body more deeply. So to say that one has less desire when one is older is wrong, but it's almost a different sort of physical experience. And there's also a backlog of disappointment and betrayal and self-protectiveness, but I think once that is broken through, the experience is enormously deep and, in many ways, I think, more satisfying than it was when one was younger.

TG: The couple in the story often talk about things like, can you know if you're a good person if you've never been tested. And there's a wonderful story . . . let me ask you to talk about the drowning story in the book.

MG: Yeah, my character is swimming with her daughter when the daughter is ten, and the two of them get caught in a rip-tide. And the mother finds herself going into a kind of trance, and the daughter is flailing, and the mother is annoyed with the daughter and in fact doesn't help her—just disappears into her own trance and somebody else saves the daughter. And the mother feels that at the point in her life when her daughter most needed her, she failed her, and this haunts her. And her lover Clement says, "No, you didn't fail, you panicked. And what you thought was a trance was not a trance; it was panic." And she doesn't quite believe him; she feels that she was tested and found wanting. And it's something that disturbs her very deeply about herself.

TG: Does this relate to a way that you've felt you've been tested as a mother and weren't sure you passed the test?

MG: It actually happened to me. I was in Martha's Vineyard with my daughter, and we did get caught in a rip-tide and exactly what I report happened to me. And I keep going up to my daughter, this is four years later, and saying, "I'm so sorry for the way I behaved in the rip-tide." And she says, "It was about three seconds, Mom. Don't worry about it." But I replay it and replay it, and I feel that this was a life and death situation, and I blew it. I really blew it.

TG: So this really stays with you. You know the character says, "You know I always used say I would gladly give my life for my child, and, you know, I don't think I can say that anymore because I didn't."

MG: Yes, "I didn't." *I* didn't either. And it doesn't matter to me that people who were watching it said it was three minutes, and if she'd really been in danger, you would have done it. I know that I didn't, and I'll never quite get over it.

TG: I really would like to know how you got saved if you were drowning in the rip-tide.

MG: Okay, this is very important for your listeners. You can get out of a rip-tide very easily. You just have to swim parallel to the shore. A rip-tide is a channel that goes straight out, and the paradox of it is that if you relax and turn and swim in a different direction, you're okay quite soon. Actually, my daughter was saved by someone coming to get her and, that was interesting, somebody came out to get her with a boogie-board, and forgot about me! And I just went out. But then I figured out how to get out of it. I was a strong enough swimmer, and I figured my way out.

TG: I'm going to move on to the second story in your book. And in the second story it's also about a couple, and it's also the woman who is afraid that she will lose her lover. This time it's because he's a foreign correspondent and is always exposing himself to revolution and coups and wars and so on. She works; she works with autistic children. In the *New York Times* interview, you said that your interest in autism was that you're obsessed with how difficult it is to live an ordinary bourgeois life, which is like the details of ordinary life. What got you thinking about that? What's the connection to autism?

MG: Well, autistic children find things that we think are very easy enormously difficult; getting dressed, eating, can be enormously problematic for them. Walking in and out of a room can paralyze them. Turning a light off and on can paralyze them. So I was interested in the fact that what is defined as easy or ordinary or customary is much more shifting that I had thought. So that, for example, I think it's really hard to keep a lot of clean clothes in your drawers at all time, but a lot of people think, of course, you just keep a lot of clean clothes in your drawers at all times, and of course, you pay your bills and of course, you don't let your mail pile up. That's just the way it is. For me, to look at my desk and not feel that there's a stack of letters I haven't answered and then to feel terror at that would be a miracle. And I think for an autistic child to one day be able to walk in and out of a door without terror is a miracle, so I think what one thinks of as ordinary, or the minimum requirement, is really very shifting.

TG: When you talk about your obsession with the difficulty of living an ordinary, bourgeois life, do you find yourself thinking about that even more when you're sick?

MG: Yes. Absolutely.

TG: The reason why I say this . . . the details of ordinary life can be overwhelming and time-consuming, and everything, but you find a way to deal with it. But when you're sick, gosh, it really saps your strength, and there's no energy left for anything else and, you know, it just becomes kind of monumental.

MG: You lie in bed and you think, "I may never buy food again. I may never answer the mail. I may never go to work. It is really possible that I will just lie here and become more and more filthy, starve, and die." And when I'm sick, that always seems very likely that that will happen, and then I get terrified, and then I think that makes you even sicker. Or when I'm extremely fatigued, I sometimes will lie in bed, knowing I have to wake up, and think, "I simply won't do it. I won't get out of bed. I will not take a shower. I will not go to work. I will just lie and then everything will be destroyed and there will be a kind of peace in that because it'll be over." It seems to me it would be very . . . the other thing I'm obsessed with when I see homeless people is at one point they decided not to keep up. They crossed some kind of line, and I'm always fascinated at what that line is. When have you gone too far to get back into the web? And it seems to me that that would be really easy to do. Like supposing you just stopped paying your electric bill, because you don't have any money in your checking account, and you're too tired to get stamps, and you just don't pay it. And then all the power goes off. And then all of the food in the house rots, and then it just goes on from there. And it seems to me it could start from the inability to buy a stamp, which, at one point very clearly to me, could seem to be too difficult. And I can see just letting one little thing go after another and ending up on the street.

TG: You know, the characters you write about are really not extraordinary people, right?
MG: Right.

TG: They're interesting, ordinary people. But, and I'm not saying this just to flatter you, I think you're an extraordinary writer, and therefore when you're writing about these kind of interesting, ordinary people, they are somehow able to think in extraordinary ways. Do you know what I mean? I think your characters are able to think more clearly and eloquently than their real-life counterparts could, because you're putting the words in their mouths.
MG: Well, I think that's the difference between thinking eloquently and speaking eloquently, and that's what a writer does. That is the gift that we have. I'm not convinced that many people aren't thinking extraordinary thoughts; they simply don't have the facility to write them or even speak them. It's something that growing up working-class as I did . . . you really understand that occasionally people who were enormously inarticulate and spoke seventy years of clichés will say a few extraordinary sentences, and you realize that in that inner life there might have been a lot of quite remarkable things that were never able to be said. Everybody dreams, for example; nobody has boring dreams. If anybody told you their dreams, they're full of details which are highly imaginative.

TG: So you kind of feel that what you could do is translate those thoughts into words.
MG: Yeah, I think that's the great lesson of Joyce's *Ulysses*. I mean, you know, Leopold Bloom was an ordinary schmuck in Dublin; he wasn't doing very well. And the entire riches of English literature and English language are put at his disposal through Joyce, and you get this extraordinary consciousness. And I think that is the task of a writer, to give articulation to what is buried and yet quite rich in, I believe, most people.

An Interview with Mary Gordon

Patrick H. Samway / 1994

From *America*, 14 May 1994, 12–15. © 1994 America Press, Inc.
Reprinted by permission.

Interview: 20 January 1994, New York City.

Could you tell me about your childhood and growing up in Valley Stream on Long Island?

I had a childhood that is wholly unlike anyone else's because my parents, Anna and David, were absolutely not typeable. At present, I am trying to find out about my father, to mine his past, and the more I try to find out about him, the more elusive he becomes. He was a Jew, born in 1899, who converted to Catholicism in the 1930s. He was 50 when I was born, and he took exactly the opposite path that most Jews took then. There is almost no one else who did what he did; he turned right politically when most Jews went left. The best way I can place him in intellectual history is that he was a good deal like Ezra Pound. He had kind of a fantasy of a great and heroic European past. He lived in a highly colored Christian world where right and wrong were very clearly identifiable. The church was at the helm. Art was great. Men were men and women were women. Excommunication was a good and ready option. He converted to Catholicism before he met my mother. So it was really an intellectual conversion. He converted, I think, because he supported Franco. His mentor was Father Leonard Feeney, who was later asked, as you know, to leave the Jesuit order.

My mother, Anna, was completely a working-class, Irish-and-Italian woman. Neither of her parents went past eighth grade. Her parents met in New York City. Her mother came from Ireland and her father from Italy. Very simple folk, yet tough. Above all, they were immigrant-survivors.

Did your father know Father Feeney personally?

Yes. And it was because of Father Feeney, who was an associate editor of *America* from 1936 to 1940, that my father wrote for *America*. And Father Feeney even wrote about my father—how David Gordon had stopped by to see him and what they chatted about.

What did they talk about?

Literature and Catholicism. They had the same fantasy of a Europe that never existed, but which they thought existed, where everything was high and fine and profound. Since everything was run by the church, there was no doubt, no equivocation, and no mediocrity. For my father, the modern world was mediocre, and thus we had lost greatness. Literature and language mattered to him in a very deep way, and that led him into an odd kind of right-wing position.

I understand from an essay you once wrote that your mother had polio?

She was a polio victim at the age of three. So she was handicapped all her life; she has no memory of not being handicapped. It is incredible when you think that my parents had virtually nothing in common except a very real spiritual life, in quite different ways. They were not fooling around. They both had spiritual lives of very high seriousness. My mother was very active in the working-women's retreat movement. My mother was also very practical, and she had a real peasant side to her.

Do you have any distinct recollections of your father?

My father died when I was seven. Since he did not work, I was with him all the time. He was devoted to me in a way that is very rare for fathers. He adored children. We were really together constantly. Although he died when I was quite young, my relationship with him was enormously intense. He was such a colorful person that it is easy to have memories of him. Yet, it was my mother who supported the family, in spite of the fact that she had polio. In those days, she could walk and get around. My mother was really incredible in terms of accomplishing tasks. She just did whatever had to be done. I might add that, if I say she is a peasant, it could sound like I am putting her down. I don't mean to do so because, even today, she is a woman of great complexity and tremendous intelligence. She has a literary gift, too, that expresses itself in writing letters. And she is funny. Both of my parents were very funny and both were storytellers. We had a life that was quite crazy but very rich during those Eisenhower years.

Did you go to Catholic schools?

I went to my parish school for 12 years—a really terrible experience because it was at the height of Catholic triumphalism, which translated itself into 60 kids in a class. We shared desks. The nuns were not particularly well educated. It is interesting to observe the fantasies that non-Catholics have about Catholic education, because they do not understand that it is not a monolithic thing. Certainly, there were some Catholic schools in the world where Ingrid Bergman was teaching students—right out of *The Bells of St. Mary's*. Our school was for working-class students. I don't think that most of my teachers had gone to college. They had few resources. The school had enormous numbers of children and did everything on a shoe-string. It was a place run by fear and a kind of perfectionism that was limited to the petty.

And college? What was Barnard like for you?

I went to Barnard in 1967; it was great, especially Elizabeth Hardwick, who was my teacher. In high school, we were still high on Vatican II, and Pope John XXIII was still shimmering in our minds; that gave us a lot of courage to move out into the larger world. I had received a scholarship to Fordham, but I didn't want to be in a totally Catholic environment. Even though I was living 20 miles away from New York City, I didn't know any non-Catholics. I knew the dry cleaner was a Protestant and the druggist was a Jew, and that was it. The reason I went to Barnard is that I read J. D. Salinger's fiction, particularly about the Glass family, and that was the world I wanted. I wanted a world of Jewish intellectuals. I thought that if I went to Barnard or Columbia I would meet Seymour Glass. Today kids choose a college after their parents have taken them to 15 different campuses; they search for a college that has the right combination of ecology and Renaissance literature. I simply wanted to meet Seymour Glass. My instincts, I believe, were completely right.

Is this when you started writing?

You have to understand I have no memory of a self that is not a writing self. Both my fathers and my teachers at an all-girls' high school taught me that it was quite possible for young women to become writers. I never experienced feeling that there wasn't anything intellectual that I couldn't do because I was female. So I already defined myself as a writer from early on, but it was at Barnard I was taken very seriously by my teachers and nurtured by them; they also set very high standards, something new to me. They were the standards of the world, not of the parish. I learned that I did not have to protect a rather fragile home territory, nor did I have to be a spokesperson for things Catholic. What was exciting to me was that the world was mine. I felt enormously free. In those days, Catholics said they were interested in the world, but they really weren't. They only put a toe in the world and extracted what would fit comfortably into a parish setting. I saw the contradiction in that. I really wanted to see everything. I was very curious. And even to see that there might be things about which the church could be wrong. And I instinctively knew I needed that; I needed to see other worlds of thought and action. As a result, I was alienated from the church for a few years. I think I needed to be. It was important to feel like I was not going home every night.

In "Immaculate Man," one of the stories in your recent collection of short stories [novellas] *entitled* The Rest of Life, *the woman narrator and Father Clement Buckley create for themselves a Hemingwayesque universe of two. Father Buckley is witnessing the dismantling of his religious order. The woman works in a home for abused women. She is very attractive to Father Buckley physically. As we see their relationship, what does she know about him personally or spiritually, and what does this tell us about the story?*

One of the things that interested me in writing about a man like Clement was the idea of innocence. How could I portray an innocent man? We usually think of most innocents in fiction as either mentally defective or women, which is the same thing for a lot of writers. One of Clement's appeals for her is something rather important: He doesn't have a pornographic imagination. He is not poisoned by a lot of what comes with being a sexually plugged-in modern person. And so she felt safe with him; sexuality wasn't toxic for her. And her femaleness was a kind of miracle to him. His goodness and lack of self-interest are a real revelation to her, something that draws her to him. She doesn't understand what a prayer life or interior life would be like. His willingness to be there for people is very moving to her, I think.

There is a flip side to this, however, in that the word "sin" does not seem to be in his vocabulary.

You're right.

If sin is not in his vocabulary, what really has replaced it?

I don't think the notion of sin was ever in his vocabulary. Evil never really interested him much. That was not his "field," though he practiced a lot of denial. The nature of the world for him was not one in which evil played a great part. He was more concerned about alleviating suffering. I wanted to create a character whose sexuality would not blast him out of the water. It is almost satanic to think that if you become sexual then you cannot be present to others. It is wrong to think that only celibates are available to others.

Does the woman have a name? I kept on looking for it.

No, she is nameless.

The woman narrator says that Father Clement doesn't really understand children. But does she really understand children? How can she face her own children as she goes off to Paris with a priest?

She does understand children, I believe, in a way that is demythified. There is a way of being a mother now that doesn't presume that you can create a perfect world for your children; it doesn't assume that everything you do will be comfortable or even comprehensible to them. A mother should be present for her children. A mother tries to give life to her children. I was interested in creating a non-idealized version of a mother. She doesn't have a model of perfection or perfectibility, which makes her very different from Clement. This woman is never totally sure that she is right about anything; she always sees a lot of different sides to any situation. She sees her children as complicated and imperfect, yet knows they are going in the right direction.

In the second story [novella] *in the collection, you have a woman doctor who deals with autistic children. Her character provides a link with the first story. Also the endings of all three stories seem linked, as if they were all companion stories. In this story, there is also a good deal of discussion about children. One of the unnamed women doctor's friends, Lydia, says something interesting: No matter how good someone may be, a person needs some firm ground in order to help children. Though the reader is constantly made to think about children, children are absent in the story. Would you comment on why you refer to absent children and then never make them active participants in the story?*

Do you mean the autistic children or her literal children?

Both.

The years when a woman is required to do hands-on mothering are, in the course of her life, not the majority—maybe 20 years of a 70- or 80-year life. Yet a woman can be a mother to children who are out in the world even when she doesn't have a lot of control over them. A mother has to get over the fantasy that she can always control her children. For a little while, children need a mother, and then there is a break, but the mother is still their mother. Sooner or later, it becomes a much looser confederation of states. Children are always present to their mothers, whether they are absent or not. This character is a mother and a daughter at the same time she is a lover. Most discussions of sexual women have assumed that when they were being sexual they were just lovers. But a woman doesn't stop being a mother and a daughter when she is a lover. I was interested in portraying that a sexual life for a woman isn't necessarily compartmentalized; it flows in and out of the other kinds of a woman that she is—a worker, a lover, a mother, a daughter, a friend—all those dimensions are woven into one another. It is enormously important to de-idealize maternity.

In this story, the woman knows and, at the same time, does not know Lauro, the male protagonist. She does not know Lauro's son, for example, or how he became acquainted with Senegalese culture. How would you respond to someone who said that talking about ambiguous relationships is the key to your short fiction?

I am really obsessed, at the moment, with the partiality of our knowing. I was brought up with so many models of perfection prevalent in the pre-Vatican II church. There was a perfect way of washing a dish; you were attentive to each dish you washed. You didn't let your mind wander. That was how you offered everything up for the greater glory of God. There was no time when you were not on the hook. So the possibilities for feeling like a failure were enormous. I felt that was a bad way to live. You nevertheless have to have high ideals and also have a great sense of humor knowing that you are going to blow most of it. Most of what you want to do is not doable; yet this does not mean that you shouldn't try to do it. If not, you end up in a suburban shopping mall saying, "There's no point to anything at all." I believe in a very non-perfectionistic, non-idealized model that has a lot of idealism in it. Why not be more like the Marx brothers?

Are your women characters, as they talk about their lives, really going through a type of therapy?

I wouldn't want to use that model because I don't know who the therapist would be.

Then, is it more a process of discovery for them?

Yes, discovery. Or explanation, or just description. When you describe your life, you discover.

I found the third story in the collection, "The Rest of Life," the most interesting. You deal with a 78-year-old woman who returns to her native Italy after being away for 63 years. A good bit of the story is interior monologue as she recalls a past experience. The story of Leo and Paula is really that of Romeo and Juliet, isn't it?

Yes, except Juliet lives.

But really aren't your women Eurydices trying to extricate the men in their lives from the dark?

That is an interesting observation because Paula writes a poem about Orpheus and Eurydice, and she gets it wrong. I think the women in these stories do tend to have a clearer and fuller vision of life than the men. Leo was a romantic boy who died stupidly by shooting himself when he was at his peak. He had this perfectionist image: To die young after love is the highest moment in love. The reason why I deliberately called it "The Rest of Life" is that there is all that rest of life that is not tragic and high but takes even the moment of greatest tragedy and incorporates it in a way that is not perfect or heroic but more incarnational.

Can we live for 63 years in a frozen life and, at the end, discover for ourselves that there is no story to tell? Would you perhaps consider this story a metaphor? If so, of what?

For me, it is a metaphor for the fact that there is no single knowable or accountable past that is the definitive version. Every time Paula tells the story, she tells it a little bit differently. It is a metaphor for the art of telling a story. Paula finds out at the end that getting the real story isn't the important thing, because there really is no real story. There is a moment when you have to break through that desire to tell the story only one way into something larger that is mysterious and beyond even story, even though you get to it only through storytelling.

It is interesting, too, that Paula's son is going off on a trip with a Nigerian woman, which is a fillip on the main story. He is going to have his own story to tell.

And his fiancée has a story that comes from a very different past, which is not European. There are many stories and many ways of narrating these stories. The world changes physically so fast that one of the ways we test our memories is to go back to a place and say, "Oh, this is where I did this." And the place would be recognizable. Yet one of the aspects of modern life is that places change in very radical ways. And so the nature of remembering will have to change, especially if, to paraphrase Gertrude Stein, there is no there to go back to. The "there" then becomes entirely a construction of the mind. We cannot really count on those physical markers any more.

Conversations with Mary Gordon

Alma Bennett / 1994–1995

From the *South Carolina Review*, 28:1 (Fall 1995), 3–34. Copyright 1995 Clemson University. Reprinted by permission.

Interviews in New York City in Mary Gordon's apartment and in her Barnard College office: 28 & 29 October 1994, 24 March 1995.

Bennett: You're in the midst of writing a book about your father. Have you decided on the title?

Gordon: It's called *Reading My Father* [published in 1995 as *The Shadow Man: A Daughter's Search for Her Father*.]

Bennett: You mentioned on the telephone that the book is pivotal. What did you mean by "pivotal"?

Gordon: Well, for one thing, it's my first book of nonfiction and my instinct is that it's an important book. I think it brings a lot of preoccupations together. "Traces them" is the word—"tracks them."

Bennett: It makes a sort of complete circle. It reminds me of your line in "In Praise of Watercolors" where you say that the retrieval of the past gives you what you conceive; in the retrieval you can see your future. Do you feel that's the kind of pivot this is?

Gordon: I don't know. It seems like it was an enormous labor that needed to be done. What will come after it I don't know, but it is an enormous labor.

Bennett: How did this start? What triggered the process of your new investigation about your father's background? You've been putting things together since his death when you were a young girl.

Gordon: I guess it was the decision to make it a book.

Bennett: When did you decide that? After "Important Houses" came out?

Gordon: I can't remember very well because it just always seemed that I was going to do it. And then "The Important Houses" came, and I don't remember which came first: the decision to write a book about him and then going back to that image or whether—I think I knew I was going to write a book about him. I don't really remember very well. Sometimes the experience of the writing and the experience of the thinking meld so much that I don't know which came first.

Bennett: But then the decision was what led you to start doing some more investigation about him? How did you start and what did you do?

Gordon: Well, I asked a couple of friends who were American historians, "How would you track someone like this?" And they kind of pointed me in the direction I would go to find the manuscript census which is not just the statistics of the census, but the actual manuscript of the original census which would give me a lot of information. So, I found that.

Bennett: Did you find that here in New York?

Gordon: Yes. And I knew I would have to go out to Ohio, so I went out there to the local library in Lorain. Actually just this morning I printed out the draft of the chapter about that, so in about a month I could send you the chapter which explains everything. Anyway, I went out to Lorain, I looked up his school records, I looked in the yearbook, I looked in the city directories. Then I went out to the Case Western Reserve Library, which has a lot of Ohio local history, and I looked up marriage certificates and necrology files. Then so many things happened in such a peculiar, peculiar way. I was giving a reading at Goucher College, reading from "The Other Deaths" in *Salmagundi.* And I said that I was going to Cleveland the next week and look for whatever. So many odd things would happen. I would give a reading and people would come up and say, "I was from Lorain." So I thought that wherever I went I was just going to open my mouth and talk about it. And who knew what connections would get to me? There was a woman rabbi in the Goucher audience, and she said, "I know a woman who does Jewish genealogy in Cleveland, and I'll put you in touch with her." Well, this woman was like one of those women that could and should be running General Motors; she was full of energy, organization, and she took my case on and was gangbusters. She found my grandfather's will, she found death notices from my aunts, she went to town. And then I had to work harder than she was working because she had been working the Jewish cause for so long. She found relatives for me. One of the relatives turned out to be the son of my aunt's lawyer who found her file in his law firm's office. It was just amazing.

Bennett: It might be interesting for you to run the question by her about the pattern of anti-Semitism among Lithuanian-Jewish immigrants.

Gordon: Oh, no, she's doesn't want to hear a discouraging word about any Jews. She actually said to me, "I was very sick this summer. I had a terrible intestinal ailment. Thank God it's a Jewish disease. It's Crohn's disease and it genetically stalemates Jewish DNA." So at least that was comforting her. *(laughing)* But she was amazing. She was a beaver.

Bennett: First of all you found out your father wasn't born in Ohio.
Gordon: Right. And that he was born speaking Yiddish.

Bennett: And do you know exactly where in Lithuania he was born?
Gordon: Vilna, near Vilna. Then I found out that he had two other sisters I didn't know about.

Bennett: But you thought he was an only child, didn't you?
Gordon: First I thought he was an only child, but then a sister of his called when he died. As it turns out, he was in touch with her all the time. She died in a nursing home surrounded by pictures of me, which my father had sent her.

Bennett: When I saw your comment about the sister in one of your essays, I thought it was either the eeriest coincidence in the world or he told her he was terribly sick.
Gordon: Well, I think he had a cousin who actually came to visit us who might have been told. But he was in constant touch with this sister.

Bennett: So you knew about that one?
Gordon: Well, I didn't know he was in touch with her! Because his thing was that the family had declared him dead. But I found out that wasn't even true.

Bennett: You mean when he converted to Catholicism?
Gordon: Yes. He was writing affectionate notes to her until the time of his death. So the mythology just goes on being layered. And then this genealogist found my grandfather's will and my aunt's address in Massilon, Ohio. The other aunt. One had died at 16, one I knew about, and this was another one. And the genealogist said, "You know that's the state mental hospital." So we called the state mental hospital. They wouldn't speak to her; they spoke to me. They gave information—it was another miracle: they were not supposed to do this—and when I tried to get more, they really clammed up. My aunt was in a mental hospital from 1922 until her death in 1959. And then I got her death certificate which said she was a paranoid-schizophrenic.

Bennett: 1922. Your father would have been how old then? Well, when was he born? You've said 1904 in essays.
Gordon: I now realize 1894.

Bennett: So he was a young man when that happened?
Gordon: And she was even younger. He was the second of four.

Bennett: Have you told your mother?
Gordon: My mother is completely gaga now.

Bennett: When did that start?
Gordon: I think it started happening *(begins laughing)* when I started writing about my father. It's really hard to track because she had been so depressed that she got very withdrawn and then the withdrawal gradually became more and more profound.

Bennett: When did the depression start? Years ago? How long did she work?
Gordon: Well, she worked until she was seventy-five; she worked until 1983.

Bennett: Her entire career was with the same law firm, right?
Gordon: Yes. You think you're doing something good, and it's totally a disaster. I thought it would be wonderful if she could retire and be with her grandchildren. Total disaster. She didn't know what to do with herself when she couldn't work anymore.

Bennett: So she made the switch at the same time—the retirement and the move to New Paltz. I noticed that in one article, a few years ago, you said that she was in a retirement home or a nursing home there. When she retired, did she live with you?
Gordon: No, she had a house two blocks away from us.

Bennett: So it turned out to be a mess?
Gordon: A total mess. She was angry, she was depressed, she had a bad fall: five days after David was born, she got herself incapacitated so I had to take care of her too. It was just terrible. And they said that I was doing a wonderful thing.

Bennett: After the fall it must have been harder to make any other option for her?

Gordon: Well, we tried until I moved down here. Then I just couldn't do it anymore. It was getting worse and worse.

Bennett: That's rough. So as far as any response about your father, there's been none?
Gordon: No, she doesn't even remember him. She can't pick his face out of their wedding pictures.

Bennett: And the son that showed up after your father's death?
Gordon: I think what it is, is a stepson. I don't think it's really a son.

Bennett: Do you know who he is?
Gordon: Oh yeah, we see each other.

Bennett: What has all this done to your intense bonding with your father? And to your continuing to deal with what you have called his anti-Semitic madness or evil? How does this new mythology change all this?
Gordon: I don't even know the answer to that yet. All I can say is it has been very sad. You know I thought my father was this big self-inventor, a kind of razzle-dazzle. I thought it was coming out of some relatively middle-class, prosperous American thing. Now I see it was just up a lot of shame and a great failure to cover up a lot of shame. It's a completely different story that's much sadder. The notion of his being full of bravado is something I have to deal with. He seems much more desperate to me.

Bennett: How did he learn all the languages if he didn't go to Harvard and the University of Pennsylvania?
Gordon: I have no idea.

Bennett: Wasn't it like eight languages?
Gordon: I know he translated from French and German. I know that he knew Latin. I know he knew Greek. A little Italian. And Hebrew. And Yiddish, which I didn't know about. Now what I don't know is how well he knew them.

Bennett: You don't have copies of the translations?
Gordon: I have copies of the translations, but, you know, he was such a liar that I just suspect everything now. But it's a great mystery that there's this man who drops out of school in the 10th grade, goes to work on the Baltimore and Ohio Railroad at sixteen. And—in however garbled a way and I think it was garbled, and it actually makes sense now because of the garbled

cultural picture—how did he teach himself? He just must have been one of those kids who sat in the library. He must have been extraordinarily gifted, which is another real sadness.

Bennett: And an amazing example of a story's becoming life or a life's becoming story. Did he go to Europe, by the way?
Gordon: No. He never even had a passport.

Bennett: Well, how did he do the essay comparing Anglican and midwestern pastors for Oxford University Press?
Gordon: He must have just sent it off to Oxford.

Bennett: So there's not much left standing?
Gordon: No.

Bennett: Do you know when his family came over and why they went to Ohio?
Gordon: I don't know. I think that my grandfather already had a married sister in Ohio. It was a booming area.

Bennett: How far is Lorain from Cleveland?
Gordon: About 45 minutes away. And there was a very large steel mill there called National Tube which later became a branch of US Steel. It was a boom city. They couldn't build housing fast enough to house all the people that they were hiring for the jobs, and they couldn't hire people fast enough to fill the jobs. Cleveland, from the turn of the century until the depression, was the center of the automotive industry in the United States too, so it was that real industrial explosion.

Bennett: On your maternal side, what about your Italian grandfather? Did he come over as an immigrant with his family?
Gordon: Yeah. Well, none of my grandparents was born in the U.S., actually.

Bennett: That gives me hope for America.
Gordon: You know how I said I wanted to undo that lie about rape? I also want to undo that lie about immigration: that all our parents came over and they were instant and flourishing successes. Maybe people were crushed by the experience of immigration, really crushed.

Bennett: I think that was what was so helpful about your novel *The Other Side*: that there were no givens about what an immigrant brings to America and what she or he is free or unfree to do and be. Ellen is a haunting character. She scares me when I look at my own mental brakes. When did your own maternal grandmother die?

Gordon: '62.

Bennett: In "The Other Deaths" you talk about nursing your sick grandmother.

Gordon: Yes. When I think about it now (and I would think about it when my daughter Anna was twelve), the kind of things I was asked to do at twelve was just unbelievable. I was changing colostomies; I was using suction machines when my grandmother was choking. Everybody just thought, "Well, she's there." It was really awful, awful.

Bennett: That seems to have been an awful decision on the family's part. It's strange that your mother would have permitted it.

Gordon: My mother, I think, was so worried that they were going to throw us out of the house, and also my mother thought I could do anything. She thought I was endlessly competent. And it was that kind of peasant thing where adolescence was already the end of childhood. So I think my mother thought that at twelve—you know, she wanted to keep me in school, but I could have gone out and gotten a job. My mother's a real peasant.

Bennett: It would be interesting to pair that article with the just-published "My Mother Is Speaking From the Desert." That's the other side of it, the depth of it.

Gordon: Well, they'll all be in the memoirs.

Bennett: After your grandmother's death, did you and your mother stay at the family home?

Gordon: Yes.

Bennett: So, all the way through the Barnard years you were still there?

Gordon: Yes, I lived there. For two years I commuted; then I got an apartment in the city.

Bennett: And was your mother still living there when she retired?

Gordon: Yes. That family had lived there from 1920 to 1983. And then she sold it.

Bennett: Was that poignant for you?

Gordon: No, I hated it. I would just torch it if I could. *(begins to laugh)* I think it would be a great boon to the world if that room were torched.

Bennett: The first thing I asked your husband about was the Gordon name; I had assumed that there had been a name change when the family immigrated.

Gordon: No.

Bennett: And then he told me about the Gordon connection, a Scot?

Gordon: Yes.

Bennett: Is there any evidence that, like your father, the rest of the Gordon family was anti-Semitic?

Gordon: No, they were not.

Bennett: And were they fairly active? I mean, did they keep up their synagogue connections?

Gordon: Well, my grandmother seems to have been very orthodox. She died in the orthodox old people's home. She could have gone to either a more or a less orthodox home and she went to the most orthodox one. I don't know about the poor mad aunt. Hattie, the oldest one, I don't think was very active, but she was buried from a Jewish funeral home.

Bennett: Do you have any known first cousins, any cousins?

Gordon: Nobody married except my father. Except poor Hattie was married late in life for almost four years. But I'm the only issue. I found some second cousins, second cousins once removed. Nobody knew my father—or any family. That family failed to leave a mark. It was really remarkable.

Bennett: Did you ever hear your father speak Yiddish? Did he use Yiddish around you a lot—you know, some of the affectionate diminutives?

Gordon: No.

Bennett: But then he gave you a Hebrew blessing every night. What was the blessing?

Gordon: All I can remember is "Baruch atah Adonai," the beginning of all Hebrew blessings. I can't remember what follows it. It's a father's blessing to his child.

Bennett: Have you ever tried to pursue the previous marriage?

Gordon: Yes. Because I'm friends with the stepson. It [the marriage] lasted only a year.

Bennett: And where was that? The Midwest?

Gordon: Cleveland.

Bennett: Then he made the shift east. Do you know when?
Gordon: '31, in the middle of the depression.

Bennett: As a little girl, what did you do in your summers when your mother was working?
Gordon: Well, we lived with my grandmother. It was a big extended family. All of the brothers and sisters were there, my aunts during the day.

Bennett: How old were you when you went to elementary school? You were a young graduate from high school.
Gordon: I believe I was six the December after I started in September.

Bennett: So you didn't skip any grades. I'll bet you wanted to.
Gordon: Oh, I think I never thought I had any choice.

Bennett: You've talked about how tremendously poor and crowded the schools were and how frustrating it was to you, you know, being bright and just "one of them." Are there any particular teachers or incidents that capture that experience?
Gordon: I had a wonderful English teacher in high school, but she was absolutely mad. She would go into these rages. She would be talking about poetry in the most delicious, exalted way, and then she would suddenly hate somebody's hair and get crazy or throw somebody's books out the window. She was the only teacher I ever made a bond with. I couldn't make any bonds with the other nuns.

Bennett: So there was no other literary fuel for you in that time? You must have been hungry when you hit Barnard.
Gordon: When I hit this place I thought I had died and gone to heaven. I am so grateful to this place. I'll tell you how I got to Barnard. Our friends, people like us—their kids go to college, they take them around to the colleges, and they have their interview, and the kids write the essay, and the parents work with the kids on the essay. The way that I got to Barnard was I was obsessed with *Franny and Zooey*. Obsessed. And I knew the Glasses went to Columbia. That Seymour and Zooey had gone to Columbia. And Buddy. So that's why I went to Barnard. I thought I'd meet the Glasses. That was my extremely well-thought-out plan.

Bennett: Well, it worked, didn't it? What kind of scholarship did you have?

Gordon: I had a regent's scholarship which is a state scholarship. Because my mother made so little money, they paid the whole thing.

Bennett: When did you meet Elizabeth Hardwick?
Gordon: She was my teacher here in the senior year.

Bennett: What about before that?
Gordon: People were wonderful to me in this department. I had a wonderful writing teacher named Janice Thaddeus. And I was a poet then. She's now at Harvard. Janice Farrar Thaddeus. She really took me under her wing.

Bennett: From the very beginning? In your freshman year?
Gordon: Sophomore year. And another teacher named Anne Prescott who was my chair when I first started here was my teacher in the freshman year. And other teachers. I was just very well taken care of.

Bennett: That must have been liberating.
Gordon: It was amazing.

Bennett: Were you reading at a tremendous rate at that time?
Gordon: Oh, unbelievable. You know, you could have told me to read anything and I would have read it. Learn another language? Sure! If only I had that energy now. Now I'm calmer. You know eighteen-year-olds—I so much wanted to live. And it was the middle of the sixties: Columbia was exploding.

Bennett: That reminds of your description of your group's having seized a hall at Columbia, but you were still worrying about whether or not you could catch the train home on time. You didn't find your Seymour at Columbia? Or were you interested in WASPS?
Gordon: Well, I seem to marry WASPs but before that I was almost exclusively in love with Jews. Catholics I've never been in love with.

Bennett: In your little essay "Looking for Seymour Glass," you describe a sort of life-changing epiphany that you and your two best teenage friends experienced in front of Monet's waterlillies at MOMA. Haven't you dedicated works to these friends?
Gordon: Yes. The first one, *Final Payments*, was dedicated to Kathleen and "The Immaculate Man" was dedicated to Maureen.

Bennett: Did either of them go to Barnard with you?
Gordon: Yes. We all went.

Bennett: Never underestimate Monet. Did they become writers?

Gordon: Maureen's a doctor, a pediatric cardiologist. She was at Harvard for a long time. Now she's at Tufts. And Kathleen is a medieval historian. She teaches at Notre Dame.

Bennett: Why the waterlillies pictures?

Gordon: I don't know. I think they were just so accessible and comforting. And you didn't feel that you didn't know what to look for.

Bennett: That was a beautiful vignette. When you decided on Barnard—of course you had your own agenda for college—what was your mother's agenda for you?

Gordon: I think my poor mother at that point—and now that I know what it is to be a mother I think how hard it must have been for her and really how amazing it was—just thought, "I don't know what to do any more."

Bennett: "With this child"?

Gordon: Yes. But she always, I think, felt a great mandate from my father to take my intellectual life seriously. And she had great respect for intellectual life.

Bennett: And she herself was very bright.

Gordon: Right. She was very bright. It's really heartbreaking now. She's suffering.

Bennett: Did she have a precise mind?

Gordon: A very precise mind. And she would write wonderful letters. She loved things like grammar. But I don't know. I think I must have been so ferocious that there was no point in standing in my way. I sometimes feel that way with my own daughter. She has a much stronger will than I do, and there's not much point fighting it because you won't win. I think Mother must have just seen that. And also there was something in her that trusted my intellect. Or, at least, that felt she didn't know what to do. But she did feel this charge, I think, from my father.

Bennett: And did it help that your girl friends were going too?
Gordon: Yes.

Bennett: What about the rest of the family at that point? You had already (always, perhaps?) felt like a child apart?

Gordon: Yes. They were very horrible to my mother after my grandmother died, so by the time I went off to college the family was completely split apart.

Bennett: You mean they wanted her out of the house?

Gordon: Half of them wanted her to leave, and half of them thought she should stay. It split the family apart. So this enormously cohesive family that had been held together by my grandmother was just *(snaps her fingers)* gone. By the end of the summer it was gone. She died in June; by the end of September it was over. A year after my grandmother died, one of her children, one of the nine, was dead, one of them had cancer, and one of them had become an alcoholic. She was a formidable, formidable person, but I admired her a lot. It's been tough.

Bennett: Later did you have anything in common with the cousins?

Gordon: I have one cousin I'm enormously close to who is very different from me. He owns a lighting store in Fort Lauderdale. He's not an intellectual, but he just saved my life because he's always been the nicest person in the whole world. We laugh a lot together. We just crack each other up. He's going to come up for my birthday. It was a funny thing: I said to Arthur (who can be exceptionally absentminded, which is why I know he'll never get to Soho this morning), "What I want for my birthday is—my cousin's name is Peppy—to send Peppy an airline ticket. I want him for my birthday." Arthur said, "O.K., I'll deal with it." I think I was out in California and Peppy called and said to Arthur, "You know what I'm going to do for Mary's birthday? I'm coming up." I said to Arthur, "Did you tell him that you were supposed to send him a ticket but you screwed up?" But Arthur—this is the difference between Catholics and Protestants: they feel no guilt—said, "But aren't you glad I forgot to tell him because if I told him you wouldn't have had the joy of knowing that he wanted to do it on his own." But we're very close. He really is like a brother to me. And he also set a model in my life for relations. I'm very good at a kind of brotherly-sisterly relationships with men. And I have great relationships with gay men. But also with straight men I'm not sexually interested in. That sort of jokey camaraderie.

Bennett: Tell me a bit more about Elizabeth Hardwick and your studying with her. Now, that was your senior year; by that time were you into your creative project?

Gordon: Yes, I didn't do it with her; I did it with Jan Thaddeus. She really kept saying to me, "You're a fiction writer, you're a fiction writer."

Bennett: Thaddeus?

Gordon: Hardwick. And I wasn't. What she did was, she kind of gave me the image of a *femme de lettres* and something to dream about and aspire to. She kind of anointed me in class. I mean, she would say, "No one else's work is interesting except yours." And she invited me over to her house, and I met Lowell and, one time, Rostropovich. You know, it was really heady stuff.

Bennett: What or who was the pivot to Syracuse?

Gordon: Working-class panic was the pivot to Syracuse. I thought I was going to get a job for a year, but I'd had too many clerical jobs. I just got scared that if I took another secretarial job or something I'd never get out. I was stupid. It was really stupid. I should have gone to Europe and worked there. I think if I had had that middle-class security—that "if you get off the ladder you can get on it again"—that's what I would have done. But I didn't have that security. I was so scared.

Bennett: Well there wasn't a lot of security at that time for women.

Gordon: No, but it was a very bad decision.

Bennett: Why Syracuse?

Gordon: Well, first of all they gave me money, and W. D. Snodgrass was there. I wanted to work with him.

Bennett: Did you?

Gordon: Oh, yes! It was a nightmare. That story that begins "The Parable of the Cave" essay—that's him.

Bennett: By the way, when you used the parable of the cave in "In Praise of Watercolors," had you read the Gilbert and Gubar essay from *Madwoman in the Attic*?

Gordon: No.

Bennett: So you came to it from Plato?

Gordon: Yes.

Bennett: For your master's thesis you did a book of poetry?

Gordon: Yes. I was in the literature program, and it was a *very* sexist place. Out of 35 full professors, there was *one* emeritus woman. Period. And it was just very narrow. All the women were getting very depressed—and those were the really heady days of the women's movement—so we formed a women's writing group outside the regular workshop. And that was where I started writing fiction. But the way it happened was a friend of mine in the group, a fellow graduate student, said, "You know, your poems are getting more and more narrative. Why don't you try a story?" I said, "I can't do that. Stories are too long; I lose control of the language. I can't have that many words. I can't control them." She said, "Well, you're very good at taking exams, so pretend it's an exam." And she gave me a blue book and said, "We'll pretend you're taking an exam and at the end of two hours you'll give me a story."

Bennett: And what did you write?

Gordon: I was engaged to Jim [Brain] at the time and he had had somebody who (she had left him, actually, just before we took up) had given him a little paperweight with a daisy on it." And I said, "I want you to get rid of it." But he wouldn't. And I wrote a story about it. But it was really quite natural after that.

Bennett: And then what happened? At that point were you still working on your collection of poetry for your master's degree?

Gordon: Yes. I don't know. I still considered myself as primarily a poet. And I just don't know. I started writing more stories and then I had this idea for a novel—supposing some young woman did what every generation of women did, which was take care of her sick relatives—and I started writing the novel and its various stories. It was no grand plan; it just happened.

Bennett: So *Final Payments* came to you as a novel project? You felt it was a big project to begin with, not a short story?

Gordon: Yes.

Bennett: Do you write poetry now.

Gordon: Very little. One a year maybe.

Bennett: Your short story "Mrs. Cassidy's Last Year" evolved into your fourth novel *The Other Side*. But not *Final Payments*? It didn't develop out of a shorter genre?

Gordon: No.

Bennett: Did you meet Jim Brain at Syracuse?

Gordon: Yes. I met him at the Post Office.

Bennett: He was a good bit older than you?

Gordon: Oh, yeah. He's the same age as Arthur. Well, I think you can look at it—I mean, the oedipal impulse is clear—*but* for a woman who is trying to start a career it's not a good bet to be with a man who is trying to start a career, too. So, I'm not saying that I did it for the absolutely best reasons, but something in me knew that that was actually a good strategy while getting my own career started.

Bennett: How long were you with Brain?
Gordon: Four years. He's still in Poughkeepsie.

Bennett: But you fell in love with Arthur Cash. Was the divorce very bitter, painful?
Gordon: I was very guilty. By the time Jim and I actually got divorced, I had been gone for two years, but it was very wrenching.

Bennett: Did your mother have opinions about that?
Gordon: Mother never liked Jim, and she loved Arthur. So, it was remarkable. No one in my family had ever gotten a divorce, and I had thought my mother would just keel over and die.

Bennett: In one of your stories you describe a man who thought you were—I should say the female narrator was—a kind of primal country to be colonized, civilized.
Gordon: That's Jim. He actually spent a lot of time in Africa. He worked in Africa, in Tanzania. Oh, he is an impressive man, but he was totally wrong for me. He could do everything. He was tremendously, physically capable and practical and strong. You know I thought I was marrying English literature. I was doing a dissertation on Virginia Woolf and his parents had been Fabian socialists. It seemed perfect, seemed like a perfect fusion of all of my interests, but it actually was about colonialism.

Bennett: When did you meet Arthur?
Gordon: I first met Arthur in 1974 when we were on a panel together, on an eighteenth-century panel. He was giving a paper called "Sex and the Sentimental Journey," and I was giving a paper called "Male Chastity in *Joseph Andrews*," my point being that Fielding really did not have a double standard for women about chastity (He's really one of the few who said that if it's good for the goose it's good for the gander.) and how unusual that was. That's how Arthur and I met. I thought he was just elegant and wonderful; he paid no attention to me. And then we met again at a party three years later because he was a colleague of my first husband.

Bennett: It started from there?

Gordon: Yes. I mean it's a funny story but it's really true. I thought Arthur was tremendously attractive, and I guess he thought I was too, but he was telling about what a good book he thought *Fear of Flying* was. And I said, "I know you don't mean that; I just know you think that's a good way of picking up women." He laughed, "That's right."

Bennett: And Arthur now?

Gordon: Well, his work. He is an internationally distinguished scholar and the world's expert on Laurence Sterne. Now he's working on John Wilkes. And his scholarship and his teaching are of an enormous quality and integrity, and I'm very proud of and sustained by the quality of his work. He's an amazingly steady, fine presence. There's an enormous fineness to him and courage and quiet. I mean he has dealt with tremendously difficult things with great and quiet courage and dignity. *(long pause)* Also, I find him completely comical. Not that I think he's funny. I don't. But he really makes me laugh because I think he's so out to lunch, and the rest of the world thinks he's totally rational. I'm always very amused by him.

Bennett: When I was here before, you worried about his making his way to Soho. Did he make it?

Gordon: Yes, I think he did.

Bennett: I think about your stories—for example, the one about your being in London with Jim Brain—and about the elusive, delicate line that separates your fiction and nonfiction. Another puzzling example is "The Important Houses" which won a short story award.

Gordon: I know, but it's not a short story. I told Louise Erdrich, "I can't take this!" But she told me I'd won it.

Bennett: Well, since you had told me that "The Important Houses" was to be a part of your book on your father, I was a bit confused. How do you differentiate? You obviously have a theory about a fiction writer's use of autobiographical and biographical details? I mean, what would you say to a class?

Gordon: *(starts laughing)* If you use the real names it's nonfiction. If you change the names it's fiction. The rest of that is total crap. Well, I was not going to turn down being in the *Best American Short Stories*. And I *did* tell her—if you noticed my author's comments in the back.

Bennett: That was '93, wasn't it? The comments that end with the great line about your taking to bed with the vapors?

Gordon: Yes.

Bennett: One of my friends who is very active with the Arena Stage in D.C. sent me their Eileen Atkins-Virginia Woolf playbill with your essay on Woolf. So, you're still using your dissertation research on Woolf?

Gordon: I feel like it won't do any harm. I don't think about her much anymore. But she allowed me to write poetic prose. And actually I'm writing something on Katherine Anne Porter that you will adore.

Bennett: Good! I think she's neglected.

Gordon: That's my—thank you!! It's a *Times* series on neglected authors, and I'm writing on Porter.

Bennett: I've always felt that she was an unsung giant. I mean, if we ranked them—Hemingway, up here, *(I gesture a high place)*, I'd put Porter somewhere just below. You'd put her up further?

Gordon: Yes. I think it's about Hemingway, and that's what I'm trying to write: that somehow, not even because of his misogyny, what he did, which was much worse, was put a heavy hoof on American prose. And he flattened it out, and he said it has to be unpoetic, its source must be journalism, not poetry. I think that's one reason why Fitzgerald's reputation went into decline and Faulkner—you can say, well, he's Southern, and they're all crazy, and we don't have to take him seriously. But Porter. I think *Pale Horse, Pale Rider* is as great as "The Dead." I really do, and you know what I think about "The Dead." But it's so poetic, so female, so open, an open, rich prose. And there was no room in American prose for that because Hemingway hoofed us *(slams her hand down)* and said, "This is it." And for about 40 years everybody believed that you could only write like Hemingway.

Bennett: Eliot did as much in poetry.

Gordon: Yep!

Bennett: I've sometimes wondered how much, if any, Hemingway was influenced by Pound's *ABC of Reading,* by imagism, other poets, by Gertrude Stein. Perhaps it wasn't just journalism.

Gordon: No, but you see, I think with both of them, it's a phobia against culture's being owned by women.

Bennett: Do you mean Hemingway? Pound?

Gordon: An association by all Americans that culture was owned by the spinster or matronly women in the town. It had to be decorous, and it was all that Victorian floweriness. It *was* very fusty. It *was* suffocating. But I really think they had to blast that female impulse out of the water so violently that it's as if they were taking all the antimacassars and making an *auto-da-fé* out of them. And they couldn't distinguish between ornament and richness and that Victorian fustiness. They couldn't distinguish. They were so phobic about the power of those women that they demanded a harsh, dry, rationale: either prose or poetry. And I think it was an act of terror.

Bennett: Well, I hate to bring this up, but there seems to be a strong recycling of that demand by some postmodern critics. The terms are different, but the rigidity is sometimes the same. For example, I notice male and female critics trying to come to terms with the lushness of your language, your foci. I see them trying to grapple with what they consider aberrant. The same fear?

Gordon: Well, it's that same desire to cut out the irrational, the emotional. And I don't mean to be foolishly anti-postmodern, but it's that same rigidity and desire for a system. And they think they're very sympathetic to the marginal, and they think they're working against rigid inclusion. But they're too easily rigid includers and excluders. And what really makes them nervous is the things that can't be systematized or held down. It's no accident that this happens after an outbreak of feminism in the way that it's no accident that this happened after an outbreak of feminism at the end of the nineteenth century. But I think [with] Hemingway—for a few historical accidents: his looks, his war record, the sports, the newspaper—a lot of icons came together in him. He was the king of the hill. And so people like Porter just got forgotten. Look how long it took for people to appreciate Welty. I mean she's amazing.

Bennett: She did well, for that generation.

Gordon: She didn't do as well as she deserved.

Bennett: And Katherine Anne Porter?

Gordon: I do think she's underappreciated. But, of course, she's one of the worst women who ever lived.You know she was escorted around by Göring. She was disappointed when he didn't pick up on her. She was an anti-Semite, a liar, homophobic; she betrayed her best friend to the FBI; she was cheap, a drunk, but so were a lot of the guys.

Bennett: Let's go back to your novels. When you started out your career, Elizabeth Hardwick evidently was a reader of your drafts for *Final Payments.* Also for *The Company of Women*?

Gordon: No, she didn't read my chapters after *Final Payments*.

Bennett: Who has remained? Have your private readers shifted through the years?

Gordon: Yes. I was very involved with Anne Freedgood for *The Company of Women* and *Men and Angels*. And then for *The Other Side* Richard Gilman helped me a lot.

Bennett: I enjoyed your review of his memoir *Faith, Sex, Mystery*.

Gordon: From *The Other Side* on, a friend of mine whom I met in graduate school—her name is Jan Schmidt—has been a very important reader. I dedicated *Temporary Shelter* to Jan. She teaches in Arthur's department, actually.

Bennett: Is she going to be your reader for the next?

Gordon: Yes. I never really let Arthur be too much of a reader because it's too hard.

Bennett: You're vulnerable then? Fighting words?
Gordon: Yes.

Bennett: I was interested in your switch to Viking for *The Other Side* and *The Rest of Life*. Why the change from Random House?

Gordon: Well, my editor was fired, and I did an act of loyalty.

Bennett: Anne Freedgood?

Gordon: Yes, she was good. So I did an act of loyalty, which didn't quite work out. It was sort of a metaphor for what they did with my collection of essays.

Bennett: So now you're back?
Gordon: Back at Random House.

Bennett: By the way, did you expect the popularity of *Final Payments*? Were you ready for that?

Gordon: No!! I was teaching at a community college. I was making $11,000 a year. I remember saying to my editor, "Do you think there's a chance I'll get reviewed in the *New York Times*?" I wanted simply to get a review and maybe to be able to get out of the community college and into a regular college. That was all I hoped for. It was an incredible shock. Of course, like everything else in my life, it was mixed. It was happening as my marriage was breaking up, so I was much more absorbed in guilt and unhappiness that I couldn't even enjoy the whole thing. Well, in a way, that was probably a good thing because it was all a little unreal, and there was something in me that knew not to take it too seriously, that it really wasn't about me.

Bennett: What was it about?
Gordon: It was about an invention. I was the right person at the right time.

Bennett: You mean by your treating Catholicism, or do you mean you were the new, the bright new artist in town.?
Gordon: Yes. Nobody had written about Catholics or Catholic women. Either that or they need a new young woman now and then. And I was very lucky. I mean I don't think *Final Payments* is a bad book. But it really was so accidental. Now, what I've done after that: that was no accident.

Bennett: Did its success inhibit you or put pressure on you?
Gordon: No, because I don't think I paid much attention to it.

Bennett: Do you think that the prepublication comments by Margaret Drabble and Mary McCarthy helped?
Gordon: I do.

Bennett: When did you meet Drabble?
Gordon: I was living in London with Jim in 1976. And I was completely lonely and depressed, just awful. I was writing fiction in the mornings and going to the British Museum in the afternoons to do my Virginia Woolf work. And I didn't talk to anybody all day. It was very lonely, and I didn't even realize how unhappily married I was. I should have known; I was crying all the time. And I saw Margaret Drabble (whose work I had adored) on TV and I wrote her a letter, in care of the BBC, saying this is what my day is like and I think of you. And she phoned me up and invited me to dinner. She's great. She is one of the best human beings that has ever lived. She was very enabling for me in many ways: giving me an idea that one can write about the lives of women in that way and then literally, she introduced me to her agent. And that was Peter Matson. I mean, talk about luck; that was luck.

Bennett: Well, you have to have something to say.
Gordon: Yes, but we all know people who have wonderful things to say, and they don't have the luck.

Bennett: When you've talked about *Final Payments* and *The Company of Women* you've described your use of Catholicism as a rubric. Are you using that word in the sense of its being directional?

Gordon: Yes, well, almost like a template or something, The structure was there, the form was there, the ritual was there, the shape was there. So it's both the shape and the terms.

Bennett: So in a sense, it's following the initial letter, a given iconography?

Gordon: Exactly.

Bennett: You've written and talked about Drabble, Woolf, and Bogan as formative influences at the start of your career. Who, if anyone, is influencing you now?

Gordon: It's different. I don't feel like I need to hold somebody's hand so much anymore. But sometimes—there's a moment in Virginia Woolf's *The Waves* when she says that Neville (when he tries to write poetry) says, "I need the tone of Byron for this poem." So he has to read Byron; then he can write something.—I still feel that, but it's a different sort of relationship. I'm very deeply into Proust. For the last 3 or 4 years I've begun every day reading Proust. And I'm now on my second trip through the whole thing. And I never will write like him. But it's a deeply spiritual exercise for me to be swimming in that tremendously dreamy ocean.

Bennett: His time-space thing.

Gordon: And memory, the way things go back and forth.

Bennett: Do you have that beautiful book *Dining with Proust* that shows all the food, the recipes?

Gordon: Yes. I would never make any of them, but I love that book. So I'm reading a lot of Proust.

Bennett: In French?

Gordon: No. God, if only. I do have the French text next to me so that when I'm particularly taken by something I'll try to read it. It would take me the rest of my life to read it in French. Although my fantasy is if I really were that nun, I'd be reading it in French.

Bennett: If you were that nun, her order might be closed by now.

Gordon: Oh, no. It would have been thriving because it would have been totally conservative. If I had been Daddy's little girl, that's what I would have done. So I'm reading a lot of Proust. Right now I'm reading a lot of Porter because I'm writing about her, but I read her a lot. She's in my heart. I always read a lot of Auden. I read a lot of the two Russian poets Akhmatova and

Tsvetaeva. They're very important to me. Theirs seem to me a purely female lyric voice. But nobody's holding my hand anymore. And Ford . . . well, he's still holding my hand. He's so comfortable. And you know, he was so good. I mean, I know he has a bad rep. for the women he slept with, but—you know how it is when you have a dear friend who acts badly with women, even though you're like a red-alert feminist, and you say, "I know, but . . ."?—I kind of make excuses. That's what I do with Ford. But when you think of the women writers he first published, it's extraordinary. He first published Porter, as well as Jean Rhys, as well as Welty, as well as Louise Bogan. He really was enormously supportive to women writers. And he wasn't sleeping with them, except with Rhys.

Bennett: Can we go back for a minute to your childhood when you were planning to be a nun? I've only seen the title of your childhood treatise, "What is Prayer?" Do you remember the titles of any more of those treatises?

Gordon: No, but I do think I have my little treatise on the Trinity. I think I could also find you my first biography of my father, which I started when I was 10. I think the first line was: "My father was the greatest man I have ever known." I know the thing on the Trinity is around somewhere.

Bennett: You don't have to answer this, but didn't you lose a baby at some time? Between Anna and David?

Gordon: Yes, I did lose a baby between my two.

Bennett: What were you writing at the time?

Gordon: *Men and Angels.*

Bennett: That's a particularly haunting since you were writing all that about safety, about Anne's obsession with trying to make things safe for her children. I've also wanted to ask what led to your focus on art in *Men and Angels*?

Gordon: I don't know.

Bennett: Did you have pressure? I know you were already fatigued with being labeled as a "Catholic writer" by the time, even before, *Company of Women* came out.

Gordon: You know, one thing about me is I do not pay that much attention to what people say about me. I don't even read most of my reviews; this is really one way I was brought up: you don't listen to what everybody says about you. You know, trying to please anybody.

Bennett: So there is no driver from what critics say about this novel versus that novel?

Gordon: No, and one of the good things about having done criticism one-self is that you say this is something somebody thinks about me; they could be wrong. I've said things and I've been wrong. So, one person thinks that; should I change something because of that? I would never do that. And also things are very accidental. You know, I've always loved looking at paintings. The genesis for *Men and Angels* was a poor, woman student I had at Amherst, then a woman that I originally thought of that I also knew at Amherst. They didn't know each other, and I had a fantasy about what if these two came together—this very fortunate woman and the other. But the first thing that got me was (in a way it was still a religious thing) if you followed what Christ said to do literally, it would be completely unlivable. And then I had the idea of having her collide with this fortunate woman. And that was what started it. Then a woman whose face came to me (when I thought of this fortunate woman) happened to be an art historian. So it wasn't any extremely well-thought-out theory. But I thought it would be fun because I love paintings. I have less artistic talent than anyone who ever lived. And I thought, "Well, these will be my paintings." And I also love learning things, so it was fun to learn more about art history.

Bennett: There seems to be an continuing inquiry, a continuing dialogue about *caritas* in *Men and Angels* and your first two novels. And Auden's a part of that ongoing question. I just located a copy of your poem "Reading Auden while nursing my daughter."

Gordon: I love Auden so much!

Bennett: He always gets around to basic things about—the coffee cups and the newspaper—domesticity. Do you plan out the continuity, the through-lines between your novels at this point, or do you just write the next work and that's it?

Gordon: Actually, when I'm finished with a book I don't think about it much anymore. I've always had good luck in that as I was finishing one thing something new was coming to me. So I've always been more interested in the new thing. Once it's done, *my* work with it is over.

Bennett: You've given it.

Gordon: Yes. I don't even mind very much anymore.

Bennett: Do you have any idea what will come after your book on your father?

Gordon: I have an idea for another novel. I actually have a new novel in my head and three more novellas. It doesn't seem to me like anything leads to anything else. I am now really longing to write fiction again; this book on my father has been so horribly painful.

Bennett: Are you ever going to use a male protagonist in your novels?

Gordon: Well, there are three basic characters that I have in this next novel, and one of them is a man.

Bennett: Of course your characters Father Cyprian in *Company of Women* and Joseph Moore in *Final Payments* are both strong, as well as the men in your novellas. That came as a surprise to me: your sudden switch to the shorter genre

Gordon: I think that *The Other Side* was an enormous structural labor; it really kind of wore me out for a larger structure. So, I wanted something that was more compressed, more lyric in its impulse, and actually more poetic and not so dependent on author or structure.

Bennett: In *The Rest of Life* novellas, I also sensed a major change in your approach.

Gordon: I'm probably more open to less linear, less thoroughly rational ways of structuring.

Bennett: What struck me the most was that the female protagonists in both "Immaculate Man" and "Living at Home" seem to embrace ambiguity, instead of a polarized or a radical approach.

Gordon: Yeah.

Bennett: Who do you talk to now about the writing process?

Gordon: Well, David Plante. He's very important in my life.

Bennett: Is he in New York?

Gordon: No he's in London. We were just in Italy together. We try to make a pact to have days together every year. He's a very important soul-brothcr. Do you know his work? No? Oh, he's wonderful. There are five books you should read: *The Family, The Country, The Woods, The Native.* Those are all about one family. And then *Accident.* I did a review of *The Family* and *The Country.* His new book *The Annunciation* is brilliant. David and also Helen Wilson are the ones I talk to about the process. And Helen really helps me with my guilt about the lack of purity in my life.

Bennett: What do you mean by purity?

Gordon: It's such a complicated thing. I guess what I mean is purity is a kind of undividedness of attention that I value very highly. Helen said, "Well, if you live like Flaubert, you write like Flaubert." She's so much more secure than I am because she's not working-class, not immigrant, and she had these parents who thought being an artist was the most important thing in the world. Edmund Wilson was tough. He was no great gift as a father, but she had an amazing mother. Helen, at one of her openings, heard someone say, "Well, it's not Corot!" And she turned to him and said, "No, it's not Corot; it's Helen Wilson." She's a great help to me in saying that you don't have to have this dualism. But David and Helen both live much more purely than I do. My life is very split up because I can't bear to give things up. For example, apparently (I don't know whether it's apocryphal or not) Márquez and his family were packed up to go on vacation. All the things were in the car, and Márquez was pulling out of the driveway, and he got the idea for *One Hundred Years of Solitude* and just drove back into the driveway and said, "No vacation." I could never, ever do that. I would have to lose *One Hundred Years of Solitude*, which is why Ford Madox Ford, I think, is so important to me because he couldn't give things up.

Bennett: Think of the meals he cooked—making an artistic production out of a recipe. And think of what he gave, for example, to Ezra Pound when he went to see Ford in Germany and gave him a copy of his *Canzoni*. Ford threw himself on the floor and started rolling around in mock pain. Pound said later that Ford's reaction to the old style he was using saved him years of work. Ford cut to the chase.

Gordon: But you know he would do it. If someone gave him something, he would put everything down.

Bennett: I think different artists have different fires. Perhaps for you, the chaos contains the fuel.

Gordon: I hope so. I have tremendous guilt about not being that nun. It wasn't just sex; sex is the least of it. *(laughing)* I mean, sex is simply a metaphor for the attention going outwards.

Bennett: Lots of artists fear complications. Ford didn't ever seem so.

Gordon: *(laughing)* No. [He] married about twelve, I think!

Bennett: Well, the productivity boiling out of artists looks good on paper, but it can mask a lot of domestic chaos.

Gordon: I have a friend who's an Irish poet, and she writes about the Irish and says that "we Irish artists always talk about all the time we give to our children and to other people and if we were really serious artists, we wouldn't, you know." But she then says, "look at all the time they're drunk! That takes up a lot of time. But they think that's feeding the work."

Bennett: If you want to look at dysfunctional relationships and neglected children of geniuses . . .

Gordon: I think you probably don't have a choice if you're that much of a genius. They don't have a choice. I'm not that gifted, but I would never do that to children. I just wouldn't do it. I would give up work, I think. Still, we're really the first generation of women who can try to do it all in some way.

Bennett: Yesterday you showed me a recent gift from Leonard Baskin. Is art an important presence in your daily life?

Gordon: I don't know what I could say that was intelligent except that art is a deep river of nurture and sustenance for me. When I'm really stuck and despairing about my work, I go to the Metropolitan Museum. And one of the things I did, one of the ways I finished *The Rest of Life* which—I could not get the end right—was just killing me, I went to the Metropolitan every morning. And I would go look at—I have two favorite paintings. I'm obsessed with Vuillard; he's my favorite. I don't know if you read my article about Vuillard in the *Times*.

Bennett: Yes, I did.

Gordon: So my two favorite paintings in the Metropolitan are a Vuillard, which has the most wonderful white ceiling in it ["Interior with Woman Sewing"]. I go look at that white ceiling. And then the Bellini "Davis Madonna." And I would go and look at them for a little while, and then I took my notebook into the restaurant of the Metropolitan, which if you're not there at mealtimes is pretty empty. And I wrote there. I would go back and forth and look at those for inspiration. I think it's the wordlessness. It seems to me just a more direct access to the world of dream without that intermediary filter of language.

Bennett: You get nurtured directly without any other complication?
Gordon: Yes. And bathed.

Bennett: Have a lot of artists given you gifts? Like the Baskin?
Gordon: Helen has given me things; other works I've bought from artist

friends. So I have a lot of things by my friends in my house. One of the nicest things in my life is that I go off to Cape Cod in the summer; there are quite a few painters and artists I'm acquainted with there.

Bennett: You have Arthur's home in New Paltz, and the West Side apartment is your home?
Gordon: Yes. It really is; you're right.

Bennett: I was thinking about your telling me that he's a country person and you're a city person. When was the move with the children to make New York your base?
Gordon: 1990.

Bennett: When you became full-time at Barnard?
Gordon: Yes, this has been a wonderful thing. And it has been wonderful to be back teaching. Although it's more splitting, it's also very nourishing. As you know, one of the things about teaching is you have to read very attentively, and if you're going to be talking about a book, you have to really be paying attention to it when you read it. I love the kind of focused reading that I have to do.

Bennett: Because of the Guggenheim, you're not teaching this semester?
Gordon: Yes.

Bennett: You're going to be off this spring?
Gordon: No, I was off last spring. So, I go back in January.

Bennett: How many classes do you teach?
Gordon: I have two each semester.

Bennett: Do you know what you're going to teach?
Gordon: Yes, let's see, one is called "Death and Modern Fiction" and the other is called "Modern Fiction's Long Stories, Short Novels, and Novellas," because I think it's a length of work that is just not being taught now. Anyway, I'm blessed enough to be able to teach only books I like. I begin with Flaubert's *Trois Contes: Un Coeur Simple*, and I go on to "The Dead." I do *As I Lay Dying*, a wonderful book by Willa Cather that I love called *My Mortal Enemy*. It's fantastic. I do Nabokov's *Pnin*, Jean Toomer's *Cane*, I do Porter, Christa Wolf, *The Aspern Papers*.

Bennett: Did you see the Argento *Aspern Papers* opera?
Gordon: No. So, I get to read a lot of things that I'm happy to be reading

attentively. I'm now really in the mood to teach Ford though, so I'll see if I can figure out which work. What I really want to do is teach the whole tetralogy, but I'm not sure that the students will sit still for it. I will at least teach *The Good Soldiers*.

Bennett: Have you had opportunities to be a mentor yet?
Gordon: Yes, and it's wonderful.

Bennett: As a mentor, are you dealing with fiction writers at both Barnard and Columbia?
Gordon: Yes.

Bennett: Are they all working on or starting with short stories? Which genres?
Gordon: Some are starting on short stories; some are doing novels. It's wonderful. But still, it's a terrible world to be published in. I mean I just think if I had written *Final Payments* in 1994 instead of 1976 it wouldn't be published. It's a very hard world to send them out into.

Bennett: Why specifically is so hard for young writers now?
Gordon: Well, I think the structure of publishing has changed so much, and the whole structure of reading has changed. Now things have to be high-concept, and things are done much more by proposal than by manuscript. And editors stay at houses for a less long time, and there's less chance that you're going to stay with one editor or have a commitment. Publishing houses are less interested in a small advance for a small novel which might lead to something else or a small collection of stories. The whole financial structure is wretched; it's so corporate now. So it's very bad now. And I think fewer and fewer people are reading now. We can't lie about that. Fewer and fewer people are reading, you know. Not like *Thin Thighs in Thirty Days. (laughing)* They seem to be reading that, including me.

Bennett: Speaking of high-concept, have you ever thought about recording your novellas or novels, marketing them on cassettes?
Gordon: No one's ever asked me. You know, you might call Manhattan Theatre Club. In January of '94 Rosemary Harris and two other actors did a dramatic reading of *The Rest of Life*, and I think they have a tape of it.

Bennett: Has your agent worked on film options? I mean, when I think of your three novellas in *The Rest of Life*, I think of tripartite films like *New York Stories*. Those novellas would give female actors incredible roles.

Gordon: Well, it's incredibly hard to bankroll a movie about a woman that doesn't involve the woman's taking her blouse off.

Bennett: Well, I actually thought the novellas of *The Rest of Life* would be perfectly cinematic. And also *The Other Side*. It would work well, and it seems timely now.

Gordon: Yeah. I've always wanted Angelica Huston to do that.

Bennett: What part of the public responsibilities connected with writing do you enjoy the most and the least at this stage of your career?

Gordon: Public responsibilities?

Bennett: You know, publicity.

Gordon: I hate all of it. I hate it. I hate it. One hundred percent unambivalent hatred. What I am ambivalent about is giving readings, which I enjoy and I think I'm actually quite good at it and I often make real connections. But they take a tremendous amount out of me, physically; I'm very exhausted and then I often—it's my anxiety about not being Flaubert. You know, was I being a public person when I should have been a private person? But when I can stop being a nut about it, I can say that I actually like giving readings. But interviews are absolutely my idea of hell.

Bennett: *(laughing)* I'm sorry.

Gordon: Not with you! But you know if the person hasn't read the book, but knows what it sounds like; you know you just have to talk to the dopes who are totally unprepared. It's enraging. It's really enraging; it's so rare that an interviewer is at all prepared.

Bennett: Do you always think of yourself as a writer in gendered terms? There have been all kinds of labels assigned to you. The last time I've found you describing yourself was some time ago, about ten years ago; you described yourself as a working-class woman writer, not European.

Gordon: I think it's kind of like what Sartre says about being a Jew, that you're a Jew if somebody calls you one. And so a lot of the time you have a label if people give it to you often enough. But what kind of label would be internally created by myself? *(long pause)* I think gender is important to me. I think it because I think I'm still read in a gendered way that, in all honesty, I have to call myself "a woman writer." I won't call myself "a Catholic writer." That's too limiting. I just won't do it because it makes me sound like this Graham Greene, Evelyn Waugh, Flannery O'Connor. I feel no affinity. I don't think that was how I was formed. But I do think I was formed as a writer by my femaleness.

Bennett: Who are the novelists, not necessarily writing on Catholic subjects but maybe spiritual subjects, working now in the Americas or in Europe that particularly interest you?
Gordon: Younger ones?

Bennett: Yes.
Gordon: I've already mentioned David Plante. I'm interested in David Grossman who wrote *See Under: Love* and *The Book of Intimate Grammar*. I'm interested in Jeanette Winterson's stuff. I don't think it always works, but I feel that she's courageous and moving. I think Denis Johnson is doing some interesting stuff. Sandra Cisneros's work interests me—well, some of these are already my age, not younger—and I'm interested in what Leslie Marmon Silko does

Bennett: March has been quite a month for your family. Anna, a ninth-grader, appeared in the last page feature of the *New Yorker*, and then last Sunday your amazing, painfully honest essay on your mother was the feature essay in the *New York Times Magazine*. What have been the responses to both? Your response to both?
Gordon: Well, I wish everything were like having my daughter in the last page of the *New Yorker*. That's complete, unabashed joy for me. She was much more cynical about it; she said, "It really had nothing to do with me, and she [Wendy Wasserstein] was really writing about herself and we [students in a production of *Heidi's Chronicles* at Brearley School] were an excuse for it. And she didn't say whether I was good or not. She just said I was in it." So Anna was very unmoved. I was *thrilled* down to my boots. My daughter's a cooler customer. *(pause)* It was very funny. There's a man who's a connection of my father's from Cleveland. This guy's a press agent. He's about 89 and is still working as a press agent. He really is out of Damon Runyon Land. I take him to dinner about once a month. He's just adorable, and he called me from California. I mean, he knew my father because when my father was a dashing, young Jewish man in Cleveland, this guy was in the Jewish orphanage and my father and the other, rich young Jews in Cleveland would take these orphans to their lake-front cottages for vacations. So this guy remembered my father as a dashing young man, and he got in touch with me. So [after the *New Yorker* article appeared] I get this message on the

phone, this little, insect-like voice of this ancient man saying, "Well, I'm just thrilled! Three generations of geniuses." It was very sweet.

Bennett: Was David jealous of Anna's publicity?
Gordon: No, David's not like that. You've seen David, haven't you?

Bennett: Yes.
Gordon: David knows that everybody in the world looks at him and adores him. He knows that about himself. *(starts laughing)* He goes through the world like, "You know, Mom, I can't go to all the people who want me." And so, I think he just looked at Anna and thought, "I'm not doing that gig. Somebody's already doing that." I think he saw that as a baby. And they're so different, and their spheres of influence are so different that they're not wildly jealous of each other. I say that but maybe I'm deeply involved in delusion. But they don't fight much. They really like each other. The other day David was worried about a test. Anna's in London, and he said, "Can I please just call Anna? I just need to hear her voice before I take this test." They really like each other. But I think I'm lucky that they're a different gender and so different temperamentally. Anna knows very clearly that, like she said, "If I went through the world walking with David in front me, every-body would talk to me. You know, people don't love me on sight the way they love David." But she thinks she's more intellectual and competent, that he's like a very good-looking dog—a *little* condescension on her part!

Bennett: What about this week? You must have gotten a lot of response to the article and the stunning photographs of your mother.
Gordon: You know, Alma, one thing that is very peculiar about me is that after I've finished writing something I'm not that interested in it. So, I was pleased that my friends responded and particularly pleased when people knew about my mother. But occasionally I just want to say to people, "Yes, I did that. Now this is the problem I'm working out. How do I cut a hundred and twenty pages down to sixty?" One of the reasons I published it where I did (and in some ways I knew it was an exposing act to my mother and to myself) was that I knew a lot of people were going through the same kinds of issues, and I thought it was important to speak truthfully about all the ambivalence one feels about this kind of degeneration. So I was happy that it did seem to touch people in that way. I got some oddly hostile comments. One friend of mine called and said, "Well, we in the mental health profession really objected to your use of the word 'rot.' That's a very harsh word to us."

And then I got a call yesterday at Barnard from somebody who had been a client of my mother's boss and remembered my mother as a very vivid presence in the office and she did all the closings and how wonderful her laugh was and that people would stop by on the way home from the station just to talk to her because she was so amusing. And that made me very sad because I then had to understand all that has been lost. And also when people praise me for the article, I want to say, "Yeah, but it doesn't take the problem away. I wrote something, but then I have to live it." I don't know. I don't know exactly what to do with praise or whatever. It's not very central.

Bennett: And not the point of the essay.
Gordon: No.

Bennett: In the past you've talked fairly strongly against Updike. Are there current novelists that you either have a very strong affinity for or some professional antipathy against?
Gordon: I don't think so. I'm kind of irritated by the whole Martin Amis mega-publicity thing for somebody I think is a genuinely minor novelist, but it's not like I think he should be suppressed like a guinea pig. I deplore what's valued. I would never say, "Don't do it." It just irritates me that everyone thinks that's wonderful. You know, I think my affinity for David Plante is very great. The other person I had a great affinity for, but I feel myself moving away from her a little bit for reasons I don't know, is Christa Wolf. I feel myself undergoing a real sea change in terms of prose now: I'm feeling very ambivalent about virtuoso prose. I'm not sure that I won't go to a more spare prose, a less embellished prose, but I haven't quite found a partner for that, the kind of thing that Willa Cather does in *My Mortal Enemy* which I'm reading carefully now. It's a very luminous but spare prose. I have a feeling I'm moving in that direction, and it's a new one.

Bennett: Do you have any other interesting new projects in mind?
Gordon: Well, at the end of the year, late in November, I think I'm going into Mexico with an organization I've been on the board of directors of for almost fifteen years called Catholics for Free Choice. And we're going to go to Mexico and do some population education, both learning and teaching. We have a branch in Mexico and others in other Latin American countries. So this will mean going to Chiapas which is so torn apart politically; that will be really fascinating.

Bennett: Any others?

Gordon: Well, I hope to start this new novel which is called *Pearl*. I never talked about that?

Bennett: You just mentioned once that it will develop characters from your story.

Gordon: "Temporary Shelter." I find myself thinking about it more and more, so I know it's in my brain.

The Writing Life: Madison Smartt Bell Hosts Mary Gordon

Madison Smartt Bell / 1995

Transcription of *The Writing Life*, HoCoPoLitSo cable television series. © 1995 by Howard County Poetry and Literature Society (HoCoPoLitSo). Printed by permission.

Taped on 19 June 1995 (Columbia, MD) and aired on 3 October 1995 (Comcast Cable 8).

Bell: Welcome to *The Writing Life*. My name is Madison Smartt Bell, and I have here Mary Gordon who is the author of a great many works of fiction including *The Rest of Life*, most recently, which is a collection of novellas; novels including *The Other Side, Men and Angels, The Company of Women*, and *Final Payments*; a collection of stories called *Temporary Shelter*; and a collection of essays called *Good Boys and Bad* [sic] *Girls*. Mary is also the recipient of the Guggenheim Fellowship and the Lila Wallace Readers Digest Award. And she is a tenured professor at Barnard College. I wanted to begin by reading a statement that you once made about your own work, and then maybe quarreling with it a little bit. "My subject as a writer," says Mary Gordon, "has far more to do with family happiness than with the music of the spheres. I don't know what the nature of the universe is, but I have a good ear. What it hears best are daily rhythms, for that is what I value, what I would wish as a writer to preserve." And the essay [" 'The Parable of the Cave' or, In Praise of Watercolors"] goes on a little later to identify that choice, on the one hand, as, again I quote Ms. Gordon, "a predilection for the [stubborn] minor" and, then in another way, to reject that, from another point of view. I have given that some thought, and it seems to me that while it is true that you have always chosen as your setting kind of small and indeed constricted domestic situations, the family romance as it is were, there is also always this involvement with the Catholic Church because the people you write about generally happen to be Catholics, and that it's that engagement with the larger issues that are sort of forced upon the subject by the Church that gives the work a larger scope.

Gordon: I think that what I was trying to respond to out of a certain

137

amount of irritation and anger is the definition of major and minor, which it seemed to me had largely been created by males for males. And so anything that happened outside or involving physical pain, violence, or unwilling sex was considered major, and anything else outside those rubrics was considered minor. And it seems to me that's been one of the most heinous umbrellas—if you can have a heinous umbrella.

Bell: *(laughing)* I'd like to see a heinous umbrella.

Gordon: *(laughing)* That's kind of an odd notion, but it's been a very constricting and crippling thing for women writers and for their readers. One of the most irritating and consistent things that gets said to me is, I will have read and a man will come up to me and say, "My wife reads your books." I'm supposed to say, "Of course, what are you, too busy killing wild animals and making nuclear war to read my books?"

Bell: Well, unfortunately, that's true. I mean, speaking as a "major" male writer I know very well that if you can't get women to read your work, you're dead. I mean, they're the only people who read in this country. Almost.

Gordon: Well, what is interesting is that a woman considers reading a male writer reading up, and a man considers reading a women writer as an act of perhaps enormously broad-minded condescension. And so women think it's kind of sexy to read something that will even describe them in quite degraded or condescending terms. But a man entering what would be the inner life of a woman feels like he's doing her a favor, that it's something he doesn't need to know. Whereas women, I think, think they need to know about the lives of men, men think they're doing women a favor to know about the lives of women. And that's sort of what I was responding to, in trying to take the word "minor" and set it on its head.

Bell: Right. Well, the idea that I had about that and about that statement in your essay is that it makes me compare your work to the work of other artists of domesticity, many of whom do happen to be women. So that if I compare your work to a really brilliant miniaturist like Anita Brookner, say, it really does seem to me that your writing has a larger scope and engages with larger issues, despite the fact that it tends to be, in terms of its plot, set rather tightly; it's "inside the house," which I think is your phrase from the essay, instead of outside the house, for the most part.

Gordon: And also I think it's inside the mind, to a certain extent. I think as I've gotten older and I've written more, that trying to get the balance between inside the mind or inside the soul and an engagement in the world is something I'm more interested in as a project perhaps than I would have been when I started out. But I think your point is well taken that, willy nilly, if you were brought up as a Catholic, particularly in the triumphalist days in the '50s, in which I was, you were in the world, and there was a sense of being part of a world-wide movement which was controlling salvation and so the stakes were very high. I think I've always written as if the stakes were very high. And maybe that creates a movement out of domesticity, because everything is at stake.

Bell: Definitely. Let me enunciate another crack-pot theory about your work. It seems to me everyone in your audience is learning more about your personal life than they used to know because of this work that you're writing about your father and your parents and your childhood which is non-fiction and autobiographical. And it occurred to me while reading and listening to selections from *Losing My Father* [published in 1995 as *The Shadow Man: A Daughter's Search for Her Father*] that perhaps—and you may not feel that this is true—your first two novels are, in a sort of covert, cryptic way, auto-biographical novels, in that *Final Payments* is almost exclusively about the relationship with a brilliant, charming, intellectual father, who may or may not to some extent resemble your own, obviously not completely, that *The Company of Women* is about a childhood spent somewhat in the manner that your childhood was spent after the death of your father, when you were ten, among aunts and a household of women, to reiterate the title. If that's so, what is the advantage for you of going back over this material in non-fiction?

Gordon: I think one of the advantages is that I could not put my father into fiction and have anybody believe him. His life is so improbable that, you know, people would think I had moved into magic realism, and since he didn't live in South America, that wouldn't wash. And there was a way in which I was taking a journey as myself, and I felt that I needed to comment upon that journey of discovery as myself in a way that I couldn't or wouldn't in fiction. Also the facts of the case were so extraordinary that I couldn't have made them up. And so I felt that in a way it was almost a spiritual exercise, that I was taking a journey and that it was a journey among facts. And a journey with one foot in fact and one foot in invention, and that fluid and unstable relation between memory and invention and fact in some way was my subject. And that had to be, it seemed to me, non-fiction, because there had to be a real "I" at the center, or that's the way it was whispered to me.

Bell: By your daemons?

Gordon: Yes, I can imagine someone else having done it another way, but it was whispered to me as non-fiction.

Bell: Would you like to read a little bit of it?

Gordon: Sure. This is a chapter called "Reading My Father." My father was a writer, so one of the ways I get to know him is by reading his texts.

(the published version of this chapter in The Shadow Man *is radically altered; the following excerpts that Gordon reads are confirmed in manuscripts Gordon sent Alma Bennett prior to final cuts and rewriting).*

[first excerpt] "Whenever and however I was living, whatever place my father took in that life, it was always important to me that he was a writer. Now it's important in a new way. His being a writer, a published writer, that is someone whose words are PUBLIC, means that others can know him as I do. What my father wrote is the property of the world.

"For the first years of my life, I thought he wrote for me.

"This is because among the earliest things I read were magazines he edited. In 1953 and 1954, he had a magazine called *The Children's Hour*. It was the size of the *Reader's Digest*, but printed on newsprint rather than glossy paper. It contained condensations and adaptations of the classics: *Aesop's Fables, Tales from Shakespeare*, Bible stories, synopses of Gilbert and Sullivan. In addition there were jokes and limericks and pages of things for children to do on a rainy day: directions for making a bank out of an empty salt container, instructions on how to make your own Halloween costume. *The Children's Hour* ran only two issues, but on both mastheads, I am listed as editor-in-chief, although in 1954 when it folded, I was not yet five years old."

[second excerpt]

"But even when I read them first, in 1953 and 1954, I had a sense of something called the past that my being born had ruined. A fragile screen, high, ornamental, and I burst through it at my birth creating as I went the modern age. The present ate up the past like an acid burning out the faces in a photograph, like spun sugar flowers on my tongue. The past was consumed before I had time to appreciate it. In becoming the present, the past grew valueless.

"The past had also happened in a place far from where I was living. It was somewhere else, but its location was fluid. Anything graceful, formal, impractical, was part of it. It was Italian, German, French, anything but American. Nothing spare or linear belonged to the pastness of the past.

"Now when I hold copies of *The Children's Hour*, I see that I collected the past right there. I looked at the pictures in it obsessively. I savored them, taking them in slowly, putting them away to tantalize myself, to strengthen myself, then looking at them again. They did what art is meant to do: they left me fully satisfied and enlarged. I had a sense of a world greater than anything I had known or seen or been a part of, and which I knew very well I had no chance of entering. But for the times that I spent looking at the pictures, looking was enough. It was everything. There was nothing desirable in life outside them."

One of my father's other publications was a girlie magazine, published in the twenties, called *Hot Dog*. This is about my coming upon *Hot Dog* as a twelve-year-old girl.

[third excerpt] "I don't know how I first learned about *Hot Dog*, knew that my father had edited a magazine with jokes and sexy pictures, but it was some time after his death. I was still a child. It was part of the story I carried in place of my absent father.

"I understood that I had a father with a split life. A life that cleft in two like a sacred oak struck by lightning, from which cleft undying flowers bloom. After my father's death people tell me the story of his life in the language of the *Lives of the Saints*. Already, before I am ten years old, I have a father who is legendary. Who leaves behind him, trails behind him, not money or property but myth which seems like an animal product, secreted from a living body. The silk from the worm. Or perhaps what's left isn't from an animal, perhaps it's manna. Or perhaps both. Both manna and silk. The product by which I was clothed and fed.

"So at a very young age I knew my father had another life. In this other life, he had money and success, but he had lost his soul. Later, he was anointed, marked; his soul burst and shone, but he was poor, a failure. And one way he had lost his soul was published in a magazine with pictures of sexy women, women I always know are nothing like me, with whom I will never have anything in common.

"I don't remember when I first heard about *Hot Dog*, but I remember exactly first coming upon it. I was twelve, looking among my father's books. Stuck in a book—a volume of *The Catholic Encyclopedia*, a study of the priesthood or the Eucharist?—is a small magazine called *Hot Dog*. I knew it was my father's, so I opened it looking for a trace of him. But I found a bare breasted woman, plaintively looking out at the camera. Underneath her body is the caption: 'Lover Come Back.'

"I was shocked and outraged. I ripped the magazine into many pieces and flushed it down the toilet, satisfied that at least I had destroyed the evidence."

Bell: Now for my most intrusive and unpleasant question. It seems to me, and again, this is a theory you may wish to dispute—I notice you're not disputing my theories and I hope it's not because you're being polite, because they certainly may be wrong—the more I hear of this book, the non-fiction book about your childhood, and bearing in mind Flannery O'Connor's remark, which you've also quoted in an essay, that everything important for a writer occurs before the age of six, it really does seem to me that a great deal of your fiction, if not all of it, has been driven by the peculiarities of a family situation. That you have, on the one hand, this very conservative and conventional Irish-Catholic world into which entered your father, a convert from Judaism with an extremely mysterious past, some of which you are still discovering. All writers, I think, have secrets that kind of give them power. Frequently these secrets are formed in childhood. I have secrets of that kind that drive my work. I would never tell them to anyone. It seems to me you're telling secrets, in a way. I would be afraid to do that. Does this worry you?

Gordon: No. Because these aren't probably the secrets.

Bell: I'm sorry?

Gordon: Probably what I'm telling are not the real secrets.

Bell: They're not the real secrets. Okay, it's a magician's trick! *(laughing)*

Gordon: *(laughing)*Yeah, it is a trick. Of course, with autobiographical writing, in a way, one is always in bad faith, because you're still only telling what you want to tell. And who knows what's being hidden? Who knows what, in fact, might be the true, dark, unsayable, unbearable story? So, I wasn't frightened. Also I think the way that these secrets drive us are as metaphors. And I think there are two things that have driven my work that are rooted in biography, two metaphors, which is early loss and my mother who was handicapped gave me the image of the brokenness of the body. That's not a secret. I can talk about that. The exploration will come, it seems to me, in traveling through these dark labyrinthian metaphors, and I think because they are rather large metaphors—loss and brokenness—I probably have quite a long way to travel in them

Bell: So, I now get the feeling that *Losing My Father* is really a novel in a way; it's sort of a Maileresque non-fiction novel.

Gordon: Excerpt that I really tried not to lie. There were some things that I would have liked not to reveal, but it seemed to me one of the subjects that I was writing about was revealing what is unbearable to reveal and then commenting on it. But nevertheless, behind or beneath what is revealable, there's always the unrevealable. I think every writer deals with that: the gap between language and what language can reveal, which is always the frustration and mystery of the whole enterprise.

Bell: Let me talk a little bit about the other side of the picture, as I see it, the Irish-Catholic side. It has occurred to me more and more as this book about your father unfolds that in some ways you are an insider, as he was, in Irish-Catholic culture, and in some ways an outsider, since you came in a way from somewhere else, coming partly from him. It seems to me that that kind of straddled position is what often gives a writer the perspective that's necessary to write about something as devouring as Irish-Catholic culture. But with that in mind, I wanted to ask you two questions. One, are you Irish and two, are you Catholic?

Gordon: Partly both, I guess. Yes, I'm Catholic, because it so formed me. And also there are parts of it that I think are irreplaceable. There are parts of Catholicism that I think the world would not be better off without. And there's nothing good, I mean I can't see replacing them with Oprah Winfrey or the Michigan Militia, which are probably your two options. And there is a way in which the Catholic Church—it doesn't exist in the world, but only in its best imagination of itself—provides an example of charity and openness, and, as I've said, things being at stake, which is of great value to me. Now the way most Catholics behave has nothing to do with that. But that's true of everything in human beings. I mean, all institutions stink, and all ways that human beings live out their ideals are usually failures. So I'm partly Irish, because I'm only a quarter Irish; I guess I'm partly Catholic, because there's so much of Catholicism in the way that it's practiced that appalls me. And so I'm a real mutt in everything that I do. I am a mutt. I was born a mutt and I guess I'll die one.

Bell: Again, bearing in mind Flannery O'Connor's remark about everything of importance happening before the age of six, I'm also reminded of something in one of your essays where you talk about being a sort of saintly little girl who would go out in the playground with the "rough" playmates and display a crucifix to try to quell their bad behavior, which you say had no effect. Did you have a happy childhood, being a Catholic? I mean, was this a good way to grow up, in your eyes?

Gordon: Was it happy? No.

Bell: Happy and good are not necessarily the same thing.

Gordon: Right. It was rich. It was a rich childhood, and it was not a foolish childhood, and it was not a wasted childhood. It was a deeply unhappy childhood, but it was a serious childhood. It's certainly not the childhood I would want for my children. But again, I keep repeating this phrase, it taught me how much is at stake, and I'm not sure a happier childhood would have taught me that. I think there was a little too much unhappiness, but there it was.

Bell: I think I better say as my questions become more inquisitorial that I am not myself a Catholic. So that's not the point. But in reading your nonfiction, it seems to me that your thinking has been in some way shaped by the Scholastic tradition that begins with Aquinas and comes on up. Is that true? Were you influenced by those writers?

Gordon: No.

Bell: So it's completely false.

Gordon: As a matter of fact, I think I'm anti-Scholastic. The tradition of Scholasticism, it seems to me, is an odd combination of excessive abstraction and excessive materialism. And I'd like to think of myself as always being hybrid, as always being a mutt, as always being a synthesizer. There's a kind of rigor that I'm very drawn to.

Bell: That's what I see.

Gordon: But I don't think it's a Scholastic rigor. There is a dualism that I think comes from being Irish, that comes from the very structure of Christianity that I both love and have to fight against, that there's a clarity of terms that I adore, but that very clarity of terms can exclude too much. I think I'm always trying to make some sort of balance between the clarity of the terms and the cruel exclusion that that clarity demands. It's tough.

Bell: There's an intellectual thoroughness in your nonfiction that I associate with the Scholastic tradition, and I think I'll have to discard this theory, but I'll declare it anyway. I went to the trouble of evolving it.

Gordon: Well, you wanted me to disagree with you!

Bell: Yes, I'm glad you did. It proves you're honest. I thought it would be an interesting irony for you with one foot in the church and one foot out, as

I've said, if the intellectual tradition with which you quarrel in many ways also, in some ways, mechanically gave you power.

Gordon: I think it demanded a sort of clarity, but I'm anti-theoretical in my nature. I'm anti-systemic. There's something about someone telling me that there's one way of describing the world that is the right way that immediately makes me rebel. And yet I am very drawn to ways to ways of describing the world that seem to be "the case" and that seem to ask the most difficult questions and to take in the most difficult evidence, and to have a kind of shapeliness about them. But I don't think those are ever large theories. I like close readings. I guess maybe I'm an intellectual New Critic. I like looking at things closely and trying to make sure, as much as possible—although, of course, this is a doomed and impossible task—that what you say is the case. And I kind of feel ferocious about that.

Bell: Perfect. I have a number of questions more that I'd still like to ask, but we seem to be out of time. So, let me thank you, Mary Gordon, for appearing on *The Writing Life*, and thank you all for watching the program.

Mary Gordon

Terry Gross / 1996

Transcription of *Fresh Air* (WHYY: Philadelphia), National Public Radio, 14 May 1996. © 1996 by WHYY, Inc. Printed by permission.

Gross: This is *Fresh Air*. I'm Terry Gross. My guest Mary Gordon is the author of several best-selling novels about the conflicts facing contemporary women, and she's written many essays relating to her life as a Catholic in conflict with the Church. In her new memoir, she writes that, at the age of forty-four, she discovered she wasn't the person she thought she was. Let me explain. The memoir is her exploration of her father's life, and doing the research into his past, she learned that he wasn't exactly who he said he was. And when she learned that, she had to alter her sense of who she is. This passage is from the beginning of her memoir, *The Shadow Man: A Daughter's Search for Her Father*:

Gordon reads from "To the Reader," xii–xiii, The Shadow Man.

 Gross: Mary, why did you want to investigate your father's life now? Why now?

 Gordon: That's the most obvious question to ask and the most impossible one for me to answer. The whole project started out of writing itself. I was writing something that I thought was about my grandmother's house. I had an image of my grandmother's house, which I followed and wrote about. And I realized in writing that that I was really writing about my father's death, because we had moved there after my father died. And then I kept writing about the moment of my father's death and how that was such an enormous break for me. And I suddenly had a great number of pages, and it occurred to me in a terrible way that I didn't know this man that was the most important man in the world to me—this man that I thought I knew so well, I really didn't know at all—and that there were ways I could know him better. So in a way that's very mysterious for me, I said to myself, "It's time now. It's time to do this."

 Gross: You know, you said in the past, and in what you read, you said that your father's death is the most important thing anyone could know about you. Why was that so important in your definition of yourself?

Gordon: I think that that moment of loss was really a defining moment for who I was, that a person who had lost at a very early age was the person whom I shaped myself around, and it was the moment all my work came out of, in a way, the recognition of loss, bearing witness to loss. It also gave me a real differentness from everyone around me; I was marked by loss at a very early age, and the loss of the person who was most beloved and important to me was also the end of joy for me in my childhood. I had to rediscover joy in adulthood.

Gross: It was the end of joy not only because your father died, but because you moved into your grandmother's house where things were much more somber.

Gordon: Well, they were much more harsh. They were somber and un-playful, and I was constantly under surveillance and constantly judged as wanting, whereas in my father's eyes, nothing I did was less than spectacular, less than glorious. So it was a tremendous shift of focus.

Gross: And at your grandmother's house, there was constant disability. Your mother had had polio, your aunt had had polio, your grandmother was around seventy-eight. You say you were always the most capable person.

Gordon: Yes. I say that one of the other important things about me is that I always feel like the most able-bodied person in any room I'm in. You know, I could be in the room with Arnold Schwarzenegger, and I would still feel, somehow, "I'll lift that for you, Arnold. Don't' worry. Don't tax yourself. I can do it." I think that's a feeling a lot of women have—of being more capable or more able to do things than other people. But with me, it was very literally inscribed at an early age.

Gross: I think one of the things that must have made your father so inter-esting to you is that he seemed to have such an interesting life. He edited a humor magazine; he was involved with soft core. I mean these are not things that typical fathers did.

Gordon: And particularly not typical working-class fathers, and class is a very important element in my history, as I think it's a very important and well-kept secret in American life. Because my mother was very working class and her mother and that family that I moved into, and my father really pre-sented me with a world that included the larger world. One of the things that differentiates the middle from the working class is how much of the larger world do you feel you have access to. And my father suggested to me that I had access to the whole world, and because he had done so much, or he had told me he had done so much—he actually did both more and less than he told me—but he did always give me a sense that other people's fathers were going to work and being responsible and respectable, and he was being adventurous and romantic, and it was very exciting.

Gross: What did you know about his humor magazine *Hot Dog* before you started researching your father's life, and what did you find out when you actually found *Hot Dog* in an archive?

Gordon: Well, when I was twelve years old, I was going through some of my father's books which were mostly very high-minded, very religious books. And I opened up one of these religious tomes, and I saw something called *Hot Dog*. I had known in some odd way that my father had edited a magazine called *Hot Dog*, and I opened it up. I was twelve. I was the most law-abiding, puritanical twelve-year-old. My entire life was based on Audrey Hepburn and *The Nun's Story (laughing)*. That was my ideal for myself, just perfection and exclusion and absolute obedience to the rules. And I opened this magazine and saw a bare-breasted woman saying, "Lover, come back." And I had to say, "My God, this is my father's magazine." So as a law-abiding and an Antigone-like twelve-year-old, I took the magazine, I ripped it into shreds, and I flushed it down the toilet. And I said, "Nobody will ever know about this again."

Well, I did look. I used all the computer-based searches and everything, and I found copies of *Hot Dog* in the New York Public Library, in Brown, and later tracked it down to some collectors. And of course looking at it as a woman in her late forties in the late twentieth century, it's nothing. But it's corny, and that actually became more embarrassing to me than the fact that it had a bare-breasted woman, which would embarrass me at age twelve. But it was so corny, and it was so provincial, and so of its time. At the same time, he was always trying to be serious. There were these one-liners like, uh, "Some guys get married. Others get by." And on the next page, there would be an article about Flaubert. And it was that same, tremendous incoherence that marked everything about my father. What did these guys think that were buying this magazine for pictures of chorus girls and all of a sudden they're reading about the temptation of St. Anthony? It was wonderful in that way of my father always trying to put things together that couldn't possibly be put together.

Gross: Had you thought when you were young that he was a wonderful writer and that you could never live up to how good he was?

Gordon: Oh, exactly. I thought he was just elegant and intellectual, and the single hardest thing in this project for me (and some of my beloved friends really had to endure a lot of abuse from me) was . . . I would show . . . the first time I wrote a draft of the chapter about what my father did there were pages and pages of his prose. And finally a friend of mine said, "You know, Mary, we're interested in *your* writing, not in his. You're a much better writer than he was." I said some unprintable—"how stupid you are!" Finally, a woman in my agent's office said, "This has to be radically cut. Nobody can read him. He's not interesting." That was the single most disturbing thing for me, having to understand that he really wasn't that good a writer, that there was a lot of incoherence, a lot of bombast, a lot of undigested or half-digested ideas. And that I was in fact the writer that he wasn't. That was terrible.

Gross: Why was it so crushing to find out he wasn't the great writer you had imagined?

Gordon: I think that he made a place for me in the world of letters, and if I had knocked him out the place that he made, then it's . . . I guess . . . I don't know how this works psychoanalytically, but it is an Oedipal moment, I guess, even for the daughter: when you have, in a way, killed the father who gave you life. If I had to say I'm better than he is, that was almost a way of killing him or stealing something from him. And I felt that he was so vulnerable in his death, and I had stolen something from a beloved dead man. I had stolen the primacy of place in the world of letters that he had created for us.

Gross: It must have been useful, though, to have thought of him so highly because that gave you . . . that helped you make a place in the world of arts and letters. I mean, you know, you kind of inherited a place there if you thought he was so good.

Gordon: Yeah, and I know that, believe me, I do know that my father was quite mad in ways that were not always benign, although the malignity did not touch me directly. But what is really a great gift that my father gave me, that a lot of women don't have, was that he said, "This world that I inhabit is yours. And there is nothing that you can't do because you're a woman. You are my heir." And he gave me a tremendous self-confidence in the world of language and thought. From the moment of my being a tiny child, he gave it to me, he brought me into it, he said, "It's ours and it's yours." And so there were a lot of things that I didn't have to unlearn that some girls did.

Gross: Your father lied about several pretty important things. He'd been married once before marrying your mother (and he never let on about that), he lied that he was an only child (he wasn't an only child), and he said he was born in Ohio (he was really an immigrant). What purpose do you think these lies served in his life?

Gordon: I think that being who he was was a torment for him, and I think he lied as an anesthetic. I think it relieved the torment. He had to make himself a person he could bear to be. I think he couldn't stand being an immigrant, he couldn't stand being a Jew, he couldn't stand being uneducated. Why he lied about being married before, I think, he just, after a while, wiped out the past, and also after his conversion, it would have created problems of canon law for him if he wanted to marry my mother. So, I think that he really found his life unbearable and his position in the world unbearable, and he had to create a new life that he could bear.

Gross: Your father was Jewish, but converted to Catholicism in the 1930s. Do you think that that was part of the changing of himself so that he could find himself and life more bearable?

Gordon: I think so. One of the sad things is that I came up against so many dead ends and so many blank walls. My father would be 102 if he were alive now, and so practically everybody that was connected with him was dead. I can only imagine that his family life or his life in the community was anguishing to him, and I think that being a Jew in the early part of the century—it's remarkable when I started to research it—how anti-Semitism was just in the drinking water. You couldn't get away from it. I think that was unbearable for him. And he wanted a place in the great cultural life of Europe that was not a marginal place. I think he saw the life of the mind, the life of art, as his way out of the tumult of this immigrant hubbub that he couldn't bear.

Gross: Did you know when you were young that he had converted to Catholicism from Judaism?

Gordon: Yeah. One thing about my father was he never tried to pass. He used his status as a convert. You kind of have to understand the culture of the Catholic Church from about 1930 to about 1960. To be a Jewish convert was a real mark of distinction, and in a way, my father picked the perfect place where he could leave his Judaism, but not have to hide it. So that as a Catholic convert you could say, "Okay, I've left that. I'm not a Jew anymore, but I was a Jew. I don't have to pretend I'm not. And as a matter of fact, it is a badge of my superiority that I have left error and found my way to truth." So he didn't have a lot of the anxieties of a name change or the terror that somebody would find out he was Jewish. He never did that. What he did was actually a little bit more complicated and a little bit more sinister, because he said, "I'm a Jew. I know what they're like, and they're really dangerous, and I can tell you the insider's story."

Gross: Well, some of his writing was really quite anti-Semitic, and he supported the Fascists in World War II.

Gordon: Yep, he did. He was very strongly a Francoist. He was an isolationist into 1943, which is really late. He was kind of denying that Hitler was very bad. You know, he said, well, he's bad, but there are a lot worse and, as a matter of fact, the English and their persecution of the Catholic Church in Ireland were just as bad as Hitler. He was pretty pro-Mussolini. Where this came from I cannot imagine, except a kind of phobic determination to embrace the Other.

Gross: Did you pick up on this hate when you were young or did you find this anti-Semitism as an adult, researching your father?

Gordon: I found it as an adult, and it was crushing for me. It was morally annihilating for me almost, because I had really loved him and still do and have to endure the truth that he was really saying hateful, wicked things. And I had had his magazines—and the way that we erase things that are unbearable to us, I think, is always very interesting—I must have known since at least my early twenties that he had written this anti-Semitic stuff, but I just didn't take it in until I sat down to read him, almost as an author who is not my father. And so it was only a few years ago and I had to look at this stuff and then research more of it that I had to confront the horror of his hatred and self-hatred and the virulence and the nastiness of what he said. And it was excruciating for me.

Gross: So what are you rewriting about yourself, knowing more about who your father really was? What changes about who you are?

Gordon: I feel that I am a less fathered girl now and more of a woman who doesn't define herself so much by him, that I'm more alone and now the next however many years of my life are a task in which he has less and less of a place. In a way that's very sad, but it's a little bit exhilarating.

Gross: Why is a little bit exhilarating?

Gordon: Because I'm grown up.

Gross: Right.

Gordon: I'm not primarily a daughter anymore. I don't define myself as being his in that way. And to say the most important thing about me is no longer my being a daughter, it does make your lungs expand a bit, however painfully.

Gross: . . . You said that you not only lost your concept of your father while writing this book, but you lost your faith in memory. And I would like to read my favorite sentence from your new memoir. You write, "I entered the cave of memory which nowadays seems like a tourist trap in high season." You go on to say, "Everyone's talking about memory: French intellectuals, historians of the Holocaust, victims of child abuse, alleged abusers." What do you mean when you say that "the cave of memory nowadays seems like a tourist trap in high season"?

Gordon: Well, kind of what I said is that there's a new industry in recovering memory, and partly it's very important and partly it's very vulgarized. I think that we believe in memory in a very unsophisticated way. So, for example, the topic that's so much on everybody's mind: abuse. Suddenly everybody you know had an abuse story, and the question is: were they really abused or were they not? This is what's anguishing, I think, about memory. In questions of justice, it's enormously important to try to figure out what really happened, but the more you try to unravel the past, the most the mix of fact and narrative overlay becomes inextricable. And people go back to the past, as we said, trying to find the golden ancestor, trying to find the criminal, and then people want, as in the case of the Holocaust, I think, to erase the past and say, "It didn't happen at all." The trouble with memory is how complicated it is, and to really confront that is a project that very few people who happen to be on *Geraldo* on Thursday morning, for example, are willing to do.

Gross: How reliable did you find your memories were?

Gordon: Oh, terrible. It was really shocking. Also for a novelist or for a writer, you believe in memory as the gilt-edged stock that you can constantly get dividends from. Then you find out you bought a swamp in central Florida. All these things that I would have sworn happened I couldn't really pin down. A lot of the times I went back and found that, you know, they couldn't have happened and that I made them up. And they were so real to me. I can tell you the smells and the tastes and some of them may not have happened at all.

Gross: Give me an example of one of those.

Gordon: Well, I had a memory of being with my father on a merry-go-round in a subway terminal. And I can tell you what the hot dog stand was like, I can tell you what the signs were like, I can tell you what it smelled like, and I know that there could not have been a merry-go-round in a subway terminal. Who would put a merry-go-round in a subway terminal? But for me I have very clear memory of being with my father in that place which could not possibly have existed. I have memories of conversations with him, which, as I try to imagine saying the things that I believe he said to a seven-year-old, are incomprehensible. He could not possibly have said them. There were just images that were so strong that I believed happened that didn't really happen.

Gross: As you were writing your memoir about your father and sifting through your own memories and trying to find out things that you never knew at all, your mother was losing her memory. She was in her eighties as you were writing this, and she was losing so much of her own memory she was already forgetting that she had been married to your father.

Gordon: Yes. She doesn't recognize his face in pictures. She asks who she was married to. What's interesting about my mother's lost of memory is that she remembers only her mother and me. So I was desperately trying to find this person, my father, and she had lost her husband, the image of him, the memory of him, the sound of his voice, with absolutely no pain and no regret. And so I was even more alone in my memories of him.

Gross: What did it make you think of in terms of the ultimate value of memory, watching your mother so completely lose hers and, really, your mother wasn't even able to recognize what it was she had lost?

Gordon: It just made the whole issue of memory more and more vexed, because I could see that without memory my mother had become less alive, not really herself anymore. And so that thing that we call a self, I understood, is so constituted by memory, and yet there she was. You would have to say she's the same Anna Gordon, she's alive, she's clearly human, she is capable of response. And so simultaneously she was herself and absolutely not herself, and I had to understand both of those things at once: the absolute essentialness of memory to the definition of a self and the fact that one could still exist as a human without it.

Gross: You say watching your mother that you realized one of the advantages for her not having any memory was that she had no dread, because she'd always forget what it was she was facing. She didn't have to relive the terror of a painful medical test. But then you say, how is pleasure judged if it can't be relived? I thought that was an interesting observation.

Gordon: It became a very practical issue, because she's in a wheelchair and she's immobile. It's difficult to get her from place to place. So I would always say: "Oh, do I take her down to the garden? Do I take her to my son's play?" Because I would go through these incredible physical machinations to arrange something pleasant for her, and literally twenty minutes later, she wouldn't remember it. She would enjoy it at the moment, but then the next time I had to say, "Am I going to get an ambulance for her? Am I going to push her down this hill?" I would question, you know, what's it worth if she doesn't remember it. And you have to really shift your focus in a radical way and say, "It is only the present, and the present is worth something." But since we're all kind of capitalists of our own expenditure, I think, it makes it very vexed. How much do I do? How hard do I work? How much do I try to make a good time for her? And I used to desperately try to make a good time for her, and I've let up on it a little bit, because since she doesn't remember it, it is worth only what it is worth at the present. And it's very strange to have to make those calculations.

Gross: Another paradox that you faced while writing this book is you say there wasn't a day you didn't wish your father was alive but, at the same time, you were beginning to think that your mother might be better off if she died.

Gordon: Yeah. It's . . . My mother is somebody I have a heartbreaking love and tenderness for. One of the things that hurts me very much is when people read what I wrote about my mother and say how cruel I am and how I angry I am at her and how much I must hate her. I don't hate her. I love her very deeply. And she breaks my heart. And her fate breaks my heart. She really sits and stares most of the day, and you know, the question is: Is this being alive? Would she be better dead? She's not in pain. She's not suffering, but she's not really alive. And so I sometimes think, "Well, it's time for her to go now. You know, she's lived enough. This is not really a life. It's time for her to go." Although I'm sure when she does die, I'll feel enormous grief. But my father is still, for me, a relatively young, vital man, because he exists in my life. And so I can fantasize about his coming back. You know, I'll walk outside the studio and there he'll be. We'll go off and have lunch together, and it will be heaven.

Gross: You know, your father is so full of surprises still for you. You're still learning things about him, because he died when you were seven and he lied so much about his life. Is your mother an already really well-told tale? I mean, do you think there are really secrets in her life and things that you'll eventually find out about that will shock you?

Gordon: I think there are secrets, but I'll never find them out. Uh, no, nothing would shock me, but I wish I had known more of her inner life. She's a heroic woman. She was a polio victim, and she worked all her life 'til she was seventy-five. But she was a woman of great imagination and dreams, which, in that working-class way, had to be repressed to get on with life. And I wish I had more access to her dreams, and I never will. So, in terms of a biography, I don't think I'm going to ever find out that she had, you know, a hot love affair with a sailor. But I wish I had known what her desires and her dreams were. Those might surprise me, but I never will know them.

Gross: There's something in your book that reminds me of what you're saying also. When she was in the nursing home, there was a questionnaire that was supposed to be administered. And you decided to ask her the questions yourself. And the questions all had to do with the quality of life and whether she was happy or not. And she responded positively to all of the questions, as if she were perfectly content and happy and comfortable. And then you said what to her?

Gordon: I said, "Do you really mean that? Are you really happy or are you just afraid of making a fuss? Do you think it's unseemly to complain?" And she said, "Yes. I don't want to seem to be a whiner." It was another heartbreaking moment for me. So, finally—I mean, talk about the questionnaire comes out the way you want it: did I want to hear that she's unhappy, and did I redo the questionnaire—but finally I said (she's a person who respected people's work so much because she importantly defined herself as a worker), I said, "Mom, it's these people's job to get the right information from you, and if you don't answer the questionnaire honestly, they're not going to be able to do their job well." And she said, "Oh, O.K." And then she talked about her own grief and her own despair. But it was so important to her to be a person that didn't complain, that kept going, that did endure. It was only when she saw that she could be helping somebody else's work that she felt the responsibility to be honest.

Gross: And confess to how miserable her quality of life was.
Gordon: Yeah. And how much she had lost.

Gross: But, you know, I was wondering if you thought that a lot of her inner life was that way when she was younger, that she wouldn't confess to anybody what she really was thinking and feeling, because it would be perceived as she was whining.

Gordon: Yeah. I think that is *the* immigrant story, in some way. You just keep going. You just do it. And it's something that I admire very much in a particular way, but it's at an enormous price. It's really what is not said just gets buried and does some terrible things to people. I do think, though, that my mother had a very deep spiritual and religious life, so that even when she's saying, you know, "I'm pretty miserable now," she believes that it's God's will and she's going to get her reward in heaven. So the despair is not thorough-going for her, because I think she enters into a very deep religious place, even now when there's not much else left of her consciousness.

Gross: With that memory does she remember much about her religion?

Gordon: Yep. What's . . . the other thing that's so amazing is what is left of her memory. She remembers every prayer that she ever said, she remembers every saint, and she remembers the words to every song written between 1910 and 1950. So, she doesn't know what her husband's name is, but if you ask her to sing, you know, "Peg of My Heart," she's got every verse. And all the mysteries of the Rosary. So, prayers and song have really remained for her. It's very strange.

Gross: You know, I think for a lot of people there's always a couple of voices in your head that are kind of directing you or helping you make decisions, or whatever, and I think, you know, a lot of us internalize our parents' voices. But sometimes you realize, you get old enough to realize, that those two voices are actually in conflict, that your mother and father would have seen this thing quite differently. And so you have these two competing voices in your head, arguing about what the correct moral or ethical or practical stance is on something. Do you know what I mean? And I wonder if you have that in your mind.

Gordon: Well, I think it is always the practical, as opposed to the impractical—you know, that my father's voice tells me, "Just follow your vision. Go as deeply as you possibly can. Give yourself over to it utterly." And my mother says, "What about your place in the world?" That is not to say fame or success, because both of them were very highly ethical people, and they didn't care about money or success at all. They cared about virtue in some way. But my mother is always saying to me, "Get on with it. Don't dawdle.

Don't dream. Get on with your business in the world. You have a relationship to other people," whereas my father's voice says, "Just give yourself to the vision, wherever it takes you." And that's a real conflict: whether I want to be a practical person in the world or a visionary.

Gross: Well, yeah. In fact you wrote a piece recently about the Jacqueline Kennedy Onassis auction, and in that op ed piece you referred to your mother. And she was always saying "It doesn't pay" about a lot of things. She'd say, "It just doesn't pay." And you say that she created a world, like an interior world, where, okay, loss was kept at a minimum, but pleasure was always suspect, and beauty was thought a waste of time. I thought how interesting it must have been for you to be brought up in a home where beauty is a waste of time and then you become a writer and artist.

Gordon: Well, one of the stories about my mother when she still had her memory—and she always had a great sense of humor that I think underscores this—was, you know, I had written, I think, four or five books at the time, and I was looking at a Bergdorf Goodman catalog, looking at things which I could never have dreamed of buying—you know, these white silk suits and things like that. I was saying, "Oh, God, I'd love to have that. Oh, isn't that beautiful? That is so beautiful." And my mother looked at me and said, "When exactly did you become such a superficial person?" And . . .

Gross: *(laughing)* And so beauty was just a sign of your shallowness, I mean, being interested in beauty.

Gordon: And so if you take that to questions of style, as I try to write beautifully, there's always something in me that's saying, "Well, why are you doing this with your life when there are children in East Harlem that can't read, and there are babies in Africa that, you know, have no food, and you are devoting yourself to beauty. And for what?" It is a very great conflict with me.

Gross: How do you resolve it?

Gordon: I just know I'm not good at anything else *(laughs)*. So that makes it a lot easier.

Mary Gordon: *The Shadow Man*

Charlie Rose / 1996

Transcription of *The Charlie Rose Show*, Thirteen/WNET, 14 June 1996. © 1996 by Charlierose.com,inc. Printed by permission.

Charlie Rose: Author Mary Gordon is known for applying intense criticism to the defining forces in her life, but there was one influence she didn't expect to find fault with: the memory of her father. For the first seven years of her life, he was her mentor, her idol, her inspiration. His influence burned its way into her life way beyond the short time they spent together. But gradually, she became aware that the father she loved and the man he was were two very different things.

The Shadow Man is the memoir of her search for the truth in his life and in hers. It speaks to the impact of memory on a person's identity and how changing the past can affect the present.

I'm very pleased to have Mary Gordon back on this program. Welcome back.

Mary Gordon: Thanks, Charlie.

Charlie Rose: This book has been received, as you are pleased about, with sort of enormous praise, in most instances. It is a very personal story. As I said to you before we started, the notion of the hold a relationship between parent and child can have through the adult's life, as the child becomes a woman or a man, an adult, is stunning to me. Did you have any sense of this all your life?

Mary Gordon: I always thought that the absolutely most important thing about me was that my father had died when I was seven, and it was as if I wore a badge, slightly like either a leper or a saint. It was both simultaneously a badge of disfigurement and a badge of honor that I thought of myself so much as the daughter of this dead man. It was the most important thing about me always, until now, perhaps.

Charlie Rose: Tell me about the journey you took, the personal story that brought you to here.

Mary Gordon: Well, the mystery is why I waited until I was about 45 to look into what I actually could have always looked into. It was suddenly time. I decided to consult archives and to look. My father was a writer, a failed writer, but nonetheless, he left a paper trail, which not all fathers do. And in looking in the archives and in the archives of his work, I found that he had lied about his place birth—he said he was born in Ohio. He was, in fact, born in Vilna, Lithuania—his date of birth, his name. He had two other sisters that I didn't know about, one of whom spent her whole adult life in a mental hospital, one of whom left me a little money at her death, and I didn't know she existed. I discovered what I probably could always have known. My father was a Jew and converted to Catholicism. I always knew that. He never hid it. But I didn't know the depth and perniciousness of the anti-Semitic articles and polemics that he devoted his life to writing, and I had to confront all these things in my mid-40s.

Charlie Rose: In your memory, in your mind.

Mary Gordon: Well, I had to find them. Most of them I hadn't known about. And the one that I had known about, I had to really look at. And what I had to do was try to understand the difference between my memories and this new evidence and try to come to terms with the gap between those two things, which was so profound.

Charlie Rose: "Come to terms with it" meaning what? Understand it?

Mary Gordon: At least witness it, if not understand it. One of the false fantasies that's very cruel is that by getting all the information, we will be able to understand what is really incomprehensible and mysterious about people. What I had to say about my father was there were, in fact, two people: a man who loved me, who was marvelous to me, who opened up the world of books and culture, and a rather mad, self-hating Jew and anti-Semite.

Charlie Rose: And how do you explain that?

Mary Gordon: I don't. I certainly mark it as a sign of madness, but I think that it's a relationship mistake to try to say there is one neat explanation. So one of the things that I do in the book is create multiple explanations, no one of which is really sufficient.

Charlie Rose: But which one rings most true for you?

Mary Gordon: What I think is that it's an immigrant's story, that it's a story of anti-Semitism, of Jewish self-hatred, of intellectual ambition on the part of a young Jewish boy—my father would be 102 if he were alive, so we're really talking about a story of the '10s and the '20s—and a child of a peddler who taught himself six languages in the Cleveland Public Library.

Charlie Rose: So this is a great American story, to do that.
Mary Gordon: It couldn't happen anywhere else.

Charlie Rose: It's a story to be proud of. It's a story to celebrate.
Mary Gordon: He was simultaneously a self-creator and a self-destroyer, and that's the part of the American dream that I think hasn't been sufficiently marked. We say that the immigrants came over. The streets were paved with gold, and they all went from strength to strength. Well, they didn't. The pressure of having to confront who you were, where you came from, in this new, cruel juggenaut of a land drove many people mad, and everybody didn't succeed. Many people failed and were crushed.

Charlie Rose: And that story's as important as the story of success.
Mary Gordon: Yes, and I think particularly in an age when we're so cruel to current immigrants and we use our fantasy of the history of past immigrants as a stick to beat the new immigrants with. We need to come to terms with the crushing failure that is also part of some immigrants' stories.

Charlie Rose: What did this do to you?
Mary Gordon: Made me very sad, to begin with.

Charlie Rose: Of course it did.
Mary Gordon: And I went around, kind of in a state of shock. My children were really wonderful to me, in keeping me centered and reminding me that my history wasn't one that only went backwards, it went forwards

Charlie Rose: And someone's deception does not define you.
Mary Gordon: That's right, exactly, and the most important thing that happened to me was that I stopped thinking of myself as primarily my father's daughter. Now, there's no one noun that can replace that. I can't say I'm a writer, I'm a mother, I'm a feminist, I'm a this or a that. Being my father's daughter was an umbrella that could define me very well, but I can't do it anymore.

Charlie Rose: Not only that, you were driven to be good in his eyes.
Mary Gordon: I was driven, but it was so easy because I couldn't do anything wrong in his eyes.

Charlie Rose: Yes.
Mary Gordon: If I did anything wrong, he wrote, rewrote the world so

that it was right. That was a great gift to give to a particular little girl in the '50s. My father was teaching me French and Latin before he died. We were writing poetry together. We would go out and, you know, we would do accents. We would do imitations of Italian barbers and Irish priests. The whole world of language and literature and the intellect was mine, and there was nothing I could do that was wrong. It's a good start for a little girl.

Charlie Rose: What's the hardest part of this to write? What was the hardest part for you to write? When were you crying into your computer?

Mary Gordon: I don't use a computer. I was crying into my fancy English notebook. Please!

Charlie Rose: Now, come on. Good writers use computers.

Mary Gordon: Yes, but not me. I think having to understand the depth of his anti-Semitism and the ugliness of it and again to say that this man who had loved me so much and had given me so much was capable of such pernicious thoughts and language and to be able to hold onto my love for him, which was true, despite the other truth of this pernicious hatefulness.

Charlie Rose: Yes.

Mary Gordon: To try to keep both at once was a great challenge.

Charlie Rose: I'm still left with this notion about this story, not just about the particulars of your story. It is why people deceive themselves and deceive those around them—a life of deception.

Mary Gordon: It's a terrible burden.

Charlie Rose: It is a burden. Exactly.

Mary Gordon: But it must be that the burden of reality is incomparably greater, so that the burden of constant self-invention seems more tolerable. It must be as if your hands were always in a fire. And you take your hand out of the fire, and even if you put it into ground glass, it seems less unbearable. I think we have to understand the unbearableness of self-hatred.

Charlie Rose: And what do we come away with from that understanding?

Mary Gordon: I think we come away with pity and, in the end, pity is a very . . .

Charlie Rose: That someone could experience such pain, and such holding their hand in the fire,

Mary Gordon: Yes.

Charlie Rose: Because of the deception, because they knew they were living a lie, even though they could isolate their life. He could isolate the fact that he loved you and he wanted you to be his partner.

Mary Gordon: That's right.

Charlie Rose: He saw in you everything. I mean, here was an opportunity almost to approach some sense of purity, to inspire, to open a mind.

Mary Gordon: Absolutely.

Charlie Rose: To give total love, to all of that. And he could say, "Here is where I'm good, and over here is where I'm . . ."

Mary Gordon: It's a very strange thing that people can put that bubble around different parts of their lives.

Charlie Rose: Categorize themselves.

Mary Gordon: And the bubbles don't interpenetrate at all. But I think it speaks to a great pain, a great sense of disassociation, a great terror. I mean, imagine waking up in the world, waking up in the morning and knowing that there are at least two people inside you that don't communicate and that don't have anything to do with one another. And that also, I think, is an American story, that incoherence, which, because we're a new country still, we allow and, in fact, encourage. It's part of our genius, but it's also part of the burden of being American.

Charlie Rose: And your mother?

Mary Gordon: My mother was Irish Catholic, a rather simple person. One of the paradoxes is I always thought my father was the educated one, because he told me he'd gone to Harvard, and I discovered he dropped out of school in the 10th grade. And she, in fact, had finished high school, so she turned out to be more educated than he. She was a simple person. She was a polio victim. She worked very hard. She was a legal secretary.

Charlie Rose: And had Alzheimer's?

Mary Gordon: She now is suffering from either Alzheimer's or senile dementia. She has no memory at all. She doesn't remember my father's face in photographs. She doesn't remember being married. And she lives in a kind of eternal present that's quite heart-breaking.

Charlie Rose: These truths, you can square them for yourself, in the end, because you write about it, which I assume is some catharsis?

Mary Gordon: I don't think it's a catharsis, because that sounds as if it's finished.

Charlie Rose: A kind of cleansing.

Mary Gordon: Yes. Cleansing. I think I like [that] better, that it's always a process of trying to understand how complicated human beings are, which is the thing I think literature gives that nothing else can give us: an understanding of how people can contain one thing and precisely its opposite at the same time. And the greatest literature, it seems, gives us a sense of enormous compassion for just how difficult it is to be a human being and get through life. So in the end, I felt like my compassion for the project of being alive was deepened.

Charlie Rose: [reading] "It is a winter afternoon, March 25, 1994. I am in a dark room, a windowless room in lower Manhattan. Varick and Houston streets, the National Archives and Records Administration—Northeast Region. I'm looking at the census for the years 1900 to 1910, looking for facts about my father and his family. I'm doing it out of some impulse of studiousness, or thoroughness, an impulse whose source is not desire, even the desire to know, but a rote habit. The habit of doing things as they should be done. In this case, it is an unfriendly habit, because in this dark room, illumined by the silver light of the screens of the microfilm readers, at the age of forty-four, I discover I am not the person I thought I was."

If you want to understand these kinds of ideas—who you are, really come from, relationships between parent and child in all of the multiplicity and complexity—*The Shadow Man: A Daughter's Search for Her Father* is for you. Thank you, Mary.

Mary Gordon: Thank you.

Sandy Asirvatham: An Interview with Mary Gordon

Sandy Asirvatham / 1997

Printed in *Poets & Writers Magazine* 25:4 (July August 1997), 50–55, 57–61. © 1997 Poets & Writers, Inc. Reprinted by permission.

Mary Gordon is not the kind to mince words. In the fall of 1995, a writer for *Newsday* asked a number of prominent New York Catholics what they'd say if given a three-minute audience with the pope during his American visit. Former governor Mario Cuomo, apparently awestruck, said he "wouldn't dare speak to the pope" but went on, in his fashion, to wax philosophical upon the difficulties and joys of modern Catholicism. Most other respondents gave solemn, respectful answers—even if they questioned the pope for his stance on birth control, or criticized modern Catholicism for producing "some of the ugliest churches in the history of Christendom," as one artist opined.

But true to form, the article's representative Catholic novelist answered in a highly unorthodox manner, if not quite blasphemously.

"I wouldn't want to say anything to the pope," Mary Gordon began, "because he doesn't interest me particularly. He's not very important to me; he's not someone who dwells in my imagination."

Readers of Gordon's fiction should probably have known to expect such a statement from her: resolute, direct, contrarian, oddly funny. As a former student of Gordon's, I immediately understood the sharp, unambiguous tone of her response to the pope question. I have watched her take a young writer's work and point out the (myriad) flaws and (occasional) strengths in plain, severe, and not necessarily tactful terms: "This is a cliché. This is a tired situation. But this, now this is something new, something we've not heard before." When I was an M.F.A. candidate at Columbia, Gordon was not a universally beloved teacher—for one thing, she didn't adhere to the workshop standard of finding something good to say about every piece of writing, no matter how weak. But in a place where it was sometimes hard to get specific, useful, honest criticism, many students valued her for being a straight shooter, even if the shots hurt.

The less-than-perfect way people really live their lives, especially in contrast to the rigorous ideals espoused by the Catholic church, has been Gordon's perennial concern in her six works of fiction. In her first book, *Final Payments* (Random House, 1978), the protagonist is a young Irish Catholic woman in Queens who has devoted more than a decade to caring for her wheelchair-bound father. Upon her father's death, 30-year-old Isabel casts about in search of a life's activity to replace the sacrificial purity of her old vocation. At first she oscillates between extremes of self-indulgence (overeating, having affairs with married men) and self-sacrifice (becoming the caretaker of an embittered, ungrateful old woman). Isabel's great struggle in this book is to find a balance, to refrain from fleeing into an idealized, nun-ish, penitential life. Completed when Gordon was only 29, the novel was a smash, a bestseller in hardcover and then, again, in paperback.

Fifteen years and a few grants later (a Guggenheim and a Lila Wallace-Reader's Digest Award), Gordon's central theme had not changed greatly. The three novellas that make up *The Rest of Life* (Viking Penguin, 1993), her most recent book of fiction, are the stories of women who seek to bridge the gap between their ideals, both religious and romantic in nature, and their real lives, full of imperfections, compromises, and tragedies.

But while her deepest concerns had not varied, Mary Gordon's writing itself had changed a great deal. Like her characters, her prose itself had learned to live, so to speak, in a less-than-perfect world. Whereas *Final Payments* is a tightly structured story that moves with wrenching, dialectical precision toward its conclusion, the novellas in *The Rest of Life* are quite the opposite: loose, static, more contemplative than narrative. And at least one of the books in between seems to represent a transition from one extreme to another. If Gordon's primary argument was anti-perfectionism, then form had learned to follow function.

I visited Gordon early this spring at her apartment near Barnard College, where she is a professor of English. We've kept in touch a little bit since our workshops in 1991–92, but it is always a shock for me to see her again: She's only about five-feet-two, but in some unrevised part of my memory, she is the large, commanding presence at the head of the classroom table, and I'm that small, intimidated student whose manuscript is about to be dismantled.

On this occasion, Gordon is contemplative rather than critical. Sitting at her unembellished wooden dining room table, we try to ignore the continual ringing of the telephone and fax machine, while we talk about the evolution of her writing.

She acknowledges right away that her writing has changed over time, has grown less severe and less formal: "When I was younger, I was so afraid of losing control and, in some ways, so uncritically in love with rigor as an aesthetic. So I think it was maturity, that I could relax a little more as I knew what I was doing, let the fear go."

Although perfectionism is a common problem for young writers, rigor for rigor's sake seems to be an occupational hazard particularly for those raised as Catholics. Some like Mary McCarthy, Gordon says, did not manage to escape that pitfall: "I do think Mary McCarthy had two marvelous books, *The Company She Keeps* and *Memoirs of a Catholic Girlhood*, and then I think she was not able to get out of that idolatry of rigor and formal perfection, so she didn't grow. There's a way in which her most stunning achievements are the achievements of a brilliant *young* woman. It's sort of sad."

In a 1994 interview with *America* magazine, Gordon described the source of her early aesthetic: "I was brought up with so many models of perfection prevalent in the pre-Vatican II church. There was a perfect way of washing a dish; you were attentive to each dish you washed. You didn't let your mind wander. That was how you offered everything up for the greater glory of God. There was no time where you were not on the hook."

Gordon's eventually loosening up as a writer was prefigured, in a way, by her transformation from lonely child into gregarious adolescent during the early 1960s: "Everybody else talks about how great childhood was and how terrible adolescence was, but for me it was just the opposite. Before age 12—I can really divide my life up like that—I had no friends."

Although she wasn't an unfriendly child, she wasn't good at small talk, and was "such a *watcher*" that it unnerved both adults and other kids. In her Catholic, working-class neighborhood, a world that valued obedient religiosity and financial security above other things, young Mary's constant reading and writing also tended to alienate people. But after 12, "suddenly I figured out that people thought I was funny. Being funny is not so much a coin of the realm for children, but it can be for adolescents."

To a great extent, Mary's mother helped her break out of her shell. Unlike Mary's bookish father, a writer who encouraged his daughter to follow in his footsteps, Anna Gordon was an assertive and worldly woman, a teller of bawdy jokes, whose example taught Mary how to function socially. In Gordon's second novel *The Company of Women* (Random House, 1981), Felicitas Taylor's spunky and wisecracking mother Charlotte was modeled upon Anna.

Leaving her fairly cloistered hometown of Far Rockaway, New York, for

Barnard College in the late 1960s was a crucial next step for Gordon—just as it was for Felicitas Taylor. Eighteen-year-old Gordon, the girl who'd once wanted to be a nun, found herself rebelling in the *de rigueur* manner of the time: losing her virginity, experimenting with drugs, becoming involved in political rallies and marches.

In those heady times, her original ambition was to be a poet: "Then what happened was, my poems just started to become more and more narrative, and longer, and what I had to overcome was my anxiety over all these words I wouldn't be able to attend to, in the way a poet attended to each specific word. It really alarmed me: I saw all these words as chaotically spinning out of my control. But then actually I did give myself over to narrative. There's a way in which you have to be a little stupider as a prose writer, you have to get lost in the story, however you define story."

She began *Final Payments* in 1975, while she was a college English teacher in Dutchess County, New York. It was not a dream job: "I had four sections of composition, and I was not good at it because I was teaching people who didn't want to be with me." In their disinterest for things literary and in their aspirations—to become police officers, nurses, dental hygienists—her students were much like the working-class people she'd known at home. While she might have enjoyed their company in other contexts, the educational setting was not ideal: "I can do anything with someone who wants to be with me. I don't require brilliance—but I couldn't fight that resistance, and it was a very dispiriting experience. I think I could do it better now, but then I was still very young."

Like most first-time novelists, Gordon says, "I didn't know what the hell I was doing, I was just writing a novel. And I had no great expectations, I really didn't." So she was "completely blown away" by the book's reception.

Even thought she has always been confident in her ability as a writer, she won't discount the role of luck, timing, and historical circumstances in her success: if she'd begun writing 20 years later, in today's far more competitive publishing world, she may never have had a career, she says. But whether Gordon's instant fame was luck or just desserts, she didn't let it disrupt her writing life: "When all the success of *Final Payments* was happening, you see, I was leaving my first husband and getting a divorce, so I didn't allow myself to experience it very much. So in a really stupid way I didn't enjoy it. But more than that—you know, this is going to sound unrealistic—but what people think of my writing, in the large sense of the public, never really makes that much of a difference."

Gordon's voice grows a little quieter, almost confessional, as she elaborates: "There are a few people whose opinion I care about tremendously." Mary McCarthy praised her work early on, and she once received a postcard from William Trevor praising her second novel, but she still dreams of hearing from certain writers she greatly admires, such as Gabriel Garcia Márquez. "But largely, the response of people who read me, or the reviews that I get from people I've never heard of, doesn't matter that much. I can be shamed by a bad review, but it doesn't ever get me where I live. Neither the praise nor the censure."

Gordon is often too involved in her next project to be concerned with opinions of her current publication. A disciplined writer, she takes about four years to get from one long piece of work to the next; she has never started a book and not completed it. In fact, the only project she considers unfinished is her doctorate in English literature. In the late 1970s at Syracuse University, she thought she'd come up with an excellent thesis topic: to explore why Virginia Woolf was capable of idealizing an independent, intellectual type of woman in her nonfiction writings, such as the classic essay "A Room of One's Own," while continually portraying such traditionally diplomatic, domestically oriented housewives as Mrs. Dalloway in her fiction: "But the men who ran the program bucked me, and bucked me, and bucked me." So when *Final Payments* hit the bestseller list, "I said *screw this* and left."

Still in her early 30s, Gordon remarried, started a family, and kept writing throughout—"except for about a four-month period with the birth of each of my two children, when I just let myself be a cow."

While her next two books displayed a deepening concern with motherhood and marriage as themes, *The Company of Women* and *Men and Angels* (Random House, 1980 and 1985) still sought to dramatize the clash between religious and secular values in an explicit manner.

Both of those books are structurally akin to *Final Payments*: well-plotted, quickly paced, and filled with sharp, pointed dialogue. It was not until *The Other Side* (Viking Penguin, 1989) that a reader might have begun to notice certain changes in Gordon's work. A long generational saga about a clan named MacNamara, complete with a family tree on the frontispiece, *The Other Side* is certainly as well-structured as the earlier books. But in this novel Gordon makes much more liberal use of flashbacks, tense shifts, interior monologues, and omniscient narration. And while several of the book's 16 characters find themselves questioning their religious faith in one manner or another, the form of the questioning is much looser than in the earlier books—more existentialist than scholastic.

"That was the real transitional book," Gordon tells me, adding that she doubts she'll ever write that kind of multi-generational story again. "I had started reading more European literature, had really started getting into Marguerite Duras and Christa Wolf and Ingeborg Bachman. In a way, you see, I couldn't use the male postmodern models [such as Italo Calvino and Jorge Luis Borges] because I felt they were too cold, and I couldn't be Garcia Márquez because I didn't have that kind of wildness in me, but Duras and Wolf and Bachman really opened up a lot of doors for me."

These three writers effectively combined philosophical abstraction with powerful emotional stories, Gordon says. As she considered different European models to learn from, she found that Calvino and Borges were usually too theoretical to be genuinely moving. But in Duras's masterpiece *The Lover*, for example, she found that the incantatory power of the narrator's soliloquy didn't overwhelm the disturbing story of a childhood love affair. Even the obtuse, lyrical, and slightly wacky language in a piece like Ingeborg Bachman's classic story "Everything" was still grounded in the circumstances of an anxious father who feels responsible for his son's death.

By the time she wrote *The Rest of Life*, Gordon had gained enough wisdom from her favorite Europeans to dispense almost entirely with plot, the traditional backbone of long-form fiction, and the main source of energy for her earliest novels. Not unlike a book by Duras or Wolf, *The Rest of Life* was grounded not in "what happens next" but in voices: the voice of intelligent but troubled female characters, each of whom simply talks, either to an imagined audience (as in the first two novellas) or to herself, in alternating third- and first-person sections (as in the last novella).

Gordon had found a solution to the problem that Mary McCarthy had, in her estimation, never surmounted: the "idolatry of rigor" than can keep a young writer from growing. Using a form of contemplative monologue, she had learned to ground a story without depending on traditional plot or overly formal structure. But here was the next challenge facing Gordon: how can a writer possible "ground" a story in which the ground itself is constantly shifting?

In Gordon's new nonfiction book, a memoir of her father called *The Shadow Man* (Random House, 1996), she has taken some big stylistic and structural risks, abandoning symmetry and straightforward chronology in favor of a fractured movement between past and present, between facts and inventions. What's clear from the opening pages of the book is that these risks are an emotional, not just aesthetic, imperative.

"I was looking for my father," Gordon writes in the prologue. "I always understood that in looking for him, I might find things that I wished I hadn't, but I didn't know the extent to which this would be the case. And I didn't know that some of the things I'd thought most essential to the idea of who I was would have to be given up."

Since childhood Gordon has known that her father, a Jewish convert to Catholicism, hid certain painful things about his past. But only in middle age did she find courage to start tracking down more of the story: that her father had never attended Harvard as he claimed, had never even finished high school; that he'd never lived in Paris or Oxford, hadn't even been to visit Europe at all. Perhaps most disturbingly, even his name and the circumstances of his birth had been fabricated: for although he claimed to have been born David Gordon in Cleveland in 1899, in truth he'd been born Israel Gordon in Vilna, Lithuania, in 1894. David Gordon—a right-wing Catholic convert who tended toward anti-Semitism, who once wrote a diatribe again André Gide, modernism, and the infection of the Jew in European culture— had grown up speaking Yiddish, not English, as his first language.

Subtitled "A Daughter's Search for Her Father," *The Shadow Man* is a disturbing and rather raw account of a man who loved his only child enormously, who taught her to read at three and encouraged her—virtually ordained her—to be a writer, but who died when she was seven, leaving behind a very mixed legacy of lies, madness, and unanswerable questions.

In direct opposition to *Final Payments*, the positivistic and fairly traditional story about a dead father that launched Gordon's career, *The Shadow Man* is a deconstructive work: a novelist's attempt, not to pin down the truth so much as to tease out the threads of a man's self-contradictions and paradoxes, to come to terms with him as a damaged person, to demythify her childhood memories of him.

Perhaps most poignantly, the book is also a successful writer's attempt to imagine what it would have been like to have failed. "I have no memory of my father that doesn't include my knowing that he is writer," Gordon explains, in the chapter entitled "Reading My Father." Although he was never able to make a living at writing or published—it was Mary's mother, Anna, who supported the family as a legal secretary—David Gordon launched a number of publications that never quite flew, and contributed to the likes of *The Nation*, *The New Republic*, and *America*. But it wasn't until age 46 that

Mary Gordon sat down and seriously assessed his work: "It startles me to
see that my father and I share stylistic tics. He couldn't have taught me to
write, and I was well formed as a stylist before I read any of his prose. Why
is it, then, that we both love the colon and the semicolon . . . Why do we both
go in for the long, argumentative paragraph that ends in a punchy accusation?"

While Gordon tried to take comfort in the few connections she found between her father's writing and her own, the disjunctions were overwhelming:
his right-wing politics, his pro-Church fanaticism, his self-hatred manifesting
as anti-Semitism—and the often tortured, pompous writing style that resulted
from this volatile mix.

After reading what she could find of her father's writings, she searched for
more details of his life, through relatives, through census data, anything she
could find. But she didn't come up with much: David Gordon had lied about
and hidden so many aspects of his life, it proved impossible to reconstruct.

So in the penultimate section of the book, Gordon applies her craft and
tries to reimagine her father's life from the inside out: "I must become my
father. I must, finally, begin to understand what it is to be a Jew." Here is
where the book departs sharply from the realistic narrative current in Gordon's fiction:

> I am a boy in Vilna, Lithuania, or Poland, or the Kingdom of Russia. The
> new century has not yet started. A figure trails me. Stalking, shadowing, hissing
> or insistent, offering me drinks in poisonous bars, tell me to sit down . . . Sit
> here, drink this, put this on, and then this. Now listen to me. I will tell you who
> you are. The Jew, he says, but he can hardly say the words because of the
> disgust they cause to rise up in him. The Jew. The Jew. Yet he seems to need to
> repeat the words the Jew, turning the J into a sibilant grown pointed, then
> spreading, from contempt. I cannot refuse this stalker.

Gordon herself calls passages like these transgressive, a little nutty. She's
a bit frightened that not everyone will want to swim in these untested waters
with her. A reader who's drawn to the book for purely personal reasons—
perhaps because his or her own father has died—may grow disinterested or
confused after the first half of the book. Even her loyal fans may not warm
to the section in which Gordon pretends to argue with H.L. Mencken and
Ezra Pound, two notorious literary anti-Semites, or the extended conceit by
which she likens her search for her father to an archaeological excavation in
a bombed-out city.

The fabulist strategies Gordon employs in the second half of the book seem very European to me, learned from Bachman and Duras, for sure, but also from Calvino and Borges, writers whom Gordon and I used to argue about when I was in her workshop—I for, she against. Although she still thinks some postmodernism can be cold, cerebral, mannered, and too much influenced by French literary theory, she says she's become more tolerant of late.

But how tolerant will readers be? "There's a kind of reader whom I value enormously and whom I'm very touched by, and I find her when I travel across the country: a middle-aged, college-educated woman—probably not a real intellectual, but a serious reader—who feels like I'm saying things that she's always had in her heart. I'm not sure that kind of reader will leap across to my thinking I'm a Jewish man in 1910, but maybe . . ."

At a reading in suburban Maryland a while back, novelist Madison Smartt Bell introduced Mary Gordon as "arguably the pre-eminent Jewish-Irish-Catholic-American novelist," which of course got a good laugh from the audience. It's probably difficult for Gordon's readers to absorb the information that she is partly of Lithuanian Jewish descent, so well-established is she as an Irish Catholic writer. Thus far, Jews have shown up only as minor characters in her fiction, perhaps a natural result of her childhood, in which the only Jew she knew was the local druggist and the only Protestant was the local dry cleaner.

But now that she's delved into her father's life, will Jewishness as a theme show up in her fiction? Interestingly, her response isn't a pithy Mary Gordon-ism: it is, in fact, quite scattered: "I don't know, it's not on my agenda right now, except it sort of is, but in ways I don't understand yet, it's in the very back . . . yes, yes, I don't know yet. How did you know that? You've been reading my mind."

As is her routine, Gordon leapt into a new project as soon as *The Shadow Man* was completed in mid-1995: "I'm doing a comic erotic novel about a woman painter, and a man who says to her, 'I'll give you everything you need to make great art—time, space, money, and sex.' It's a kind of of utopian look at sexual life." After dwelling in the dystopia of her father's life, Gordon "just wanted to do something really different."

Asked if the knowledge of her father's lies and omissions ever led her to rebel or to question herself as a writer, Gordon responds with a resolute "No." When she sees the surprise on my face, she elaborates: "The fact that he was born speaking another language blew me away. That he dropped out of high school"—she pounds on the table three times—"Blew. Me. Away. There were other parts of his life that didn't affect my self-image and my formation of self, and I was perfectly happy for him to lie about those." But having become a writer, a reader, an educated person because of her father, she naturally found some revelations more troubling than others: "I thought I might find out, yeah, so what, he dropped out of Harvard. But not the tenth grade!"

Yet her father's love as so strong, undivided, and uncritical, that however flawed and mad it was, she never doubted its sincerity: "I was a very beloved child, and I think that gets you through anything."

Although Gordon grew up with a strong sense of herself as her absent father's daughter, her mother's vivid presence was crucial. As she says at one point in her 1991 collection of essays, *Good Boys and Dead Girls* (Viking Penguin), "I am the kind of writer I am because I am my mother's daughter. My father's tastes ran to the metaphysical. My mother taught me to listen to conversations at the dinner table; she taught me to remember jokes."

Gordon tells me that her mother never once discouraged her writing, even if it was beyond her ken: "She did send me to typing school when I was 12 and shorthand school when I was 13, because you always have to make a living, but she never said, 'Don't write, you'll never make a living at it.' I think it's very touching for a mother to step back and let her daughter do something she doesn't quite understand." While one chapter of *The Shadow Man* is devoted to Anna—who now suffers with Alzheimer's disease— Gordon will probably start writing about Anna more, now that she's finally put David's story to rest.

Gordon knows she has been given a wonderful gift—the certainty and support her parents provided, despite their flaws: "So I never wonder about the worthwhileness of the enterprise, I just sometimes wonder if anybody cares any more. And yet it seems to me a very beautiful thing to do with your life, if you can. Somebody once said to me, have you ever gone anywhere, for even a weekend, without paper? And I panicked. Why would I do that? So in some ways that are probably not entirely good for my moral, mental, spiritual development, I cannot divide a self from a writer."

Mary Gordon

Terry Gross / 1998

Transcription of *Fresh Air* (WHYY, Philadelphia), National Public Radio, 12 March 1998. © 1998 WHYY, Inc. Printed by permission.

Gross: This is *Fresh Air*. I'm Terry Gross. What artist doesn't feel that his or her work would improve if only they had more time, more space, and more money? In Mary Gordon's new novel, a woman painter meets up with an admirer who offers himself as her patron, muse, model, and lover. The novel explores the impact this relationship has on the painter's work and every other aspect of her life, from money to parenting to sex. In fact, one of the issues we'll talk about is the dilemmas Gordon faced in writing about sex.

Gordon is the author of the novels *Final Payments*, *The Company of Women*, and *Men and Angels*. Her recent memoir, *The Shadow Man*, was about discovering that her father, who died when she was seven, had fabricated much of the story of his life.

Here's a reading from the first chapter of *Spending*. The painter, Monica, is in the gallery giving a slide talk about her work. She's discussing one of her paintings called "The Artist's Muse," which shows a man in his underwear in a state of arousal.

Gordon reads from Chapter 1, pages 15–16, Spending.

Gross: Thanks for reading that, Mary Gordon. That's from Mary Gordon's new novel, *Spending*. Well, this gentleman who stands up and says "right here," he not only wants to be this painter's muse, he wants to be her lover; he wants to be her benefactor. What made you think about what it would be like for a woman to have a male muse-benefactor?

Gordon: I think the general crabbiness that my friends who are artists of one stripe or another have kvetched . . . where . . . it's made us crabby, and we've been kvetching for years about . . . you know . . . why do these guys get this and we don't? When is the balance going to be tipped? And I simply couldn't wait for life, and so I . . . I decided to just . . . just make it up in art.

Gross: What connotations does the word "muse" have for you?

Gordon: Well, it has the connotation, of course, of inspiration, but also of . . . of that nest of things that is required for an artist to be helped in her or

174

his work. That is to say, someone who provides not only inspiration, but makes a space in the world; gives you space and time and says, "You know, what's important for you is your work. I'm going to make it possible for you to do your work." That's what I think a "muse" is, or should be.

Gross: And what does this guy do to make it possible for her to work?

Gordon: Well, he gives her money and . . . so she can quit teaching and she can feel that she can paint absolutely on her own schedule. She can do whatever she wants. She can travel wherever she wants in case she needs to look at paintings in a particular place. He provides a space for her to live and work in. He provides pleasurable objects for her to be nourished by. And he also is her lover.

Gross: When she has the . . . the space and the time and the money to devote herself completely to painting, the artist in your novel ends up painting a series that she describes as the "spent male." These are also Jesus paintings. Do you want to describe the work that she does?

Gordon: Yeah, my painter, whose name is Monica, is looking at her lover one night after they've made love, and the posture in which he's sitting seems familiar to her in a puzzling way. And it occurs to her that the way that he's sitting reminds her of a painting by Carpaccio of the dead Christ. And she has a revelation. She says, "My God, maybe these dead Christs in Renaissance paintings weren't really dead; they were just post-orgasmic." And she decides to do a series of paintings, based on the Italian masters called "spent men," of her lover is a post-orgasmic condition, but using the iconography of Christ in the Renaissance paintings.

Gross: What made you think of this?

Gordon: I was looking at a show of Pontormo drawings in London, and I said: this guy's not dead. This guy's just been worn out from a hot night. And it was an absolute perception that . . . that amused me. What's really interesting is that the northern Christs look much more dead than the Italian Christs. And I just had fun thinking about that.

Gross: Mary Gordon, your early novels seems to be mostly about characters who were . . . were very repressed and very guilt-ridden . . . about responsibilities to family, about other responsibilities. This character just wants to be totally absorbed in her paintings, and she . . . there's a lot of sexuality in the new book, many scenes where the painter and her lover are engaging in acts of passion. And I'm wondering, it seems to be your characters are becoming less inhibited and more sexual. And I'm wondering what that says about you as a writer as you're writing more about sexuality.

Gordon: One of the things that I, again, wanted to rewrite, and I think maybe one of the things that I feel I stand for or wish to stand for more as a writer and, I don't know, a human being—although the two are not necessarily unlinked—is I am very tired of duality. I'm very tired of an either/or.

And it seems to me if literature gives us anything, it's the opportunity to say not either/or, but yes/and. And so this character is . . . she's really committed to her work. She loves her work. She gets irritated if people get in the way of her work. But when her daughter gets mono, she puts down her work. She's a little crabby about it, but she does it. When her lover throws his back out, when her lover loses money and gets depressed, she is there for him . . . not without ambivalence. But I guess I wanted to undo what I think is a particularly male fantasy about the artist, which is that there's this tremendous split between life and art, and that being a good person or a responsible person necessarily cuts into . . . your artistic life. And I think that that's a myth.

Gross: Let's get back to sex, though.

(Both begin laughing)

Gordon: Okay.

Gross: Your character has a lot more sex than, I think, most of the previous characters . . . most of the characters in your previous books have. And she is very comfortable with that. And I'm wondering if you are more comfortable as a writer writing sexual scenes than you would have been early on as a writer.

Gordon: I think that writing about sex is a little bit hard, and you have to feel your oats a little bit as a writer to feel that you have a right to do it. One of the things that I didn't realize until after I was finished was worrying about not being seen as a good girl writer anymore; that everybody had sort of thought of me as, you know, really serious and really taking the moral high ground. And I was really writing about pleasure—particularly sexual pleasure.

And while I was doing it, it was an interesting formal problem for me, in a way, and something I was interested in writing about, so I wasn't worried about it. And it was only after the book was finished that I realized that I was worried about not being seen as a serious good girl anymore. I think I probably couldn't have done that when I was younger. I think one of the hopeful things about getting older is you get less worried about being thought of as a good girl.

Gross: Now your character Monica says that she hates talking about sex. She says, "most words that connect up with sex have one kind of bad effect or another. Either I laugh or I want to become a Carmelite." Slang is not good. Scientific names are not good either. Then she runs down some of the names used for female genitalia. She thinks one sounds like a gum disease and another sounds like it was invented in the men's room of a bus station. How did you find the right words that you wanted to use, that you were comfortable with, that sounded sexy and not . . . not condescending or insulting to you? Because—so many words—slang words that are used to describe women's bodies end up sounding nasty.

Gordon: They do. And it was a real problem. I had to go through a lot of revisions and finally I did do the slightly cop-out thing of saying, "I'm not going to use any of these words because they're tainted." But I realized that in my own conversations, I rarely would use those kinds of words. So I . . . I fudged it in that way.

But I also was very interested in creating a new erotica that was really female, and it seems to be that female erotica is . . . are much more contextual than male erotica. And one of the things I did was I read a lot of Colette. And Colette very rarely names anything, but she creates a situation in which the objects surrounding the events are so erotically charged that they begin to give off a kind of musk of their own. And I realized I could be more explicit than Colette could be, but I wanted to create a sexual, an eroticized, a richly voluptuous context, so that the sex came from a place, not just sort of appearing from nowhere. And yet I didn't want to be coy. I didn't want to say: "Now, we're going to draw the curtain." And so, that was kind of a challenge.

Gross: Now, you're writing about a comparatively older couple in this. The woman has already gone through menopause, so, you know, birth control isn't an issue for her; pregnancy isn't an issue. She says, "I was too old now to lose anything by it"—to lose anything by sex. "I almost certainly couldn't even get pregnant anymore. One of the things we could both count on was that we were past many things that once might have been at stake." Talk to me a little bit about that—about writing a couple that's older and is engaged in first-time sexual encounters with each other.

Gordon: This is something that I'm actually rather hopeful about. And you know my nature is not to be so hopeful. But I think that—and again I'm talking about people who are fortunate, and I understand that a lot of people have had terrible situations—but I think that there is a cohort of us who went through the sexual liberation of the '60s; went through the women's movement. We have our own identity through work, not just through . . . not just through who we are in the eyes of men. We're . . . we're not young, but we're still peppy, and we might even look good. Some of us, oddly enough, look better than we did at 20. And I think that because, you know, a lot of us know even if you make a sexual mistake, your life is not going to be ruined by it. I mean, unless you get killed, which is another popular motif in writing about women and sex. But supposing that you don't get killed, you have too much in your life that's in place to have ruined it by sex. And that, in conjunction with some of the other good things that have accreted through life, gives you an odd freedom and energy, sexually, I think.

Gross: So you're talking about the anxiety that was involved for a lot of women in their early sexual encounters . . .
Gordon: Yeah.

Gross: . . . where it was related so much to their personal identity and to fear of getting pregnant; fear of being found out; fear of being hurt by . . .
Gordon: The fear of being hurt; fear of marrying the wrong person or not marrying the wrong person or not getting married; or you know, getting, as you say, getting pregnant or not getting pregnant. And once you . . . being beloved . . . and if you're not beloved, then you were a whore. All those things are . . . if they're out of the way, there's a lot of nice open space.

Gross: Over the past year or so, there's been a lot of controversy about the form of the memoir. Are writers being honest when they write about their lives? Are the memories they have accurate memories? Do the writers become exhibitionists by, you know, not only revealing intimate details about their own lives, but intimate details about the lives of friends and family, who are unwillingly being drawn into a public eye? Is there no longer any discretion about issues that should remain private?
You wrote a memoir before writing this new novel, and I'm wondering if you felt that there were any surprising after-effects from having revealed very personal things about yourself and your family?
Gordon: Well, I was in the odd situation with my family in which practically everybody was dead that I was writing about. And my mother is suffer-

ing from a very advanced form of dementia. And so, she had no memory and really no awareness that I was doing this.

The fallout from this book was surprisingly positive and wonderful—extra-literary—in that I found a new family. I hooked up with some distant cousins of my father's and . . . who have really embraced me and taken me in and given me a kind of connection to that Jewish part of my life that I hadn't had.

So again, I was very lucky. I didn't . . . I didn't feel that I was revealing anything that could hurt anybody. And so the fallout from it was completely positive. And some people were shocked about things that I said about my mother, but on the other hand, many people who were experiencing the kind of thing I had experienced with my mother (which is seeing somebody . . . somebody falling apart through dementia or Alzheimer's) were very, very grateful to me for having named the thing.

So again, I had this odd . . . you know, I'm often in very odd situations in my life which are lucky. So, is it lucky that practically everybody in your family is dead? You know, maybe that's an odd kind of good luck, but for writing a memoir, the dead are a lot less trouble than the living. And then I got this wonderful, wonderful gift of a new family.

Gross: You mentioned that with these new-found family members who have embraced you, you've learned more about the Jewish aspects of your family. Your father was Jewish, and, as you later found out when you were writing your memoir, he had written some very anti-Semitic things. Your mother was Catholic. Your father died when you were seven, and you were raised Catholic and spent a lot of your girlhood, I think, expecting to become a nun.

Gordon: Mm-hmm.

Gross: So, what has it been like for you to learn more about the Jewish side of your family?

Gordon: As I get older, I'm really interested in a life of amplitude. And so, as I explore the part of my history and connection that's Jewish, it's not . . . it doesn't seem to be a conflict with the Catholic part. It seems to me they're in dialogue with each other and their very contradictions are, for me, enriching and opening up. And one of the things I was trying to write about in *Spending* is a world of enrichment and a world of complexity, and I guess, what William James called "the buzz and gloom and implication."

And it's something that I feel literature can do that nothing else can do, because the opposite of literature is not life, but the soundbite. And this . . .

what does the soundbite do? What do religious fundamentalists do? But flatten the world and make it less complicated. And I think ideally as you grow older, you see how complicated it is and how much more rich it is than you ever would have dreamed when you were a kid and you were really, you know, on a mission.

Gross: Is religion for you now a kind of cultural intellectual expression? Or do you practice any aspects of Catholicism or Judaism?

Gordon: No, I . . . I do go to church. And you know, I try to go to churches that aren't going to put me into a murderous rage, which if you're Catholic is not always easy. I go to the synagogue on the high holy days as a kind of witness and touching in, but I definitely think of myself as a Catholic, having been estranged for many years and coming back, largely through meeting like-minded people who offer me, again, a more complicated and, I think, more mature and richer and more humane and more humorous version of the church than is coming out of the Vatican right now.

So, I have a religious life that's important to me. One of the things that I like about a religious life is . . . in church you see people that can all be together in one place that wouldn't be together in a building for any other reason. And I like being in a place where you don't have to be distinguished to get in; you don't have to earn your place there. You don't have to be good looking. You don't have to be smart. You don't have to be rich. You don't have to be successful. You don't even have to be sane or clean. You just have to be there. And I like being sort of under a roof with people who are very different, who are all aspiring to, in general, the same thing.

Author Mary Gordon Says She Wanted to Be Celebratory

Charlie Rose / 1998

Transcription of *The Charlie Rose Show*, PBS, 18 March 1998. © 1998 by Charlierose.com,inc. Printed by permission.

Charlie Rose: The heroine of Mary Gordon's new novel, *Spending*, is Monica Szabo. She is a divorced, 50-year-old artist who is fiercely independent. When faced with the prospect of taking on a male muse who will not only be her lover and novel but her patron as well, she's forced to question the values of art and money and the relationships between men and women.

I am pleased to have Mary Gordon here to talk about these ideas and this book. Welcome back. It's great to have you here.

All right, now. What's going on here? Is it because there are very few heroines that you have seen—or certainly none that you have created—who sort of have this world in which they act a little bit like Picasso did with women?

Mary Gordon: Well, you know, you would have to work so hard to catch up with Picasso that I would have had to have written a 900-page novel.

Charlie Rose: That's true.

Mary Gordon: But it seems to me that in the history of literature every woman who has sex dies. So that, if you get to page 3 and she's gonna have sex, you know she'll be dead before . . .

Charlie Rose: Yeah, the death warrant.

Mary Gordon: And it occurred to me that, in life, I have known women who have had sex and not died.

Charlie Rose: And lived to tell about it.

Mary Gordon: They certainly have and told and told and told. But I thought it would be fun to allow a woman in literature to have both love and work and not be punished for it, because I'm really tired of this strain of punishment that goes through literature and film and popular thought whenever the themes of women and sex come together. And if you put women and sex and work together, you get a triple-decker of punishment. So, the woman

181

has to die. Her children have to die. There has to be dismemberment. And I really wanted to play with the idea of a woman having the freedom that, as you said, a male artist might have.

Charlie Rose: Or, if you love sex and you enjoy it and you find it enormously satisfying, you are treated as if—frequently female characters are—as somehow without standards and something like a slut.

Mary Gordon: That's right. There's no word.

Charlie Rose: There's no appreciation of a woman's eroticism, I guess is what I'm trying to say.

Mary Gordon: No, there's no word that would be the counterpart of "slut" for a man.

Charlie Rose: Right.

Mary Gordon: So, a man who's sexually active—we're supposed to say, "Isn't he just wonderful?"

Charlie Rose: That he loves it so much.

Mary Gordon: That's the only synonym, "Isn't he just wonderful?"

Charlie Rose: Primarily comes from women, too.

Mary Gordon: I'm not sure about that.

Charlie Rose: I know. I know.

Mary Gordon: But it seemed to me that we've made . . .

Charlie Rose: Catholicism in you coming out, Mary.

Mary Gordon: Sorry, Charlie.

Charlie Rose: Go ahead.

Mary Gordon: We've made so much progress in the way that women have actually lived, and yet there's a lag, it seems to me, in this culture in general. There's a lag between the way that we live and the way that we can talk about it. I'm also distressed that for all that we are purported to be a very pleasure-loving culture, in fact we're not a pleasure-loving culture. We have a great deal of trouble valorizing pleasure. There has to be some notion of suffering built in. Our puritan ancestors were busy little creatures.

Charlie Rose: Why is that? I could not agree more. Why is that? We have trouble with pleasure.

Mary Gordon: You know, we think that pleasure is consumerism, and it's not. We don't mind consumption, but we really dislike pleasure—I think because it makes us feel so alive that it frightens us.

Charlie Rose: If it's this good, it must be something wrong with us.

Mary Gordon: Right. And if it's this good and we're this alive, maybe we'll die. I think it's a terror that we'll be punished. I don't think other cultures do this. Look at the way that we deal with food, for example. You know, Italy has created pasta. We've created the Big Mac.

Charlie Rose: Or pizza.

Mary Gordon: Yes, that's right. We did that for them, too. And then we brought it over there. But we eat quickly. We don't eat beautifully. We don't have wonderful accoutrements.

Charlie Rose: We don't take two hours for lunch.

Mary Gordon: No, we don't.

Charlie Rose: And other cultures create mechanisms for pleasure, like the siesta, like in the Mediterranean culture there's something called the *passeggiato* where people just walk around and look at each other—of all ages, grandparents, grandchildren, as well as courting couples. You're out on the street. You're looking. You're being looked at, as if to say, "Life is good, and it's O.K." We have a tremendous amount of trouble with that in this culture.

What has been the reaction of the critics to Mary Gordon writing about this subject? Because she has written about family before. She's written about relationships among members of a family. She's written about Catholicism and lots of other subjects, from *Final Payments* to whatever the last one was.

Mary Gordon: *The Shadow Man*, which was about my father.

Charlie Rose: Exactly. Right.

Mary Gordon: I think they want me to sing "Melancholy Baby," you know? If I wrote *Final Payments 13*, I think everybody would be thrilled and delighted. I have to tell you, I can't listen to what critics say. I do have a good way of dealing with negative criticism of this book.

Charlie Rose: Which is?

Mary Gordon: I simply assume that anyone who doesn't like this book does not have, never has had, and never will have a good sex life, and anyone who likes this book is terrific in bed. So, that's the way I deal with it in a very mature and, I think, sophisticated way.

Charlie Rose: Okay. This is a test here.
Mary Gordon: That's a test.

Charlie Rose: If you like this book, then you are good in bed.
Mary Gordon: Right.

Charlie Rose: Or you like being in bed with someone who is good in bed.
Mary Gordon: Right. And, if you don't like, we know everything about you.

Charlie Rose: We know everything there is to know.
Mary Gordon: So, I hope the critics will agree then.

Charlie Rose: This is the litmus paper test right here.
Mary Gordon: Absolutely.

Charlie Rose: So, go buy this book. If you want to know whether you're really good in bed, go buy Mary's book.
Mary Gordon: It's much easier than hurting the lives of strangers.

Charlie Rose: That's exactly right.
Mary Gordon: Absolutely.

Charlie Rose: Now, what is it about this book that will be the test for you?
Mary Gordon: I am really sexually explicit in a way that I never have been before. I'm talking about sex. I'm talking about a woman saying, "I like sex. I am not married to this man. There are times when I like work more than I like him," which is a little bit threatening for a man to hear, I think.

Charlie Rose: Yeah, well, we've been reading some stories about that where people are saying, "I find more satisfaction at work than I do at home," regardless of what their home life is.
Mary Gordon: But she's not saying that. She likes both. And I think that's one of the interesting things about going into your 50s, having come of age during the women's movement, because now there are those of us who have claimed a space and claimed a voice. It's not as good as it could be, God knows, but there are those who have done things. We have achieved things. We have power, and now is a time, it seems to me, for us to say, "Here I am." I want people to pay attention to the subtitle of this novel. It's called "a utopian divertimento."

Charlie Rose: Which is?

Mary Gordon: Which means, "wouldn't be great if?"

Charlie Rose: And so it's a fantasy.

Mary Gordon: Yeah, it's a fantasy.

Charlie Rose: But it wouldn't be a fantasy if the genders were switched, though, would it? It'd be reality. No?

Mary Gordon: I don't think so.

Charlie Rose: Men are all talk and no action.

Mary Gordon: Well, I don't want to talk about what happens to men. It's very sad. But nevertheless, it's not so easy to incorporate love and work, whatever gender you have.

Charlie Rose: Yeah.

Mary Gordon: And it seems to me, oddly enough, that as women get older, I think we're doing better than men who are getting older right now, because we've known how to integrate life.

Charlie Rose: Speak for yourself, Mary.

Mary Gordon: Well, we know how to have friends. Many of us have had children.

Charlie Rose: Right.

Mary Gordon: We've just had to be doing so many things. We were so tired for so many years that now we have these very rich lives in a way that I think it's harder for men to have the kind of full lives that women have. They're not so good at being a person who works and a person who has children and has friends and just kind of hangs-out or goes swimming. I think that the very pressures that women had to work with—if we're lucky, and many of us are not, but if we are—have given us very rich lives. And, in some ways—although it's a very dire time for women—it is a time of expansion.

And I wanted to say [in the novel], "You know, there are things to celebrate." And I did want to be celebratory, which is a big change for me.

Charlie Rose: Most of the women you know who are contemporary of yours are happy?

Mary Gordon: They're a lot happier than they were when they were 30, and at 30 they were a lot happier than they were when they were 20. And I think they're a lot happier than the men my age going into their 50s.

Charlie Rose: And why are the men unhappy?

Mary Gordon: Because I think that they have, you know, been on a single track at lot of their lives, and they're suddenly looking around and work isn't exactly what they thought it was going to be. And they look over their shoulder and there's a 28-year-old that's taking their place.

Charlie Rose: Yes.

Mary Gordon: And they haven't made that kind of nest. Women are awfully good at, I think—if they're lucky, again—at making a nest where there's a place for work, but there are other things too. I think it's a lot harder for men to make a nest for their own lives. And, as they get older and they look around, a lot of them are feeling that maybe there are some other things that they wish they had, that they don't have, that women have had to have.

Charlie Rose: What's the attraction between Monica and B [in *Spending*]?

Mary Gordon: One of the things I wanted to write about that I think is a very well kept secret is how wonderful it is if a man desires a woman for her work.

Charlie Rose: And this is a case of a man who's a patron, who meets her at a gallery, and he desires her because of her art.

Mary Gordon: He bought her paintings before he ever saw her. So, he's, in fact, drawn to her for the combination of her work and herself. I think it's a great fear that women have: if we're accomplished, that will make us less desirable. And I wanted to explore the possibility that perhaps accomplishments, with some men, could give you the same erotic charges as a man. So, you know, Picasso can be 85 and look like a bald bull and everybody's supposed to, you know, fall madly on their backs. And everybody believes that doesn't happen for women. I would like to at least explore the possibility that accomplishment can begin to have an erotic vector for women. And that's what happens with my characters. He really is drawn.

Charlie Rose: Accomplishment can be an erotic vector for women?

Mary Gordon: Yeah. Just as it has been for men.

Charlie Rose: Did anything happen in your life, and I mean by this a conversation with someone, something personal, to cause you to want to explore this subject and to cause you to say, "where are all the sexually adventurous literary heroines?"

Mary Gordon: My English editor was putting together a series of erotic novellas by women, and she challenged me to do it. And then I began to think as—you know, I teach literature, and I was just so tired of these women that died. And I would watch films with my daughter, who is 17. And she said she was really tired of my saying at the beginning of the film, "She's gonna die. She gonna die. She's gonna die." So, I thought for my daughter and for her generation and the women who come after her, I wanted to undo that. But it was the impulse of my editor's challenging me, saying, "Try to do this." And also I'd never done comedy, and I thought that formally would be a challenge.

Charlie Rose: And how much of a stretch was it?

Mary Gordon: It was really hard because the way that I have written in the past is always to go deeper and deeper and slower and slower. And comedy's about velocity. You have to really move across a narrative. And so a lot of the skills that I had didn't help me.

Charlie Rose: Writing about sex, how was that?

Mary Gordon: It was very hard, because you don't want to do a lot of "place A on B." You know, nobody wants that, and if they want it they can call it up on the Internet much better than I can give them. So, the question was to, again, create a context in which all the objects would be sexualized, so that you didn't have to do so much actual naming of parts. But I wanted to create a kind of sexual shimmer in the scenes, so that what was sexual would almost come out of it automatically. And also the challenge was that much of what has been written sexually is from the point of view of a man, and I firmly believe that what is erotic to men is very different from what's erotic to women.

Charlie Rose: What? How is it different?

Mary Gordon: I think that men don't need as much narrative or context for their erotic lives. You know, *Playboy* really does just fine for a lot of men.

Charlie Rose: What do you mean by "narrative" and "context"?

Mary Gordon: I think that pornography, which is geared mainly for men, is mainly visual and rather static. And I think that the imagination, the sexual imagination, of women is more contextual. And so again, objects become eroticized. One of the sexiest scenes—ask any woman in the world—is where Robert Redford washes Meryl Streep's hair in *Out of Africa*. Every woman in America gets a hot flash.

Charlie Rose: Every woman remembers this?
Mary Gordon: Yeah. Now, probably bathing is not . . .

Charlie Rose: We need to know this, Mary.
Mary Gordon: I know.

Charlie Rose: We do.
Mary Gordon: You really do. And that's why . . .

Charlie Rose: That's why this is an important book. We need to know that Robert Redford washing Meryl Streep's hair in *Out of Africa* is a turn-on for a lot of smart women.
Mary Gordon: Of course. And dumb women. I don't think you have to be smart to get it.

Charlie Rose: To get it. *Now* you tell me.
Mary Gordon's novel, is a must-read for everybody, because it is a kind of test for your own sexuality, in terms of where you are and what . . . how far you've got to go. The book is called *Spending*. Lots of people are talking about it. Alice Adams said on the back, "A total delight. Fun and incredibly sexy. And, as always with Mary, brilliantly and incisively intelligent." Thank you.
Mary Gordon: Thank you.

Mary Gordon: The Art of Teaching and Writing

Amy Callahan / 1998

From *Columbia University Record*, 23:18 (27 March 1998), 3. © 1998
by Columbia University Record. Reprinted by permission.

Somewhere in another room, an answering machine picks up a call. Mary
Gordon, in the midst of an interview in her Claremont Avenue apartment,
pauses, straining to hear the young women's voice rising from the speaker.
She recognizes it's one of her students and picks up the receiver.

Unlike the main characters in her new novel, *Spending*, Gordon does not
struggle with the dual job of being an artist and teacher; with the often con-
flicting demands of earning a living and the passion to create. In the novel,
when Gordon's character is presented with a benefactor's proposition—
allowing full-time devotion to her art—she eagerly sloughs off the shackles
of teaching to blossom in the productive, sunlit life of an artist with funding.
Gordon is hardly so constrained. During the past 20 years, through teaching
freshman English at a community college in Poughkeepsie to her current
position as Millicent McIntosh Professor of English, she has produced nine
books—two of them *New York Times* bestsellers. Yet her day job—
teaching—she approaches with no less passion.

Gordon is working to strengthen that voice she strains to hear. "It's harder
for young women, even now, to feel that they have the right to their own
voice," she explains, referring to the writer's ultimate task of developing a
genuine voice on the page. "And I feel like that's my job." She says, "I love
teaching. And I feel like I have the best job in America."

With that job comes scores of students annually for whom, in some degree,
Gordon is responsible. Gordon does not take that responsibility lightly, particularly because her students are primarily Barnard students. "I can deliberately attend to the needs of the female voice, which I think is unattended to
in most co-ed institutions," says Gordon, herself a Barnard alumna. "Now,
I'm talking about training writers. I'm very aware of what writers need to be
taught, and I think that one of the most important things you can do is give
them a lot of voices in their ears. And for young women writers, it's very
helpful to be listening to older women writers."

So in her literature and writing classes, she introduces female authors who have been overlooked in many classrooms. "I'm not interested in bean counting—insisting there's got to be a certain number of women in the curriculum," says Gordon, a professor of both literature and writing at Barnard who also teaches in Columbia's School of the Arts graduate Writing Division. "But one of the things that happens is that the same two or three women always are taught if they are being taught by people who are doing it because they feel they have to. I think it's wonderful that Emily Dickinson and Virginia Woolf and Toni Morrison are taught, but they tend to be taught over and over and over again. And there are enormously important, evocative women writers that simply don't get taught." Gordon cites Katherine Anne Porter, Jean Stafford, Colette, Anna Akhmatova, Eudora Welty, Tillie Olsen and Louise Bogan. "I want to put rich, interesting, quirky, profound, funny female voices in the ears of young women writers," she says.

And what does Gordon, the bestselling author, get out of it? The teaching of writing and the teaching of literature nurture her own work in different ways. "Teaching literature is wonderful for my writing," she explains, "because I always read over a text that I teach—I don't have one lecture that I've been giving for fifteen years. And if you're going to talk to students about a book, you have to read it in a very intense way. And that is nourishing for my own writing."

As for dissecting student stories in her writing workshops, she says: "I do get surprising ideas and new ways of looking at things from my students, but what it mainly does is give me hope. Hopelessness is a great paralyzer, and my students give me hope that what I'm doing isn't some anachronistic, marginal thing that's going to die with me. For me, students give me a great gift of hopefulness, and that gives me energy to go on with my own task in a way that's very valuable."

Her energetic writing life has most recently produced *Spending*, an erotic comedy playfully subtitled *A Utopian Divertimento*. It is about a struggling painter offered the freedom of money and the inspiration of a muse from a wealthy commodities broker who admires her work. While many reviewers have noted this book about sex and pleasure is a departure from the dark themes of her former bestsellers, such as *Final Payments*, the work does reflect Gordon's commitments to feminism and risk-taking. But, despite this departure and despite the fully chronicled sex life of the main character,

Gordon does not expect the book to be controversial. And that is because the story, from beginning to end, is like a fairy tale in the good fortunes enjoyed by its characters.

"I think I'm doing something quite radical, but people won't get it," Gordon explains. "My radical act is that a woman has good sex and nobody dies. And that, in fact, is something you don't see much in fiction. Nobody dies. Nobody's punished. Good sex for a woman without punishment is rare. So that's my radical act, but nobody's going to get much up in arms about it. I don't think people care that much about fiction about women unless it involves mutilation of the body."

Taking two years to write a novel about pleasure was a welcomed change for Gordon. And a challenge.

"The challenge was comedy. Velocity was very important. So it wasn't deeper, slower, darker anymore. There had to be movement. So the aesthetic was not an aesthetic of depth, but an aesthetic of movement."

Gordon said the book also allowed her to examine pleasure.

"I'd just finished writing this book about my father (*The Shadow Man*). And for four years I was in a place of great sadness. I think I was hungry for an atmosphere that would be more pleasurable, but also I was interested in just the idea of pleasure. And particularly for women. Why is pleasure the big taboo? We're a very un-pleasure-loving culture. We think we're very pleasure-loving, but we're not. We're consumers, but we're actually very puritanical. So, I wanted to write about pleasure. I wanted to explore that. I was interested in talking about the pleasure of food, the pleasure of weather, the pleasure of movement, being a body in this world, which is a good thing. Or can be."

The title of this new book refers in part to the series of paintings created by Gordon's main character Monica, but also to what Gordon explains as the action needed to induce pleasure, as in spending rather than hoarding, enjoying the moment rather than working and worrying about the future.

"I think people are working like crazy," she explains. "And I think that you can't get away from it. For example, home used to be a place where you could veg out. Now you walk in the door: Is there a fax? Is there an email? Is there a message on the answering machine? There is no place anymore that is free of work. And I think that has made us much less able to take pleasure because there is no space that is reserved for non-work, and I think it's making us very crazy."

So, a kind of divertimento could be what we all need, whether found in the pages of a new book or at the end of a salad fork:

"I'm a great lover of Italy, and when you go there, having a tomato is an event. Go to the market. It's fun to buy it. It's fun to put it on a dish. It's fun to cut it up. It's fun to put olive oil on it. It's fun to eat it. And I feel like we don't have that. It's very impoverishing.

Hidden at the Heart of the House

William L. Hamilton / 1999

From the *New York Times*, 23 December 1999, F1, F4. © 1999 by the
New York Times Company. Reprinted by permission.

The house, like a family, has its secrets. The domestic surfaces lie, until you
start listening to your memory of them, until you look at their commonplaces
as clues.

When Mary Gordon, the best-selling author, was 13, she went through the
drawers of a boarder renting a room in her mother's house, an incident she
recounts in her new memoir, *Seeing Through Places* (Scribner), to be published next month.

"I opened his drawers, "Ms. Gordon recalls in the book. "Found handker-
chiefs, perfectly folded. A few shirts. Two sweaters, in a drawer of their own.
And then, in the bottom, a collection of books I knew were there because
they needed to be hidden."

For a pubescent snoop, she hit the jackpot. It was pornography: 10 explicit
books of it. Though what provoked her invasion was the "sexual curiosity of
well-behaved girls," she writes, what she discovered "crushed my imagination." She continues, "It wasn't the feather touch of titillation, or the quick
chase of arousal, but the paralyzing force of a puzzlement so deep that the
mind feels like a locked machine."

The room revealed a story, too. The boarder was never in it; he was having
an affair with the Gordons' married neighbor. It was as empty as a broken
vow.

Places can be accomplices, as culpable as people.

At 50, with what could be described as a moral challenge in her eyes, Ms.
Gordon still looks like a Long Island girl, born in Queens, brought up in
Valley Stream, who might go through a drawer to get at the "mystery that
can surround or locate itself at the center of a house's life," as she writes,
that exists in the lives of the people who live there.

Ms. Gordon lives on the Upper West Side with her husband, Arthur Cash,
an author and retired professor of English; their 16-year-old son, David Cash,
and a white-muzzled, 12-year-old Labrador retriever, Peggy, who passes like
time through the narrow corridors of the apartment, securing each room. A

193

daughter, Anna Cash, 18, is now at Columbia University. Ms. Gordon teaches at Barnard College.

The issue of place became important "because I'm finally in the place I want to be," Ms. Gordon said recently, dressed in a black suit and white blouse, sitting at her dining room table drinking coffee. "I'm in New York— 'the city,' as we called it—which was always the great, good place to me, where you were free and the trivial was burned away."

The relationships between people have been the structure of both her fiction, like her debut, *Final Payments* in 1978, and her memoirs, like *The Shadow Man*, a 1996 portrait of her father, David Gordon.

Now, in *Seeing Through Places*, the houses and places of her experience are characters and family members. They have an emotional life, which is a kind of alternative architecture that Ms. Gordon inhabits in her book. They open doors.

There was, in the house she lived in as a girl with her young parents, the empty attic "meant to be our storage space, but we had nothing to store," Ms. Gordon writes, not even a sense of history. Her father, an intellectual and writer, lied pretentiously about his past as a French aristocrat who was educated at Harvard and Oxford, concealing his birth as a Lithuanian Jew who converted to Catholicism and who dropped out of high school.

Imprisoned by deceit, he stripped his life like a cell.

"He took pride in ignoring his surroundings," Ms. Gordon recalls in her book. "To care about things like furniture would have been for him a proof of an inferior nature."

On summer evenings, her mother, Anna Gordon, a legal secretary, whose income supported the household, ironed in a sleeveless dress, "freckled like an early apple." Ms. Gordon was an only child, the single fruit of an unhappy marriage. As she listened from the living room, the iron hissed; there were gunshots on the radio.

Undecorated, unembarrassed, furnished for comfort with favorite things, Ms. Gordon's New York apartment lacks the sophisticated relationships of design. "I was brought up to think that things were not important," she said. "And yet I love them. But I had to discover it on my own. We never talked about them in my family."

In the dining room, a William Morris fruit-pattern fabric, laminated for spills, covers the table. On the wall is a drawing by Vuillard, whom Ms. Gordon has defended against the charge that his art was minor because he painted interiors. He spoke "the deep, secret language of home truths," she wrote in a 1990 article. In the long hallway is a bright Mexican carving of a creature that is half insect and half woman and a discolored decoupage table that belonged to the writer Katherine Anne Porter.

When called a materialist, Ms. Gordon giggled quickly, like a young girl hearing an obscenity.

She writes with a black enamel, gold-trimmed Waterman pen in notebooks she collected on travels in Paris, Dublin, and Rome. It is a recognition of what Katherine Anne Porter called, at the end of her 1939 novel, *Pale Horse, Pale Rider*, which Ms. Gordon teaches, the "art of the thing."

Whether stockings or a sentence, there is a "fineness and goodness," she said, and a power of revelation to the craft of things "that can give you a tremendous sense of hope." She added, "And bad things are despair in-ducing."

Ms. Gordon told a story about her mother.

"I'd written five books, I'd had my children, I'd really been a fairly re-spectable person," she said. "I was looking at a catalog from Bergdorf Good-man. I was saying: 'Oh, look at that jacket. I love that jacket.' My mother looked at me in all seriousness and said, 'When exactly did you become such a superficial person?' "

Ms. Gordon's father died when she was 7. He had a heart attack in the main reading room of the New York Public Library, a place Ms. Gordon treasures because it is charged with the atmosphere of her memory. "It makes me incredibly happy," she said. Her father took her there every Saturday; she learned to read at 3.

"I think, if I just go to the reading room, he'll be there reading," she said. They might be there together.

In her grandmother's house in Valley Stream, where she moved with her mother when her father died, there were frightening "unmodern smells," ammonia and lavender, that turned the air dark to a child. An unmarried aunt lived upstairs, and an unmarried uncle slept on an unheated porch with an unplayed piano. It became her mother's house after Ms. Gordon's grand-mother died.

"It was not a loving house," Ms. Gordon writes.

But her grandmother washed her silver hair outside in the summer, in the sunshine of the backyard, with a white pitcher and a blue towel and a battered tin basin, while the children watched, with a ritual that was "inexplicably celebratory," Ms. Gordon recalls in *Seeing Through Places*. If the routine of domestic habit is a ring of fire, it is also a magic circle.

For Ms. Gordon, the home is a vexed place, with an ambiguous halo. She spoke of Virginia Woolf, whose photograph hangs in her hallway.

"She was terrified of domesticity," Ms. Gordon said. "She said that the woman writer had to kill the 'angel in the house.' She saw it as a complete threat."

Ms. Gordon said that she also saw it as a threat.

"One of the things I dislike about domesticity is that it makes people so anxious," she said, "because they feel so judged, about the way their home is constructed. Particularly women; if you feel you're always on trial, that your worth is being proved by the state of your abode, it makes for a lot of shame." Ms. Gordon mentioned Iris Murdoch, another favorite writer, who lived in a "filthy house," she said, undisturbed by housekeeping, which for a woman was an indication of "spritual squalor."

"If your house is not tidy, even if you've happened to finish *War and Peace* that day, you would still be judged by it," Ms. Gordon said. Proust lived like a pig, "because he's a genius," she added.

"I'm trying to reclaim some of the pleasures," she said. "It's a way of understanding who you can be in the world, and what you were told you couldn't be, and what you were told you must be. I'm fascinated by the way houses make people behave, in very practical ways, and I think that's a particularly female focus."

Seeing Through Places is something of a response: a creation—like a room of one's own—that carves security from fear, by giving it shape.

Writing of the sitter's house, where she was left each day while her parents worked, Ms. Gordon recalls, "The darkness of her house was in itself a kind of architecture." Inside boxes, under tables, children contain the anxieties of abandonment. At home, Ms. Gordon played in her father's closet, fragrant with his clothes.

In her New York apartment, she has built a life in which she can write in the morning, read in her red, velvet slippers and be with her family, the things that are important to her.

"It's a place to be quiet, and a place to be private," she said of the idea of a home. "These things seem so endangered. You need a refuge."

Ms. Gordon's husband woke from a nap and left the bedroom for the bathroom. Peggy, at her post by the front door, got up to see who it was.

The writer offered to show a visitor her office, down the hall. She is finishing a biography of Joan of Arc, to be published next year.

"I do have a room of my own," she said, lowering her voice as she walked in, "and I close the door."

A Sense of Place: Looking Into the Life of Mary Gordon

Alden Mudge / 2000

From *BookPage*, January 2000, *http://www.bookpage.com/0001bp/ mary_gordon.html.* © 2000 by BookPage. Reprinted by permission.

It's a relief, really. Mary Gordon seems no more inclined to answer deeply personal questions than I am to ask them. Of course, the questions flutter at the periphery of our conversation about her collection of meditative, autobiographical essays, *Seeing Through Places: Reflections on Geography and Identity*. How can I not wonder about the pain of a child who dreams of fairy princesses and kisses the knee of "Grandpa" Haubrecht in hopes of forming some sentimental connection with the old man, only to recognize in his unbending silence that she is not the magical child of her imagination, and probably not even a child at all? Or the desperation of a 15-year-old living alone with her alcoholic mother in increasing dishevelment, who hears a bird trapped in her closet struggling toward death and reacts by pulling her clothes from the closet, laying them on a chair, and never opening the closet again until it is time to go to college?

But, really, what more could I actually learn by asking Gordon about her implacable grandmother or her cruel aunt? Her mother and the priests who "embodied her idea of the desirable male"? Or the fact that her father, who died when she was seven, was the only person she liked to play with?

In these eight linked essays about the places that have shaped her sensibility—as in her recent memoir about her father, *The Shadow Man*, and her novels, *Final Payments* and *The Company of Women*—Gordon writes with such brilliant specificity and with such sensitivity to the fine gradations of human emotion that readers simply infer the answers to such questions. To actually ask them is a betrayal of one of the deepest pleasures of reading writers as good as Gordon: that sense of one mind and spirit connecting with another's. To ask also invites a kind of reductive pop psychologizing. Or worse, the commodification of spirit, which is a sorry trademark of our era, and an increasing concern for Gordon.

"What makes me nervous," she says midway through our conversation, "is that even people's interest in religion has become a commodity. I mean, the corporate world is now getting spiritual advisors so that their executives can be more productive, because they need to be in touch with their spiritual roots in order that they can make a better Web page . . . There's no other narrative, except commodity and profit. I find myself wondering, is there anything that is not commodifiable?"

Religion has never been a commodity for Gordon. She was raised in a family that "took deep pleasure in the liturgical world of the church" and assembled at her grandmother's on Tuesday nights to watch Bishop Sheen on television. But in the 1960s, in a moment described in the essay "The Architecture of a Life with Priests," a young priest's well-meaning remark "demolished the walls of the confessional," and led her to believe that she "would have to leave the church, because to live with this new sense of lightness and clarity I would need a dwelling that let in the light."

Thirty-some years later, Gordon has returned to the church. "Those sacred spaces were very formative, and irreplaceable," she says. "I began to understand that the habit of mind that was generated by those sacred spaces was very important to who I am, and that if I didn't honor my hunger for that, I would be less than truthful about who I really am. This is another reason why the metaphor of place is so important to me. I needed to be in the psychic space that only church ritual and the ethical framework that is expressed in ritual could give me. Nothing else would substitute for that."

But sacred spaces are not the only places Gordon reflects on in *Seeing Through Places*. There are also the houses of her grandmother and her babysitter and the neighbors next door, the public places of New York, and a forsaken house on the Cape. *Seeing Through Places* developed "without an intentional arc," Gordon says. At some point she realized that the essays she was writing were about place and that she wanted to "talk about where I am, I mean literally where I am and metaphorically where I am. So I organized the book around the motif of a journey." That journey spans only a short distance in miles—from Valley Stream, Long Island to Manhattan—but it is an immense psychic journey from a seemingly cloistered life in a working class neighborhood to public life as a best-selling novelist and English professor at Barnard.

"I really wanted to meditate on a place being at the center of a consciousness," Gordon says. "The accidents of place, the pressure of place that enables certain kinds of behaviors and makes other behaviors impossible. So that place becomes an agent in ways that are practical, in ways that can be tyrannical, and in ways that are very atmospheric and hard to pin down. . . . Often when people write about place it's from a sensibility that believes that place is divorced from people and has a kind of life of its own. I was brought up to think that people were more important than place and more important than things. I was even brought up in a sensibility that said that the invisible is more important than the visible. So the way that I come at place is not the way that Protestant males come at place. If this were an equation, I would be talking about place minus Thoreau."

In the most poignant essay in the book, "Places to Play," Gordon writes that as a child, she was not good at playing and always felt that she "was only masquerading as a child." Desperate to be taken seriously, she couldn't wait for childhood to end. Gordon later writes that she graduated from college younger than when she entered, and credits Barnard and the 1960s for teaching her the value of play.

"Far from being a '60s basher," she says, "I am so grateful for them. Because we were all allowed to play and to be serious. . . . The playful and the serious were able to flow in and out of one another in a way that for me was extremely freeing. And at Barnard, my mind was given play. I was given tremendous attention, a debt I can never repay."

Little wonder, then, that she has returned to Barnard to teach and that she writes of the place in her final essay with such affection. "I'm always afraid that with one false move, which I can't predict or name, I could be back at that old place I was in when I was young," Gordon says near the end of our conversation. "But I also feel a tremendous sense of gratitude and amazement that life has had so much more pleasure and amplitude and graciousness than I ever believed it would have when I was a child."

Index